The
AGING
PARENT
HANDBOOK

Virginia Schomp

HarperPaperbacks
A Division of HarperCollins*Publishers*

![HarperPaperbacks logo]

HarperPaperbacks
A Division of HarperCollins*Publishers*
10 East 53rd Street, New York, N.Y. 10022-5299

HarperCollins®, ![logo]®, and HarperPaperbacks™
are trademarks of HarperCollins*Publishers* Inc.

HarperPaperbacks may be purchased for educational, business,
or sales promotional use. For information, please write:
Special Markets Department, HarperCollins*Publishers*,
10 East 53rd Street, New York, N.Y. 10022-5299.

ISBN: 0-06-101032-4

Cover illustration by Frank Cezus/FPG

First printing: June 1997

Printed in the United States of America

Library of Congress Cataloging-in-Publication Data

Schomp, Virginia, 1953–
    The aging parent handbook : the directory of everything you
    need to know as relatives and friends grow older /
    by Virginia Schomp.
      p.   cm.
    ISBN 0-06-101032-4 (trade pbk.)
    1. Aging parents—Care—Handbooks, manuals, etc.
    2. Aging parents—Family relationships—Handbooks,
    manuals, etc. 3. Adult children—family relationships—
    Handbooks, manuals, etc. 4. Caregivers—Family
    relationships—Handbooks, manuals, etc.
    I. Title
    HQ1063.6.S36   1997
    362.6—dc21   97-12625
                                      CIP

Visit HarperPaperbacks on the World Wide Web at
http://www.harpercollins.com/paperbacks

97 98 99 00 ❖ 10 9 8 7 6 5 4 3 2 1

To Ruth Schomp,
who makes 5'2" look tall,
eighty look young,
and giving look easy

Table of Contents

Preface   **xiii**

Introduction: To the Caregiver   **xv**
   Recognize Yourself?   xvi
   Tools for Caregiving   xviii

Chapter One: First Steps   **1**
   Should You Step In?   1
   Communication Guidelines   2
   Developing a Support Plan   3
   Tapping into the Support Network   4
   Geriatric Care Management   6
   Your Part in the Support Plan   8
   Checklist #1: Health Warning Signs   9
   Checklist #2: Needs and Solutions   10
   Directory of Resources   16

Chapter Two: Staying at Home   **21**
   In-Home and Community Services   21
   Checklist #3: Evaluating Home Health
     Care Agencies   26
   Checklist #4: Hiring Home Care on Your Own   28
   Checklist #5: Evaluating Adult Day Care   30
   Checklist #6: Home Safety & Security   32
   Directory of Resources   35

Government Programs for At-Home Seniors 36
Other Helpful Free or Low-Cost Publications 51

Chapter Three: Housing Options **53**
Moving On 53
Alternative Living Arrangements 54
Joint Living with Adult Children 54
Staying Home by Scaling Down 55
ECHO Housing 56
Homesharing 57
Accessory Apartments 57
Adult Foster Care 58
Congregate Housing 58
Retirement Communities 59
Assisted Living Facilities 59
Continuing Care Retirement Communities 60
Nursing Homes 62
When Problems Develop with Nursing
Home Care 66
Checklist #7: Pros & Cons of Alternative
Housing Options for Older Adults 66
Checklist #8: Evaluating Assisted Living Facilities 69
Checklist #9: Evaluating Continuing Care
Retirement Communities 71
Checklist #10: Evaluating Nursing Homes 73
Directory of Resources 80
Other Helpful Free or Low-Cost Publications 93

Chapter Four: Financial and Legal Concerns **95**
Time to Talk 95
Information Gathering 96
Planning to Pay for Care 97
Income: Public Benefits 97
Income: Private Sources 99
Tax Facts 102
Insurance: Government Programs 103
Private Insurance 107
Other Private Insurance 113

Rating the Insurance Companies 114
Managed Care Plans 115
Legal Arrangements 116
Wills 117
Living Trusts 118
Letter of Instruction 118
General Power of Attorney 119
Durable Power of Attorney 119
Durable Power of Attorney for Health Care 119
Conservatorship and Guardianship 119
Joint Ownership Accounts 120
Checklist #11: Financial Inventory 121
Checklist #12: Personal and Financial Records 122
Checklist #13: Choosing a Medigap Policy 132
Checklist #14: Choosing a Long-Term
Care Policy 134
Checklist #15: Evaluating Managed Care Plans 139
Checklist #16: More Money-Saving Options 141
Directory of Resources 142
Other Helpful Free or Low-Cost Publications 163

**Chapter Five: Healthy Aging and
Common Disorders** **167**
What's Normal, What's Not 167
One Note of Caution 168
Predictable Age-Related Body Changes 168
Common Diseases of Aging 171
Arthritis 171
Cancer 172
Diabetes 173
Hearing Impairments 174
Now Hear This! 177
Heart Disease 178
Hypertension (High Blood Pressure) 180
Incontinence 181
Mental Health 182
Osteoporosis 187
Visual Impairments 188

Getting a Good Night's Sleep 191
Checklist #17: Managing Medications 191
Directory of Resources 195
Other Helpful Free or Low-Cost Publications 265
Publications for the Visually Impaired 269
Lending Libraries 275
Specialty Catalogs 277
Toll-Free Health Helplines 282

Chapter Six: Enriching the Later Years **289**
Active and Involved 289
Enrichment Through Education 291
Enrichment Through Employment 292
Enrichment Through Volunteerism 292
To Drive or Not to Drive? 293
Checklist #18: Boredom Beaters 294
Directory of Resources 296

Chapter Seven: Facing Final Days **307**
Breaking the Silence 307
Advance Directives 308
Hospice Care 310
Funeral Planning 312
Checklist #19: Selecting a Hospice Program 313
Directory of Resources 315
Other Helpful Free or Low-Cost Publications 321

Chapter Eight: Care for the Caregiver **323**
Caregiver "Maintenance" 323
The Support Network 324
Long-Distance Caregiving 328
Using Your "Weekly Planner" 330
Weekly Planner 331
Directory of Resources 339
Other Helpful Free or Low-Cost Publications 344

Appendix A: Parent Profile **347**

Appendix B: State Units on Aging   359

Appendix C: State Long-Term Care
  Ombudsmen   371

Appendix D: Sources of State
  Inspection Reports for Long-Term
  Care Facilities   383

Appendix E: Self-Help Clearinghouses   395

Bibliography   399

For Further Reading   405

Index   413

Preface

In one of life's less happy coincidences, just as research for this book began, my own mother experienced some very trying health problems. Mom has lived alone since my father's death over a decade ago, and though she's weathered a few illnesses, she has remained generally strong and remarkably active. At seventy-eight, she enjoyed doing volunteer work at her church, delivering Meals-on-Wheels to shut-ins, buzzing around town for errands and social gatherings, gardening, and spoiling the grandchildren. A condition called spinal stenosis—a form of arthritis of the spine—put a rude and sudden stop to this busy schedule. Weeks of pain and worry were followed by diagnosis, treatment, therapy, and finally, after six months, a relief of symptoms. At this writing, my mother is working to regain her lost mobility. She is able to stand and sit for increasing periods of time, but bending over, lifting, driving, and many other former activities are still out of the question.

The illness that so disrupted my mother's life prompted my first extended experience as a caregiver. In combination with the readings and interviews that went into the preparation of this manuscript, it encouraged me to take a long-overdue look at the future. For the first time, my mother and I discussed her priorities and preferences. What would she do if the condition recurred and she became incapacitated? What supports might we put in place to keep her at home as long as possible, and where would she want to live if a move became necessary? Does she have the financial resources to pay for long-term care? Has she prepared an advance directive to give her family and doctors guidance if she ever became unable to make her own health care decisions? Tackling these difficult questions, attending to my mother's physical and emotional needs, and at the same time juggling responsibilities to a husband, young son, home, and full-time career gave me a profound respect and compassion for the thousands of family caregivers who are struggling with similar and more difficult challenges. The experience also was an education in the kinds of information and guidance caregivers need. The result, I hope, has been the creation of a practical and useful resource.

Acknowledgments and sincere thanks go to the staff and volunteers at hundreds of organizations who contributed their knowledge and special insights to ensure this book's accuracy. Many caregivers also graciously shared their time and their personal stories to enrich these pages. To them, my deepest gratitude. Your work is demanding, often frustrating, always vital. This book salutes your accomplishments. May it also help to lighten your load.

Introduction:
To the Caregiver

You've heard the numbers. Modern medical technology has increased the average life expectancy in the United States from forty-seven years in 1900 to about seventy-two for men and seventy-nine for women today. The percentage of Americans over age sixty-five has more than tripled since the turn of the century, to 12.9 percent of the population, or 33.6 million, in 1995. As the older population grows, it itself is growing older. By the year 2030, according to Census Bureau projections, there will be about seventy million Americans age sixty-five and older, including nine million in our fastest-growing population segment, those eighty-five and up.

Chances are good these statistics have touched your life in profound and unexpected ways. Longer life span carries with it a greater potential for chronic health problems, and the older a person gets, the more likely it is that she or he will need some measure of long-term care. Most older Americans have their care needs met by a family member. In fact, about three-quarters of disabled elders receiving home care services depend entirely on family or other unpaid help.

An estimated eighteen million family caregivers spend an average of ten hours a week tending to the needs of a frail, ill, or disabled relative. Three-quarters of all caregivers are women. Most work outside the home. Many are raising children; some have grandchildren. Caught between the responsibilities of caring for both older and younger generations, these overextended, stressed-out, guilt-plagued, emotionally drained, and financially squeezed individuals belong to a growing group that has been dubbed the "sandwich generation."

Recognize Yourself?

- Rosemary has a teenage daughter, an older son living at home, a hardworking husband, and a full-time teaching job. Two years ago her mother, Elma, was hospitalized suddenly with a neurological condition that overnight robbed her of all feeling in her lower body. Since then life has been a grueling cycle of surgery, home care by two different agencies, nursing home care, and rehospitalization for dangerously infected bedsores. The home care agencies provided shockingly negligent care. Today Elma lives in an adequate if far from perfect nursing home. Rosemary visits for a few hours every afternoon after work and every weekend. It's exhausting, but she feels "like I have to be there. My mother is her own worst enemy because she doesn't speak up. I can't even imagine the people who have no one."

- Ruthie was looking forward to her husband's retirement. After forty years of raising five children, paying off a mortgage, and putting their own needs last, she and Russ finally would have the time to relax, do a little traveling, and rediscover the pleasures of privacy and spontaneity. When Ruthie's mother was diagnosed with inoperable ovarian cancer, the couple put their plans on hold. They moved Ruthie's bedridden mother into their home and devoted themselves to her care. It was a hard, confining, joyless year that "just went on and on and on. I don't think I even knew there was any way to get help. The doctor never suggested it and I didn't know where to go. I just figured this was what we had to do."

- Donald took a leave of absence to move in with his mother, Marion, after she was diagnosed with terminal cancer. For six months he kept her company, coordinated the care provided by home health aides, and, when those services proved inadequate, took over many of his mother's personal care tasks himself. "You know your parent better than any stranger could," he says. "I could tell her moods and know what she needed." It was a tiring and sometimes lonely stretch of time, but he "never thought of it as a burden. I was happy to be able to do it for her."

No one job description fits the family caregiver's role. You may provide round-the-clock attention to a chronically ill or disabled parent, grandparent, spouse, life companion, or dear friend. You may live on the opposite coast from a loved one and spend vacation time and hours on the phone arranging and monitoring care. In between these two extremes are countless different combinations of care-receiver needs and caregiver responsibilities. Despite their differences, though, family caregivers have a lot in common. All share in similar emotional, physical, and financial strains. Again and again, in interviews with caregivers, we heard about these common feelings and concerns:

Frustration
"I wish I could do more. I guess if life were simpler and we were home like we used to be, it would be easier. But life isn't what it used to be."

Fatigue/Stress
"Some days I just wish that I didn't have to face it. It would be nice just to go home after work and maybe veg out for fifteen minutes. It's like another job."

Resentment/Anger
"I didn't . . . I don't think I . . . well, yes, I did resent my mother, but I gave her the best care I could. There were times I disliked her, when she snapped at me, when she was critical of me when I was doing everything I could."

Sadness
"There's such sadness inside me for her. She was such a good mother and such a caring person. And for her to be there, with

nobody there for her . . . I know that, the kind of person she is, she would rather just close her eyes and be gone."

Guilt

"I can spend the weekend with her, clean the house, run her errands, do everything possible, and I still feel guilty driving away Sunday night. She's standing in her front porch, this tiny little figure, and I feel like I'm abandoning her."

Isolation

"The main thing was that my husband and I were restricted a lot, that we gave up our friends and our lives. About maybe once every ten days we had a friend of hers come over and stay with her so we could go out. The rest of the time we stayed home with her."

Satisfaction

"I feel good that I do this. There's not much else I can do except be there each day for her."

Tools for Caregiving

The Aging Parent Handbook is written in recognition of the challenges you face as a caregiver. Our goal is to give you, in one easy-to-use package, a variety of tools to help make your job easier.

A large and growing network of programs and services has sprung up in recent years, addressed to the needs of seniors and family caregivers. In nearly every community, government agencies, charitable organizations, and private companies offer information, services, and support for older adults and the family members or friends who care for them. Often, though, it can be difficult to tap into this "hidden" support network. You may not know what help is available, and you may have no idea where to look for it. Too often your efforts run smack into a brick wall of misinformation, dead-end referrals, and phone operators whose only proficiency seems to lie in pushing the hold button.

This book can steer you past the brick wall. We've sifted through hundreds of reports, fact sheets, articles, books, and brochures to extract practical information on locating and evaluating needed resources. We've included the medical, financial, legal, and home care tips caregivers told us they wanted. Checklists and fill-in forms are designed to enable you to quickly assess your loved one's needs and target your energies toward filling them. Most important, each chapter's directory provides key data on resources that are ready to lend you a helping hand, by phone, by mail, and in your own community.

All information in the directories came from the agencies and organizations themselves. Not included are groups involved solely in research, advocacy, or professional membership services. While many of these organizations do good and important work, we chose to list only resources equipped to provide services directly to you, the consumer. Also listed are some of the many publications these organizations offer. Available free or at low cost ($5.00 and under), these materials can be an excellent source of comprehensive, up-to-date information. In the "For Further Reading" section at the back of the book, you will find an additional list of more costly publications targeted to specific areas of concern. You may be able to find copies of some of these titles at your local library, government resource center, or senior center.

All addresses, phone numbers, and services described in this directory have been checked and rechecked. As we found when tracking down sources, however, organizations relocate, merge, and disband at an alarming rate. If you have trouble reaching a listed resource, try another organization on the list that provides similar services. Also see the agencies and information clearinghouses listed in Appendices B through E. These often can point you in the right direction.

Chapter One

First Steps: Assessing Needs & Seeking Solutions

I would see my mother once a month or so. The house was starting to fall apart. She had never been the greatest housekeeper, but things were really dirty. She had always been a thin person, but she seemed to be losing weight. I suggested she see her doctor, but she said she was fine. I wavered for a long time about what I should do. After my visits I would talk it over with my husband and worry about it. I finally sat down and had it out with her. She herself had come to the conclusion that the house was getting to be too much for her. She didn't know her neighbors anymore and the neighborhood wasn't as safe as it used to be. So we found a very nice senior housing complex and moved her there. She's very happy. It's a little apartment, but she's comfortable. She's made a lot of new friends. There's a dining hall where she has her meals. There's a cleaning service. I was sorry I agonized over it for so long.

Should You Step In?

Sometimes it's obvious a loved one needs care. The news may come through a doctor's pronouncement or that dreaded late-night phone call. Mom has fallen and fractured her hip. Dad has suffered a stroke that has left half his body paralyzed. A husband, wife, or dear friend has been diagnosed with a disabling illness or life-threatening disease.

Just as often, there is no call to action. Instead, the adult child of an aging parent hovers in an uncomfortable gray zone, nagged by worries about that former paragon of strength and self-sufficiency who has begun to show a few cracks in the armor. Mom or Dad seems to be losing weight or acting listless or depressed, letting the housekeeping go or forgetting to pay the utility bills. The small warning signals are accumulating, but do they add up to a significant problem? Should you say something? Is there something you should do?

Uncertainty, embarrassment, or the fear of humiliating or angering your loved one can make it easy to put off the conversation you know is coming. Following are a few guidelines that can help you decide when it's time to face the issue, along with tips for opening the lines of communication. Also look over Checklist #1, which lists physical and mental health warning signs that health professionals tell us should not be ignored.

Communication Guidelines

1. When you can't decide whether your concerns about your parent are justified, try asking other family members or your parent's neighbors, friends, clergy, or doctor for their perspectives on the situation.

2. If still in doubt, speak up. You may find that your loved one is relieved to talk about a troubling problem or that the problem has a surprisingly simple explanation or solution. Whatever the outcome, the paths of communication you open today will make it easier to speak your mind next time.

3. Pick an unhurried time and a quiet, private place for your discussion, and organize your thoughts beforehand. Have a clear goal in mind—reaching agreement on a specific problem—and steer the conversation in that direction. It may help to make a list of concerns to be addressed and questions to be answered.

4. Present your concerns calmly and without criticism. Family Service America suggests improving communication

skills by "always *speaking for yourself,* not for the other person. . . . When you are explaining what you *think* and *feel* and *why* you feel that way, support your statements with what you *saw* and *heard.*"

5. Listen carefully to what your relative says. Avoid arguing, interrupting, or offering blanket solutions. Simply present your concerns and offer your assistance in exploring options.

6. If you anticipate strong resistance or resentment, enlist a non-family-member such as a friend, doctor, clergy, or social worker to help with the discussion. Often the presence of an outsider will keep discussions calm and on target.

7. Be patient. Except in cases where you suspect a serious medical problem, it does no harm to state your case, then step back to give your relative time to think things through. If you don't see results in a reasonable period of time, you can try again or ask a sibling or family friend to reinforce your message.

8. Be respectful of your parent's right to control his or her own life. Only if your loved one's physical or mental well-being is endangered should you consider taking over the decision making.

Developing a Support Plan

Through careful advance planning or by simply making up solutions as problems arise, every caregiver develops a support plan. The goal of the plan is the basic mission of caregiving: to help ensure a loved one's comfort and safety while enabling that person to function at the best possible level.

In developing a support plan, you will first need to pinpoint your loved one's needs. Checklist #2 can help you zero in on the areas in which services and support might be helpful. It's a good idea to go through the list by yourself, checking off your areas of concern, then review it a second time with your parent to make sure you both agree on where help is needed.

Next you and your relative must consider how needs will be met. What services will you provide yourself? How will other family members and friends help out? When will you depend on community programs and services? Keep in mind that there often are several possible solutions to a problem. Let's say your mother lives alone and is losing weight because she finds it difficult to prepare nutritious meals. Your options might include taking over the grocery shopping and cooking; filling her freezer with home-cooked meals; working out a schedule for siblings, friends, and neighbors to drop off meals; arranging for a local restaurant to deliver meals; contacting Meals-on-Wheels or a similar community nutrition program; or arranging for her to eat at a local nutrition site or senior center. The course you take in this and similar situations will depend on many factors: how close you and other family members live to your parent, your work hours and other responsibilities, how much outside help your parent is willing to accept, financial resources, the availability of good community services, and so on.

As you consider all your options, refer to Checklist #2 again for listings of the types of community resources designed to assist in particular problem areas. The chart tells you where to turn in this book for more detailed information on specific problems and resources. If you're *really* in a rush, see the "For Fast Action" column, with phone numbers of organizations that can get you off to a running start. Complete listings for these groups may be found in the appropriate chapter directories.

Tapping into the Support Network

Help is out there, but finding the right services can be frustrating and time-consuming. As you ply the phones and pound the pavement investigating the service organizations in your parent's community, you may well be shuffled from one wrong office to another, ignored, or put on hold indefinitely. You'll leave messages that are never returned, battle rudeness and incompetence, and wade through a sea of red tape. You'll also meet people who are compassionate, knowledgeable, and helpful; discover lifesaving services

4

right in your backyard; and find that the time invested in researching your options pays lasting dividends.

Here are some suggestions that can ease your journey through the social service network:

Before you make the first call, set up a system for organizing resource information. Some caregivers use a loose-leaf notebook or a notepad, with a separate sheet for each agency; some prefer index cards in a file box. Top each sheet or card with the agency's name, address, and phone number.

Pull together the information you'll need about your relative's personal affairs, including date of birth, Social Security and Medicare numbers, names and phone numbers of doctors and other health professionals, and a chronology of health problems, medical tests, and treatments. Take the time to fill out the "Parent Profile" in Appendix A. You'll find that the information you gather to complete this form will come in handy as you make calls and answer queries. In many cases you'll also need financial and health insurance information. See Chapter 4, "Information Gathering," for tips on assembling that data.

Set aside a generous block of time for phone calls. You'll need all the patience you can muster, and you're more likely to lose it if you're pressed for time. Keep a pleasant, calm tone when speaking, but be persistent. Stay on the line until you get what you want.

Organize your thoughts before each call. Jot down an opening line describing what you're looking for; keep it brief, as you'll probably repeat it several times before reaching the right party. On each organization's sheet or card, note the questions you want to ask, and leave space for the answers. Your questions might include:

- What services does the agency provide?
- What are the qualifications and training of the staff?
- What are the eligibility requirements?
- What is the application process?
- Is there a waiting period?
- What are the fees?
- Is financial aid available?
- Are there brochures or other literature describing the program?

Make a note of the date you call and the name and phone number of each person you reach. Without that information, you're back to square one if you have to make a follow-up call. If you must leave a message, note the name and number of the person who is supposed to call you back so you can follow up if that call never comes.

If a face-to-face interview is required or you decide to check out a facility in person, find out what information and documents you'll need to bring along. Confirm appointments a day in advance. Bring a notepad with a list of questions to ask, and jot down the information you gather. If the person you meet with cannot help you, ask who can, and don't leave without a concrete referral—name, address, and phone number—in hand.

If you run into a worker who is rude, incompetent, or otherwise unhelpful, phone that person's supervisor with your complaint. Follow up with a letter to the supervisor or the administrator of the facility. By the same token, sending a thank-you note to someone who was particularly helpful may pay off in special attention to your relative's needs in the future.

Making phone calls and accompanying your relative to interviews is one of the areas in which a family member or friend may be able to save you valuable time and energy. Consider putting together a file folder of places to contact and questions to ask, then delegating that responsibility to someone who has offered to lend a hand.

Geriatric Care Management

Geriatric care (or case) management is a new, fast-growing profession that specializes in evaluating an older person's requirements and locating and organizing the best possible combination of services to meet them. A geriatric care manager (GCM) will visit your parent at home to assess needs. Then the GCM will design and help put in place a long-term care plan that weaves together community services such as in-home aides, Visiting Nurses, homemakers, transportation services, home-delivered meals, social programs, financial planning, and institutional care if needed. Most families use a care manager to make an initial assessment, discuss care and payment options, and help arrange for services to begin. Others, especially those who live at a distance from their loved one or have particularly heavy work or family responsibilities, hire a GCM on a retainer basis to supervise care and periodically reevaluate the older person's needs.

There are no specific licensing requirements for geriatric care managers, but most of those specializing in the field are licensed professionals such as nurses or social workers. Some nonprofit social service agencies, hospitals, and managed care health plans also offer geriatric care management. About one-third of local Area Agency on Aging offices (see Appendix B) offer free geriatric care management; those that don't usually can refer you to a local private GCM. Other sources of referrals include the National Association of Professional Geriatric Care Managers (see Directory of Resources) and local geriatricians, elder law attorneys, senior centers, or nursing homes.

Here are some questions to ask when shopping for a geriatric care manager:

- ***What are your qualifications?***
  Look for a professional (a nurse, social worker, geriatrician, counselor, etc.) who is licensed in your relative's state and has extensive experience working with the elderly. Ask for and check references from other clients.

- ***What services do you provide?***
  Make sure you understand how each service is defined. Does assessment include in-home visits and a written evaluation of the older person's strengths and weaknesses? How many visits, family consultations, and periodic reports can you expect? Will the GCM work with your parent's doctor? Will you receive a written contract spelling out services and fees? Look out for potential conflicts of interest. For example, does the GCM or agency have contracts with outside service providers or facilities that might limit or bias recommendations?

- ***What hours are you available?***
  Is the GCM on call twenty-four hours a day for emergencies? How promptly can you expect return phone calls? Who substitutes when the GCM is unavailable?

- ***What is your caseload?***
  Private GCMs generally have smaller caseloads than those in publicly funded programs, so they may offer more extensive services and greater continuity of care. According to the American Association of Retired

Persons, a full-time care manager ideally should handle no more than fifty to seventy-five clients.

- **What are your fees for the initial consultation and subsequent services?**
  Social service agencies may offer their services free or on a sliding scale based on income. Private GCMs may charge from $50 to $150 an hour or negotiate a flat monthly fee. Ask about eligibility criteria for publicly funded services, and check your parent's health or long-term care insurance coverage. Medicare and other health insurers generally do not pay for private care managers but may cover some or all of the services they recommend. Many care managers will explain Medicare and Medicaid rules, complete insurance forms, and work with financial and legal professionals to protect your parent's assets.

Your Part in the Support Plan

The family is the main support system for most older adults. As a family caregiver you may wear many hats: chauffeur, housekeeper, cook, nurse, companion, financial adviser, advocate. But you cannot, should not, and do not have to do it all. Keep the following facts in mind as you piece together a support plan that draws on all available resources:

1. According to the National Family Caregivers Association, more elderly people enter nursing homes because of their caregivers' burnout than because of a worsening of their own physical condition.

2. The quickest path to burnout is taking on too many responsibilities. Don't try to be superhuman, a hero, or a martyr. Take a hard, realistic look at your capabilities and time constraints before committing yourself to new caregiving tasks.

3. Your first responsibility is to take care of your own physical and mental health. Try to eat a balanced diet, get enough sleep and exercise, and allow some personal time for relaxation

8

and activities you enjoy. Chapter 8 includes tips on reducing and coping with stress and managing your time.

4. Ask for help when you need it and accept it when offered. Chapter 8 has suggestions for building a support team of family, friends, and outside resources.

5. Don't expect your support plan to solve problems once and for all. Your relative's situation will change, as will your own, and you must be open to periodically reworking your plan to suit evolving needs.

6. Try to anticipate crises and plan ahead. Consider your relative's current situation and what types of services might be needed if existing problems worsened. By gathering information and considering options now, you lessen the risk of having to make hasty decisions later.

✔ CHECKLIST #1: HEALTH WARNING SIGNS

If you notice any of these red flags, it's time to tactfully but frankly state your concerns and make certain your loved one gets appropriate care.

- ❑ Significant unexplained weight loss or gain
- ❑ Sudden loss of appetite
- ❑ Excessive thirst or water consumption
- ❑ Frequent trips to the bathroom
- ❑ Persistent coughing, hoarseness, or shortness of breath
- ❑ Unexplained bruises, burns, or other injuries
- ❑ Severe loss of hearing or vision
- ❑ Changes in speech
- ❑ Unusual skin color or skin growths
- ❑ Dizziness or loss of balance
- ❑ Persistent fatigue or increase in daytime sleep
- ❑ Swollen feet or legs
- ❑ Limping
- ❑ Increased use of alcohol or other drugs or medications

- ❏ Inability to take prescribed medications as directed
- ❏ Inability to keep self and home reasonably clean
- ❏ Unsafe driving (i.e., a number of fender benders or minor traffic violations)
- ❏ Sudden or increased confusion
- ❏ Sudden or increased reclusiveness or preoccupation with health
- ❏ Lack of interest in matters once considered important
- ❏ Talk of hopelessness or suicide

 ## CHECKLIST #2: NEEDS & SOLUTIONS

WHERE TO TURN			
MY RELATIVE'S PROBLEM	IN THIS BOOK	OUTSIDE RESOURCES	FOR FAST ACTION
Needs help but won't listen to reason	Ch. 1: Communication Guidelines	Ask family, friends, clergy, or doctor to back you up in presenting concerns	
Often feels bored, lonely, or isolated	Ch. 2: In-Home & Community Resources, Evaluating Adult Day Care; Ch. 6: Active & Involved, Enrichment through Education, Enrichment through Employment, Enrichment through Volunteerism, Boredom Beaters	Friendly visitors; senior companions; telephone reassurance; senior centers; adult day care; crafts, hobbies, & other interests; continuing education; part-time work; volunteer activities	Eldercare Locator (1-800-677-1116): referrals to social & recreational programs

National Senior Service Corps. (1-800-424-8867): referrals to volunteer programs |
| Is unable to shop or prepare nutritious meals | Ch. 2: In-Home & Community Resources | Home-delivered meals, congregate meals, transportation services, home-delivered groceries | Eldercare Locator (1-800-677-1116) or National Meals-on-Wheels Foundation (1-800-999-6262): referrals to nutrition programs |

My relative's problem	In this book	Outside resources	For fast action
Cannot drive or use mass transit	Ch. 2: In-Home & Community Resources; Ch. 6: To Drive or Not To Drive?	Transportation & escort services	Eldercare Locator (1-800-677-1116): referrals to local transportation programs
Needs help cleaning or maintaining home	Ch. 2: In-Home & Community Resources, Evaluating Home Health Care Agencies, Hiring Home Care on Your Own	Home maintenance, repair, and chore services, homemaker services	Eldercare Locator (1-800-677-1116): referrals to local homemaker & chore servies
Cannot be left alone at home all day; needs help with personal care (bathing, eating, dressing, etc.)	Ch. 2: In-Home & Community Resources, Evaluating Adult Day Care, Evaluating Home Health Care Agencies, Hiring Home Care on Your Own	Home health care, personal care aides, senior companions, adult day care	National Association for Home Care (202-547-7424) or Foundation for Hospice & Homecare (202-547-6586): referrals to home care agencies
Lives alone & fears health emergencies or crime	Ch. 2: In-Home & Community Resources, Home Safety & Security	Emergency response systems, home observation programs, telephone reassurance, commercial alarm system	Eldercare Locator (1-800-677-1116): referrals to local phone reassurance & home observation programs
Lives at home & needs nursing services or rehabilitative therapy	Ch. 2: In-Home & Community Resources, Evaluating Adult Day Care, Evaluating Home Health Care Agencies, Hiring Home Care on Your Own	Adult day care, home health care services, Visiting Nurses	Visiting Nurse Associations of America (1-800 426-2547): referrals to local visiting nurses

Foundation for Hospice & Homecare |

MY RELATIVE'S PROBLEM	IN THIS BOOK	OUTSIDE RESOURCES	FOR FAST ACTION
			(202-547-6586): referrals to home care agencies
Is no longer able to live alone at home	Ch. 3: Moving On, Alternative Living Arrangements, Pros & Cons of Alternative Housing Options for Older Adults, Evaluating Assisted Living Facilities, Evaluating Continuing Care Retirement Communities, Evaluating Nursing Homes	Living with children, ECHO housing, homesharing, adult foster care, congregate housing, retirement community, assisted living facility, continuing care retirement community (CCRC), nursing home	American Association of Homes & Services for the Aging (202-783-2242): lists of accredited CCRCs Assisted Living Facilities Association of America (703-691-8100): lists of assisted living facilities
Has unmanageable health care costs	Ch. 4: Planning to Pay for Care, Tax Facts, Choosing a Medigap Policy, Evaluating Managed Care Plans, More Money-Saving Options	Medicare, Medicaid, QBM, SLMB, Medigap, Medicare HMO, veterans' benefits	Medicare Hotline (1-800-638-6833): information on Medicare, Medicaid, QMB, SLMB, HMOs Department of Veterans Affairs (1-800-827-1000): information on veterans' & survivors' benefits
Has substantial assets to protect & is concerned about the potential costs of long-term care	Ch. 4: Planning to Pay for Care, Choosing a Long-Term Care Policy	Long-term care insurance, elder law attorney, accountant, financial planner	National Academy of Elder Law Attorneys (602-881-4005): attorney referrals Institute of Certified Financial Planners

My relative's problem	In this book	Outside resources	For fast action
			(1-800-282-7526): financial planner referrals
Needs assistance with legal matters	Ch. 4: Legal Arrangements; Ch. 7: Advance Directives	Elder law attorney, community legal aid program	National Academy of Elder Law Attorneys (602-881-4005): attorney referrals Choice in Dying (1-800-989-9455): advance directive forms and information
Has aches & pains, fatigue, vision or hearing problems, or other physical complaints	Ch. 5: What's Normal, What's Not; Predictable Age-Related Body Changes; Common Diseases of Aging	Family doctor, geriatrician, or specialist; organization serving people with specific illness or disability; self-help group	American Geriatrics Society (212-308-1414): geriatrician referrals American Self-Help Clearinghouse (201-625-7101): self-help group referrals
Is depressed, irritable, confused, or acting strange	Ch. 5: What's Normal, What's Not; Predictable Age-Related Body Changes; Mental Health	Family doctor, mental health specialist or clinic, organization serving people with mental illness or dementia	Alzheimer's Association (1-800-272-3900): information on Alzheimer's Disease American Association for Geriatric Psychiatry (301-654-7850): psychiatrist referrals

MY RELATIVE'S PROBLEM	IN THIS BOOK	OUTSIDE RESOURCES	FOR FAST ACTION
Seems to be taking an awful lot of medications	Ch. 5: Managing Medications, Medications Record	One family doctor to monitor all medications	National Council on Patient Information & Education (202-347-6711): information on use of prescription drugs
Is having sleep problems	Ch. 5: Getting a Good Night's Sleep		
Is having difficulty communicating, because of hearing impairments	Ch. 5: Hearing Impairments, Now Hear This!	Audiologist, hearing aid center, assistive listening devices	American Hearing Research Foundation (312-726-9670): referrals to hearing aid clinics & specialists American Speech-Language-Hearing Association (1-800-638-8255): referrals to audiologists & speech-language pathologists
Has been diagnosed with a terminal illness & wants to die at home	Ch. 7: Hospice Care, Selecting a Hospice Program	Local hospice program	Medicare Hotline (1-800-638-6833): referrals to Medicare-certified hospices HospiceLink (1-800-331-1620): hospice referrals

WHERE TO TURN

My needs & concerns	In this book	Outside resources	For fast action
I'm not sure if I'm overreacting or if my concerns about my relative are justified	Ch. 1: Should You Step In?, Communication Guidelines, Geriatric Care Management, Health Warning Signs; Ch. 5: What's Normal, What's Not, Predictable Age-Related Body Changes	Discuss with family, friends, neighbors, doctor, clergy; consult a geriatric care manager for in-home needs assessment	National Association of Professional Geriatric Care Managers (502-881-8008): geriatric care manager referrals
I'm trying to check out community resources but I'm getting the run-around	Ch. 1: Tapping into the Support Network, Geriatric Care Management	Turn over research task to family member or friend; hire geriatric care manager to arrange services	National Association of Professional Geriatric Care Managers (502-881-8008): geriatric care manager referrals
I need to help my relative manage finances but don't know where to begin	Ch. 4: Time to Talk, Information Gathering, Financial Inventory, Personal & Financial Records	Medicare or Medicaid office, Area Agency on Aging, financial planner or accountant	Medicare Hotline: (1-800-638-6833): information on Medicare & Medicaid Institute of Certified Financial Planners (1-800-282-7526): financial planner referrals
I need to plan or help my relative pre-plan a funeral	Ch. 7: Funeral Planning	Local funeral directors	Funeral Service Consumer Assistance Program (1-800-662-7666): publications on planning a funeral

My needs & concerns	In this book	Outside resources	For fast action
I feel over-whelmed by my caregiving responsibilities	Ch. 8: Caregiver "Maintenance", The Support Network, Organizing Your Day, Weekly Planner	Informal support network of family & friends, com-munity resources, respite care, adult day care, caregiver support group	National Adult Day Services Association (202-479-1200): adult day care referrals Eldercare Locator (1-800-677-1116): referrals to adult day care & respite care American Self-Help Clearinghouse (201-625-7101): support group referrals
I am worried about my parent who lives at a distance	Ch. 1: Developing a Support Plan, Tapping into the Support Network, Geriatric Care Man-agement; Ch. 8: Long-Distance Caregiving	Informal support network of family and friends, com-munity resources, geriatric care manager	National Association of Geriatric Care Managers (502-881-8008): geriatric care manager referrals

Directory of Resources

These organizations either provide geriatric care management or can help you locate and/or evaluate others that do. Also contact the local Area Agency on Aging (see Appendix B) for geriatric care management services or referrals.

NATIONAL

Organizations on this list offer their services nationwide or over a sig-nificant area of the country.

Aging Network Services (ANS)
4400 East-West Highway, Suite 907
Bethesda, MD 20814
301–657–4329

Serving adult children who live at a distance from aging parents, this private agency will assess the family's needs, then match the older person with a qualified local geriatric social worker for comprehensive care management. ANS's fees are based on an hourly rate comparable to private-practice social workers.

Council of Better Business Bureaus (CBBB)
4200 Wilson Boulevard
Arlington, VA 22003
703–276–0100
Fax: 703–525–8277

Your local Better Business Bureau can tell you whether there have been complaints about the services provided by a geriatric care manager and how any complaints were resolved. Contact the national office for the phone number and address of your local BBB.

National Association of Professional Geriatric Care Managers (GCM)
1604 North Country Club Road
Tucson, AZ 85716
502–881–8008
Fax: 502-325-7925

Contact this professional association of geriatric care managers for the names and credentials of GCMs in your parent's area.

National Association of Social Workers
750 First Street NE, Suite 700
Washington, DC 20002–4241
202–408–8600

Contact this professional association of social workers for referrals to social workers and therapists who can provide geriatric care management services.

REGIONAL

Organizations on this list provide services in limited geographic areas. You may be able to find groups offering similar services in your relative's community.

Aging in America
1500 Pelham Parkway South
Bronx, NY 10461
718–824–4004

For a small annual membership fee, older people and their families in the Bronx receive geriatric care management services, including in-home assessment of needs, development of a plan of coordinated services, and assistance in accessing services provided by the agency and through government entitlement programs.

Council for Jewish Elderly (CJE)
3003 West Touhy Avenue
Chicago, IL 60645
773–508–1000
Fax: 773–508–1028

Care managers at this private nonprofit organization offer a variety of programs and services for older people in the Chicago area. CJE will serve as a liaison to families and caregivers living nearby or at a distance, alerting them to changes and problems, coordinating service delivery, and monitoring care. Phone for information on services and fees.

Fairview/Ebenezer Caregiver Support Program
3400 West Sixty-sixth Street, Suite 190
Edina, MN 55435
612–924–7039 or 612–924–7040

The Care Source is a joint program of Fairview, a regional health care provider, and the Ebenezer Society, a community service organization. This for-fee program offers Minneapolis-area seniors and their families a detailed assessment of needs, development of a care plan, help in arranging recommended services, and continuing care management as needed. Care coordinators also will help area families seek out resources for older loved ones who live out of state.

Jewish Association for Services for the Aged (JASA)
40 West Sixty-eighth Street
New York, NY 10023
212–724–3200

This service agency with offices and social workers in New York City's five boroughs provides in-home needs assessment and referrals to local medical, social, and legal resources. Outside Manhattan the service is free to low-income adults age fifty and older of all faiths; in Manhattan there is a sliding-scale fee based on income. Staff speaks English, Spanish, and Yiddish.

ALSO HELPFUL:

"Care Management: Arranging for Long-Term Care." Order #D13803. Free 20-page booklet on selecting and evaluating geriatric care management services. Contact: AARP Fulfillment, 601 East Street NW, Washington, DC 20049 (1–800–424–3410).

Chapter Two

Staying at Home

We had two home care companies. The first was a large agency. They were recommended to us by the hospital, and we used them because we assumed that the hospital would know if there were complaints. I tried to set up times for them but they could never stick to a schedule. There were mornings they didn't show up. There were mornings they came late. They didn't do what they were asked to do. Every time I called they would change their story, change the aides. After three weeks of this horrible care my mother had a bedsore four inches across and two inches wide, infected all the way down to her bone. I took her to the hospital and they admitted her immediately. I learned that even though the social workers may recommend "Brand X," it may not be the best. If you're really not happy about the type of care you're getting, then you should change, try another agency. You have to go through the hassle of having another nurse come to evaluate. You go through the whole thing again, so it's a bit of a nuisance, but it can be worth it.

In-Home and Community Services

Given a choice, most people would keep their independence and continue to live at home as they age. Today a broad range of home care services can make that choice possible, even if the older person develops some physical or mental limitations.

Home care is a broad term covering services that range all the way from free transportation for doctor visits to round-the-clock skilled nursing care. Most home care services are designed to assist frail, ill, or disabled people with the daily activities of independent living. Your parent may need assistance with a single activity or many. By exploring the available options, you can help stitch together a combination of services that meet the care-receiver's individual needs and free you from some of the worries and chores of caregiving.

Following is a description of widely available in-home and community services:

Nutrition programs

There are two types of nutrition services for older adults living at home: meals delivered to the home and congregate meals. Home-delivered meal programs provide hot, nutritionally balanced meals for older adults who are unable to shop for groceries and/or to cook. As a side advantage, the delivery volunteers ensure a daily check on the meal recipient's well-being. Congregate meals are served in a group setting such as a senior center, often with recreational activities before or after. Both types of nutrition programs usually can accommodate special needs such as low-salt or sugar-free diets. In most cases services are available free or at minimal cost.

Transportation

Many communities provide special transportation for seniors. Staff or volunteers driving their own cars or specially equipped buses or vans transport riders from their homes to doctors' offices, hospitals, nutrition sites, senior centers, grocery stores, and pharmacies, and on other essential errands. Some programs also will provide an escort to accompany an older person to medical appointments. Transportation programs may be available on a first-come first-served basis or by advance reservation. Most publicly funded services are free or low cost. If you are using a private service, the American Association of Retired Persons recommends checking the service's references and asking about driver requirements, training, and vehicle equipment and maintenance.

Home maintenance, repair, and chore services

Community volunteers perform minor household repairs and home and yard maintenance chores such as fixing stairs and windows, winterizing the home, seasonal heavy cleaning, installing handrails and other safety features, cutting down branches, mowing lawns, and removing snow. Major repairs and cosmetic improvements such as replacing a roof or installing siding usually are not included. Costs vary, with some programs providing services free or on a sliding scale based on income, some charging for materials but providing free labor, and others charging relatively low fixed fees or offering no-interest or low-interest loans for home repairs.

Home observation

In some communities postal carriers or meter readers will watch for indications that a homebound older person is in trouble—accumulating mail or trash, unmowed lawns, etc.—and pass on word so a family member can be notified. Ask your relative's public utility or post office about arranging for this free service.

Telephone reassurance

A volunteer makes a daily phone call to an older person who lives alone, providing social contact and checking on well-being. Some programs are set up to remind the older person about medication, meals, or other needs. There usually is no charge for this service.

Friendly visitors

A volunteer from a local religious, civic, or social service group will regularly visit an older person at home, providing companionship and emotional support. The visitor may play cards, help write letters, read aloud, or simply ease loneliness through friendly conversation. Keep in mind that even though this is a free, volunteer service, you are entitled to request a different "friend" if your parent and the first assigned visitor don't hit it off.

Senior companions

Companions provide social stimulation, supervision, and light meal preparation for an older person who lives alone but cannot function completely independently. They generally will not perform medical services, heavy housecleaning, or extensive personal care but may provide some assistance with activities such as feeding and toileting. Free service is available in some communities through government-funded or volunteer programs. You also can hire a senior companion privately or through a home health care agency to help out for a few hours a day or all day. For tips and precautions on hiring in-home caregivers, see Checklist #3, "Evaluating Home Health Care Agencies," and Checklist #4, "Hiring Home Care on Your Own."

Emergency response systems

Emergency response systems (ERSs), also called personal response systems, provide reassurance and emergency assistance to older people who live alone and worry about health emergencies, accidents, or crime. By pressing a button on an electronic device worn as a pendant or wristband or clipped to clothing, your relative can signal for help. A central monitoring station will receive the signal and call prearranged emergency numbers. Some models allow the wearer to speak through the device to the monitoring station. Some have an inactivity alarm, which signals for assistance if the wearer has not contacted the center after a predetermined period of time. ERS costs and availability vary, but there usually is an initial equipment and sign-up charge plus a monthly monitoring fee. Some new models may be hooked into the 911 emergency phone lines instead of a monitoring station, eliminating monthly fees. The Directory of Resources lists a few of the largest national ERS suppliers. You also might contact a local hospital, your Area Agency on Aging (see Appendix B), or ABLEDATA (see Directory of Resources) for referrals to local suppliers.

Senior centers

Senior centers provide a variety of daytime social and recreational activities for older people who are mobile and able to function independently within the community. Services may include educational and cultural programs, financial and legal counseling, health screenings, meals, and travel and volunteer opportunities. Many centers also act as a clearinghouse for information on community programs. Services are generally free or low cost.

Adult day care

Operated by hospitals, nursing homes, local government or religious groups, and private agencies, adult day care centers offer social and health care services in a protective setting for older people who need some special assistance. Centers may provide health monitoring and personal care; physical, occupational, and speech therapy; nutritious meals and snacks; medication dispensing; exercise programs; and social activities. Many will work with people who are in wheelchairs, demented, and/or incontinent; some are set up especially for individuals with Alzheimer's disease or other specific health problems or disabilities. Centers usually are open weekdays during normal business hours and offer the option of attending for a few hours or all day. Costs vary, with sliding-scale fees available in many community-sponsored programs. For referrals check with your Area Agency on Aging (see Appendix B), local senior center, or family doctor. See Checklist #5 for guidelines on selecting adult day care services.

Homemakers and personal care aides

Homemakers help with light housekeeping, laundry, meal preparation, local errands, and other household duties. Personal care aides, also called home health aides, give nonmedical assistance with daily living activities such as eating, bathing, dressing, grooming, toileting, and walking. Some home caregivers combine the two roles. Government and charitable programs may offer these types of services free or on a sliding scale. You also can hire a personal care aide or homemaker privately or through a home health care agency. See Checklist

❏ *Is the agency accredited?*

Accredited agencies voluntarily submit to reviews by a national accrediting organization, which determines if they meet specific industry standards. Accrediting organizations include the Community Health Accreditation Program, the Joint Commission on Accreditation of Health Care Organizations, and the Foundation for Hospice and Homecare (see Directory of Resources).

❏ *Is the agency certified by Medicare?*

Medicare certification means the agency has met the minimum health and safety requirements established by the federal government. Medicare will not reimburse for services provided by a noncertified agency. Absence of certification does not necessarily reflect on quality. Some agencies accept only private payments, in order to avoid the complicated process of seeking Medicare certification.

❏ *Will a nurse or therapist conduct an in-home assessment of your relative's condition and needs?*

Provide a copy of your completed "Parent Profile" (Appendix A) to help the staff learn more about your parent as an individual.

❏ *Does the agency create a plan of care for all new patients, detailing recommended types of services and frequency and duration of care?*

The care plan should be periodically updated as patient needs change. Ask if you and your relative will have input in the care plan and receive copies of the initial plan and updates. Also find out how often a supervisor will visit your parent's home to make certain the plan of care is being carried out.

❏ *How are employees selected and trained?*

Ask if employees are bonded, to protect you in case of theft, and covered by workers' compensation, in case of

on-the-job injuries. Find out if the agency will send a substitute if your parent's caregiver doesn't show up for work.

❑ **Will the agency provide a written description of services and fees?**
A good agency can tell you which charges Medicare, Medicaid, or private insurance will cover.

❑ **Is there a phone number you and your parent can reach twenty-four hours a day with
problems, complaints, and emergencies?**

✔ CHECKLIST #4: HIRING HOME CARE ON YOUR OWN

Privately hiring a personal care aide, homemaker, or other in-home caregiver
may save 30 percent or more off agency fees. There are drawbacks, however. Without the benefit of an agency's oversight, you must carefully screen
prospective employees and assume the responsibilities of an employer: hiring, firing, negotiating salary and benefits, withholding Social Security payments, and setting up your own backup care plans. The following steps can
help simplify the process of hiring in-home care without an agency:

1. **Begin your search for applicants** by asking for recommendations from friends, doctors, clergy, and caregiver
   support groups. You also might contact employment and
   referral services, school placement offices, and senior
   employment programs; place ads in the local newspaper;
   and post flyers at hospitals, senior centers, college dormi-
   tories, and houses of worship.

2. **Save time by screening prospects by phone.** Ask
   about former employment and training and describe your
   parent's needs in detail. Schedule face-to-face interviews
   with those who sound qualified.

3. **Arrange interviews in a public location** such as a
   restaurant, for safety and security. Ask prospects to fill out

28

an employment application, listing their name, address, education, work history, and at least two personal and two employment references. You can make up an application form yourself or buy preprinted forms at an office supply shop. During the interview describe the job honestly and in detail. Run through a list of questions prepared beforehand, and note the prospect's responses. Your questions might include:

- Why are you looking for work?
- What were your responsibilities at your previous job(s)?
- Why did you leave your previous job(s)?
- How soon would you be available for this job? For how long?
- Are there any duties involved in this job that you feel you cannot perform or would feel uncomfortable performing?
- What about this job interests you?
- What would you do if . . . ? (Evaluate the applicant's judgment by asking about hypothetical situations involving care problems or emergencies.)
- How would you get to work? Do you have a backup plan in case your regular means of transportation fails?

4. **Check all references**, verifying the information provided and asking about the job seeker's work history, dependability, and suitability for your needs.

5. **Check for a criminal record**. Local law enforcement officials can tell you how to access arrest records in your state. Some states also have abuse registries, with records on people involved in elder abuse or neglect.

6. **Draw up an employment agreement** that details names, addresses, and phone numbers; employee's Social

Security number; hours to be worked; services to be performed; holidays and other time off; rate and schedule of pay; benefits such as meals and mileage reimbursement; and grounds for dismissal. You may want to consult an elder law attorney for advice on negotiating an employment agreement, tax withholding requirements, and proper insurance coverage.

7. **Supervise the caregiver you hire**, praising good job performance and promptly and tactfully pointing out problems, with suggestions for improvements. Ask friends or family to make occasional unscheduled visits to check on the quality of care. Keep a copy of your "Parent Profile" (Appendix A) at hand to help the caregiver remain mindful of your relative's personal needs and preferences.

✔ CHECKLIST #5: EVALUATING ADULT DAY CARE

Before enrolling your loved one in an adult day care program, check out these quality considerations:

❑ *Is the center certified and/or licensed by the state?* Check with the Area Agency on Aging (see Appendix B) about your state's requirements.

❑ *Will the staff assess your relative's condition and needs before admission?* To ensure quality care, an initial assessment should cover physical condition, medical history, activity and cognitive levels, and personal interests. Share a copy of your completed "Parent Profile" (Appendix A) with staff members doing the assessment to give them a personal view of your loved one. Also ask if the day care program regularly monitors participants' condition and progress.

❑ *Does the program meet your relative's social and rehabilitative needs?* Some centers are medically oriented, while others focus more on social activities. Look for an active, stimulating program that suits your loved one's physical, intellectual, and social requirements. You also might look for staff membership in professional associations, such as the National Association of Activity Professionals, that encourage the development of high-quality, life-enhancing activities in adult care facilities.

❑ *What are the staff's credentials?* Staff at adult day care centers usually include a professionally trained director and/or social worker, at least one registered nurse or licensed practical nurse, nursing aides, licensed therapists, and a recreation therapist or professionally trained activities director. Some centers hire only social workers, in place of nurses. If that's the case, make sure the staff is trained in CPR and other emergency procedures.

❑ *Will the staff work with you and your parent to develop an individualized program of care and activities?* Find out what activities are included in the program and how often. The staff also should be able to make referrals to other needed community services.

❑ *What is the ratio of staff to patients?* The National Council on the Aging's Institute on Adult Daycare recommends a minimum staff-participant ratio of one to six.

❑ *What are the criteria for terminating service?* Ask about the conditions and terms under which you would be expected to make other care arrangements if your parent's condition deteriorated. Would the staff be able to assist you in finding a care alternative?

❑ *Is the facility safe, clean, odor free, well lighted, and comfortable?* Check out dining areas and bathrooms, and make sure there are adequate accommodations for any physical limitations.

❑ *What are the fees, and what services do they include?* You may want to ask about eligibility criteria for sliding-scale fees or state or local aid.

✔ CHECKLIST #6: HOME SAFETY & SECURITY

Accidents at home are a serious threat for older adults. As we age, we're more likely to suffer falls or burns, and the accident that might result in minor injury for a forty-year-old may mean broken bones or permanent disability at age seventy. It's a wise precaution to spend a weekend safety-checking your parent's home. Use the following checklist to identify hazards and the accommodations that can help ensure comfort and safety.

Bathroom

❑ Place nonskid strips, appliqués, or a rubber suction mat on the tub or shower floor.
❑ Place a nonslip bath mat next to the tub or shower.
❑ Install bathtub grab bars at both standing and sitting heights. A grab bar next to the toilet also may be helpful.
❑ Sliding glass doors on the tub add an extra inch to step over. Consider removing these and replacing them with a shower curtain.
❑ Make sure hot and cold water taps are clearly labeled.
❑ Replace small knobs with long-handled faucet turners if gripping or turning faucets is difficult.
❑ Check that towel bars are well secured.
❑ Make certain electrical appliances are stored away from water.

Kitchen

❑ Check for loose handles on pots and pans.
❑ Store heavy pots and pans on lower shelves.
❑ Store sharp knives away from other utensils.
❑ Store electrical appliances away from the sink.
❑ Make sure step stools are stable and in good repair.

❑ Make sure towels and curtains are kept away from the oven and cooktop.

❑ Check that ventilation systems and range exhausts are functioning properly and are used during cooking.

❑ Place a fire extinguisher in the kitchen and make certain your relative knows how to use it.

❑ Review these safe-cooking tips with your relative:

- Keep pan handles turned toward the back of the stove.
- Keep a lid handy for smothering pan fires.
- Fold back long, loose sleeves while cooking, and fasten them with pins or elastic bands.
- Use pot holders or oven mitts, not dish towels, when handling hot utensils.
- Set a timer as a reminder to turn off burners.

Stairs and Halls

❑ Make sure the coverings on all steps are in good condition. Check for worn treads, protruding nails, and worn or loose carpeting.

❑ Install handrails along the entire length of staircases, or tighten existing handrails.

❑ Highlight the first and last step of staircases with bright, contrasting paint or tape.

❑ Place nonskid strips on uncarpeted steps.

❑ Vertical stripes on the wallpaper lining stairways can reduce the risks of falls; horizontal stripes increase the risk.

❑ Keep stairs and hallways clear of clutter, including wobbly furniture and low-hanging plants or light fixtures.

❑ If climbing stairs becomes too difficult, consider helping your parent move needed living supplies to the first floor.

Bedrooms

❑ Make sure your parent keeps a lamp, flashlight, and telephone by the bedside.

❑ Consider installing handrails between bedroom and bathroom to make it easier to navigate the hallway at night.

Outdoors

- ❏ Check for broken or uneven concrete steps, walks, or driveway.
- ❏ Install railings on outside steps.
- ❏ Make sure walks are kept clear of leaves, snow, and ice.

Security

- ❏ Post easy-to-read emergency numbers beside all phones.
- ❏ Make sure all window and door locks are secure and easy to operate.
- ❏ Install door chains and an optical viewer in the front door.
- ❏ Consider installing an emergency response system or a commercial alarm system monitored by a central station, to give your relative quick access to emergency services.

Around the House

- ❏ Install smoke detectors and regularly check batteries.
- ❏ Check electrical outlets, cords, and equipment for frayed or cracked wires and loose connections. Make sure cords are placed out from beneath furniture and rugs or carpeting.
- ❏ Make sure lightbulbs are the appropriate size and type for lamps and fixtures.
- ❏ If fuses are used, check that they are the right amperage for the circuit.
- ❏ Check furnaces and exhaust systems, and replace filters as necessary.
- ❏ Set the hot water heater to 120°F or lower to prevent burns. (If the water heater does not have a temperature setting, use a thermometer to check the water temperature at the tap.)
- ❏ Make sure carpets or rugs are securely anchored to the floor.
- ❏ Rearrange furniture to clear main traffic areas.

❏ Make sure cleaners, bleaches, detergents, and other poisons are clearly marked and stored away from food.

❏ All areas of the house should be well lighted, especially stairs, hallways, entryways, and kitchen and basement work areas. Several diffuse lights distributed evenly throughout a room are better than a single bright source of light. Install light switches outside rooms and at both the top and bottom of staircases.

❏ Use blinds or curtains to reduce glare in rooms that receive bright sunlight.

❏ Install night-lights in bedrooms, bathrooms, and hallways.

❏ Your relative should have a fire escape plan, with at least two alternative, clutter-free routes to safety.

Directory of Resources

The following resources provide services for older adults living at home or can help you find organizations that provide these services. In addition, to seek resources in your parent's community, you might try contacting:

- the Area Agency on Aging (see Appendix B)
- your relative's or your own doctor
- a community information and referral service
- the county or city department of health, consumer affairs office, or family services department
- a local senior center
- a local YMCA
- the social services or geriatrics department at an area hospital
- the retirees' association at your relative's former workplace
- your own employer (some companies offer caregiving-related employee assistance and counseling)
- the reference librarian at your parent's local library
- the local phone directory (look under "Social Services," "Human Services," "Senior Services," or "Aging")
- an organization that provides referrals to health care

professionals or one that offers information and services related to a specific illness or disability (see the
Directory of Resources in Chapter 5)

- a national or regional self-help clearinghouse for referrals to mutual-aid self-help groups for individuals coping
with chronic illness, disability, or other concerns (see
Appendix E)

Government Programs for At-Home Seniors

The Older Americans Act of 1965 established entitlement
programs for older adults and led to the development of a
network of agencies to serve them. At the head of the network is the Administration on Aging, which advocates for
older people at the federal level. At the state level are the
State Units on Aging (also called State Agencies on Aging
or State Departments on Aging), which administer federal
funds and coordinate services statewide. Serving older people directly are the Area Agencies on Aging (AAAs), a network of 664 local offices. Some AAAs are private nonprofit
organizations, while others are a unit of state, county, or
city government. All have been designated by the State
Unit on Aging to serve as its local arm in a specific geographic area. The AAAs are the older consumer's front line
of service, developing community-based federally funded
programs to help older people live independently at home.
Appendix B lists addresses and phone numbers for the
State Units on Aging, which provide statewide referrals to
programs for seniors. Some State Units publish useful
statewide directories of programs and services, available
free for the asking. Your State Unit also can refer you to
your local AAA for local information and referrals.

NATIONAL

Organizations on this list provide their services nationwide or over a significant area of the country.

ABLEDATA/Information for Independence
8455 Colesville Road, Suite 935
Silver Spring, MD 20910
1–800–227–0216 (voice/TTY) or 301–588–9284
(voice/TTY)
Fax: 301–587–1967

This is a good place to start your search for products and devices that can help your relative maintain independence. An information specialist will search the ABLEDATA database of more than 21,000 assistive technology products and give you detailed descriptions of each product, including price and manufacturer information. Searches can be tailored to a functional need such as eating, bathing, or food preparation; to a recreational activity such as crafts or gardening; or to a specific device such as emergency response systems or powered wheelchairs. Simple information requests or referrals are free; a listing of fifty or fewer products costs $5.00. Lists can be sent in large print or Braille, on audiocassette, or on PC-compatible diskette.

ABLE/INFORM BBS provides direct access to the ABLEDATA database via computer modem. Phone 301–589–3563 (line settings of 1200 to 9600 baud, N=8=1).

American Federation of Home Health Agencies (AFHHA)
1320 Fenwick Lane, Suite 100
Silver Spring, MD 20910
1–800–234–4211 or 301–588–1454
Fax: 301–588–4732

AFHHA is a trade association of Medicare-certified home health care agencies. Contact for referrals to agencies providing services in your area.

American Nurses Association
600 Maryland Avenue SW, Suite 100 West
Washington, DC 20024–2571
1–800–274–4ANA (1–800–274–4262) or 202–651–7000
Fax: 202–554–2262

Phone this professional society of registered nurses to locate your state nurses association, which will provide referrals to local organizations that recommend home care nurses.

American Red Cross
2025 E. Street NW
Washington, DC 20006
703–206–7090

Many of the nearly two thousand local Red Cross chapters offer health and safety programs helpful to family caregivers, including first aid, CPR, and home health care training. Contact your local chapter for information about programs in your area.

B'nai Brith
1640 Rhode Island Avenue NW
Washington, DC 20036–3278
202–857–6625

Many local lodges of this international organization for members of the Jewish faith perform volunteer services for senior citizens. These may include home-delivered daily meals or holiday meals and assistance with household tasks. Phone the national office to locate your local lodge for information about local service programs.

The Caring Network of B'nai Brith
1640 Rhode Island Avenue NW
Washington, DC 20036–3278
1–800–222–1188

The Caring Network is a membership program offering referrals, information, and support. Members who phone the toll-free number speak with a geriatric social worker or nurse who will discuss their problems, questions, and financial concerns related to the care of an older relative or friend. The phone counselor then reviews the resources available in the caller's area and phones back with the names of three pre-screened local service agencies providing the services needed. Annual membership fee: $54.00.

Catholic Charities USA

1731 King Street, Suite 200
Alexandria, VA 22314
703–549–1390

About 1,200 independent agencies nationwide offer home-delivered and congregate meals plus a variety of social and recreational programs at senior centers. Services are free and available to all, regardless of religious affiliation. Catholic Charities agencies often can refer you to community resources providing additional services. Look in your phone directory under "Catholic Charities" or "Catholic Social Services," or phone the main office to locate a nearby agency.

Center for the Study of Aging

706 Madison Avenue
Albany, NY 12208
518–465–6927
Fax: 518–462–1339

Consultants from this nonprofit foundation help develop health, wellness, and physical activity programs for older adults throughout the country. Program areas include home care, transportation, nutrition, physical and mental fitness, and more. Contact the center to locate quality senior programs and resources in your area.

Christmas in April USA

1536 Sixteenth Street NW
Washington, DC 20036
202–483–9083

The national office of this nonprofit, nonsectarian organization coordinates the work of about 160 local Christmas in April programs throughout the United States. (A handful of these programs go by related names, such as Christmas in July or Christmas in October.) Volunteers with local programs rehabilitate the houses of low-income homeowners, particularly those who are elderly or disabled. The work usually is performed on a one-day National Rebuilding Day late in April and may include painting, cleaning, weatherizing, carpentry, plumbing, electrical work, and other repairs, all free to the homeowner. Each program has different criteria for homeowner selection. Contact the national office for information on local programs.

Community Health Accreditation Program (CHAP)
National League for Nursing
350 Hudson Street
New York, NY 10014
800–669–1656 ext. 242 or 212–989–9393

CHAP accredits home and community-based health care agencies that voluntarily agree to meet its quality standards and submit to periodic on-site inspections. Contact for information on accredited organizations in your area.

Council of Better Business Bureaus (CBBB)
4200 Wilson Boulevard
Arlington, VA 22003
703–276–0100
Fax: 703–525–8277

Contact the CBBB for the location of your local Better Business Bureau, which can give you information on consumer complaints about local businesses providing home care services.

Eldercare Locator
1–800–677–1116

Operated by the National Association of Area Agencies on Aging, this nationwide directory assistance service will help you locate local support resources, including nutrition programs, home care, Visiting Nurses, transportation, home repairs, assistance with shopping, and telephone reassurance. Phone with your relative's county and city name or zip code, and an operator will help identify the kinds of services your relative needs and refer you to state or local information and referral sources for those services.

Foundation for Hospice and Homecare
513 C Street NE
Washington, DC 20002–5809
202–547–6586
Fax: 202–546–8968

The foundation accredits home care aides through its National Certification Program. Contact for referrals to local home health care agencies.

Generations United
c/o Child Welfare League of America
440 First Street NW, Suite 310
Washington, DC 20001–2085
202–638–2952
Fax: 202–638–4004

This national coalition of more than 130 organizations can provide information on intergenerational programs in your relative's area, which may include projects in which young people volunteer to provide services to help frail, homebound older people live independently.

Joint Commission on Accreditation of Health Care Organizations
One Renaissance Boulevard
Oakbrook Terrace, IL 60181
630–916–5800

This independent agency evaluates and accredits U.S. health care organizations, including more than fourteen thousand home health care agencies, health care networks (HMOs, PPOs, and physician networks), hospitals, hospices, and long-term care facilities. To earn the Joint Commission's seal of approval, an organization must meet certain performance standards and undergo periodic on-site surveys. There are different levels of accreditation, reflecting the degree to which an organization meets standards. Phone the number above to ask about a specific home care agency's current accreditation status and history. If you have a complaint about an accredited organization, phone 630–916–5642.

Helpful Publication:
"Helping You Choose Quality Home Care." Free leaflet.

Medicare Hotline
1–800–638–6833
TTY: 1–800–820–1202

Phone for the number of your state's Home Health Hotline, which you can call to register a complaint about the care provided by any Medicare-certified home health agency.

National Asian Pacific Center on Aging (NAPCA)
Melbourne Tower
1511 Third Avenue, Suite 914
Seattle, WA 98101
206–624–1221

For names and phone numbers of Asian-language-speaking information and referral sources across the country, contact this nonprofit agency, which serves Asian and Pacific Islander seniors. NAPCA also has a library of brochures and articles in various Asian languages. Tell them the aging-related topic and the language you need, and they will send free copies of relevant publications.

National Association for Home Care (NAHC)
228 Seventh Street SE
Washington, DC 20003
202–547–7424
Fax: 202–547–3540
E-mail: celiap@nahc.org

This is the largest trade organization representing home

#3 for tips on evaluating home health care agencies and Checklist #4 for guidelines on hiring caregivers on your own.

Home health care

Home health care services include nursing care, special medical treatments, and rehabilitative therapies. Routine checkups, blood tests, intravenous feeding, administration of special medications, catheterization, wound care, and physical, occupational, and speech therapy all can be provided at home by licensed nurses and therapists working under the supervision of your relative's physician. A home health care agency will assess your parent's needs and coordinate a customized package of in-home services, which may include visits by registered nurses, licensed practical nurses, personal care aides, homemakers, therapists, and social workers. Agency fees vary and usually are charged by the visit or by the hour. Some physician-prescribed home health services provided to homebound patients are covered by Medicare, Medicaid, and other health insurance. That may include the use of durable medical equipment and assistive devices such as hospital beds, oxygen, wheelchairs, and walkers. The Directory of Resources lists several of the largest national home health care chains, along with organizations that provide information and referrals. See Checklist #3 for quality considerations in selecting a home health care agency.

 ## CHECKLIST #3: EVALUATING HOME HEALTH CARE AGENCIES

Even if a doctor, social worker, or hospital discharge planner recommends a particular home care agency, the final choice is up to you and your loved one. Find out as much as possible about a recommended agency by reviewing these quality considerations:

❑ **Is the agency licensed?**
Most states require licensing of home care agencies. Check with your Area Agency on Aging (see Appendix B) about your state's regulations.

health care agencies, home care aide organizations, and hospices. Contact the national office for the address and phone number of your state NAHC office. Most state offices maintain directories of home care agencies and can help you find appropriate providers.

Helpful Publication:
"How to Choose a Home Care Agency." Free brochure.

National Association of Meal Programs (NAMP)
101 North Alfred Street, Suite 202
Alexandria, VA 22314
703–548–5558
Fax: 703–548–8024
NAMP members include home-delivered meal programs such as Meals-on-Wheels, congregate meal programs, food banks, and organizations and businesses providing meal services to people in need. Phone for the location of meal programs in your area.

National Association of Nutrition and Aging Services Programs
2675 Forty-fourth Street, Suite 305
Grand Rapids, MI 49509
616–530–3250
Fax: 616–531–3103
If you are having trouble finding a local source of nutrition-related services, this professional organization of nutrition and other community-based care programs for the elderly may be able to help. Its main agency is the National Meals-on-Wheels Foundation (see below).

National Association of Professional Geriatric Care Managers (GCM)
1604 North Country Club Road
Tucson, AZ 85716
502–881–8008
Fax: 502–325–7925

Call or write this professional association of geriatric care managers for the names and credentials of care managers who can assess your relative's needs, design a care plan based on available community resources, and arrange for services to begin.

National Association of Social Workers
750 First Street NE, Suite 700
Washington, DC 20002–4241
202–408–8600
This professional association of social workers offers referrals to local social workers and therapists providing services to older adults and their families. Social workers can help older people who live alone maintain their independence with the use of community services and support. They also may be able to advise on income assistance for seniors as well as services designed to support family caregivers.

National Council on the Aging (NCOA)
Information Office
409 Third Street SW, Suite 200
Washington, DC 20024
202–479–6653 or 202–479–6654
Senior volunteers in NCOA's Information Office will answer questions on issues related to aging services and adult day care or refer you to organizations that can, within the council and elsewhere. NCOA is an association of organizations and individuals that work with or on behalf of older adults.

National Meals-on-Wheels Foundation
2675 Forty-fourth Street SW, Suite 305
Grand Rapids, MI 49509
1–800–999–6262
Meal-on-Wheels programs serve more than a million meals a day to the homebound and at congregate sites. Home-delivered meals may be available free or for a small charge, once or twice a day, weekdays only or on weekends too, all depending on the local program. Meals-on-Wheels programs are supported by federal and/or charitable funds

and usually are organized by community religious or social service organizations. Call the 800 number to locate the program serving your relative's area.

Presbyterian Church USA

100 Witherspoon Street
Louisville, KY 40202–1396
502–569–5000

The Presbyterian Older Adult Ministry Network is made up of healthy, active retirees who volunteer to provide services and spiritual support for older people who are living in their own homes and need help to remain independent. Phone for information on support programs in your parent's community and for the name and number of the local Older Adult Ministry resource person.

PRIDE Foundation

391 Long Hill Road
P.O. Box 1293
Groton, CT 06340–1293
860–445–1448 or 860–445–7320

For the older person who has difficulty dressing, this nonprofit agency will modify off-the-rack clothing, for example, by replacing buttons with Velcro fasteners, attaching easy-grip zippers, and adapting styles for the comfort and ease of wheelchair users. Also available are custom-designed clothing patterns, plus advice and assistance for solving special problems with sewing, crafts, grooming, and home management.

Helpful Publication:
"Resources and Clothing for Special Needs." Listing of services, catalogs, books, and other resources devoted to special clothing and grooming needs of the elderly and disabled. $3.50.

Shepherd's Centers of America

6700 Troost Avenue, Suite 616
Kansas City, MO 64131
1–800–547–7073 or 816–523–1080

E-mail: shepherd@qni.com

via Internet: http://www.qni.com/~shepherd

If you are having trouble finding needed services in your area, this organization may be able to help. Ninety Shepherd's Centers nationwide try to fill the gaps in community services to seniors and caregivers. Phone the 800 number to locate a nearby center, which will help you find local sources of assistance.

United Methodist Communications InfoServe

P.O. Box 320

Nashville, TN 37202–0320

1–800–251–8140

Phone this toll-free information and referral service of the United Methodist Church for the names and phone numbers of local Volunteers in Mission—retired registered nurses who volunteer to provide short-term in-home care. The service also will give you the addresses and phone numbers of local clergy, who can tell you about other community programs for seniors.

United Way of America

701 North Fairfax Street

Alexandria, VA 22314–2045

703–836–7100

Many local United Way organizations operate or support information and referral services designed to put callers in touch with community resources that provide services for the elderly and for people with disabilities. Your local United Way may be able to help you locate family counseling services; medical, rehabilitation, and mental health programs; emergency food and shelter; and programs providing help with housing, rent, utility payments, and a range of other individual and family needs. Look in your phone directory or contact the national office to locate your nearest United Way.

Visiting Nurse Associations of America

3801 East Florida Avenue, Suite 900

Denver, CO 80210

1–800–426–2547 or 1–888–866–8773

46

More than 580 nonprofit community-based Visiting Nurse Associations (VNAs) operate in forty-five states. Visiting Nurses, working with the patient's doctor, provide an array of home health care services, including skilled nursing care, therapy, mental health nursing, nutrition counseling, administration of medications, medical social work and counseling, homemaker and chore services, and hospice care. Many local VNAs also work with community groups to offer special services such as volunteer senior companions and home-delivered meals. Phone the 800 number to locate a nearby VNA office.

REGIONAL

Organizations on this list provide services in limited geographic areas. You may be able to find groups offering similar services in your relative's community.

Aging in America
1500 Pelham Parkway South
Bronx, NY 10461
718–824–4004
A wealth of in-home services are available free of charge or for a small annual membership fee to older people in the Bronx through Aging in America's seven senior centers. Staff will assess clients' individual needs, develop a plan of coordinated services, and help clients access services provided by the agency and through government entitlement programs. These services may include home care attendants, home-delivered meals or congregate meals at senior centers, nutrition counseling, adult day care, transportation, telephone reassurance, and information and referrals for dealing with legal and financial problems.

CARIE (Coalition of Advocates for the Rights of the Infirm Elderly)
1315 Walnut Street, Suite 1000
Philadelphia, PA 19107
215–545–5728
Fax: 215–545–5372

CARIE operates a free telephone consultation service that assists Philadelphia-area callers who need information about obtaining services and benefits or resolving health, legal, or financial problems. Telephone counselors will help you locate transportation for seniors; local health, mental health, nutritional, and in-home care services; and caregiver resources. Counselors speak English and Spanish. In addition, CARIE's Home Care Advocacy Project investigates and resolves complaints from area consumers of home and community-based long-term care services.

Citizens for Better Care
4750 Woodward Avenue, Suite 410
Detroit, MI 48201–1308
1–800–833–9548 or 313–832–6387
This nonprofit consumer advocacy organization will provide statewide referrals to adult day care programs.

Council for Jewish Elderly (CJE)
3003 West Touhy Avenue
Chicago, IL 60645
312–508–1000
Fax: 312–508–1028
This private not-for-profit organization provides a range of services to older people and their families in the Chicago area. Home and community-based services include care management, consultations and counseling, in-home health care by registered nurses, housekeeping, personal care aides, home repairs, friendly visitors, home-delivered kosher meals, transportation, and in-home shopping. Phone for information on services and fees.

Jewish Association for Services for the Aged (JASA)
40 West Sixty-eighth Street
New York, NY 10023
212–724–3200
Serving adults age fifty-five and older of all faiths in New York City's five boroughs, JASA provides home-delivered kosher meals; referrals to local medical, social, and legal services; in-home counseling to resolve family problems and tensions; and

information on many topics related to aging and caregiving. Staff speaks English, Spanish, and Yiddish.

SageNet (Senior Action in a Gay Environment)

305 Seventh Avenue
New York, NY 10001
212–741–2247
Fax: 212–366–1947
E-mail: sageny@aol.com

SageNet is a network of twelve independent affiliate groups across the country committed to providing community services to older gay men and lesbians. The flagship organization in New York City offers free and/or low-cost services including geriatric care management and assistance in accessing medical, legal, and community services; friendly visitors and telephone reassurance; escort services; individual, family, and group psychotherapy; benefits counseling; and social and support programs. Contact the New York City office for information about the Sage network and the location of your nearest Sage office.

Supportive Older Women's Network (SOWN)

2805 North Forty-seventh Street
Philadelphia, PA 19131
215–477–6000
Fax: 215–477–6555

A nonprofit agency dedicated to helping women over age sixty cope with the issues of aging, SOWN establishes and maintains support groups for older women throughout the Philadelphia area.

Home Health Care Agencies

Following are addresses and phone numbers for several of the largest private home health care agencies. Inclusion on this list is not intended as an endorsement or recommendation of any particular company. See Checklist #3 for guidelines on evaluating private home health care agencies.

Integrated Health Services/
First American Health Care
4541 Altama Avenue
Brunswick, GA 31520
1-800-777-6876

This organization has four hundred and fifty agencies in twenty-three states across the country.

Interim Services
2050 Spectrum Boulevard
Fort Lauderdale, FL 33309
954-938-7600

There are more than four hundred offices throughout the United States.

Kelly Assisted Living Services
999 West Big Beaver Road
Troy, MI 48084
1-800-541-9818

Kelly has ninety-eight branch offices nationwide.

Olsten Kimberly QualityCare
175 Broadhollow Road
Melville, NY 11747
1-800-666-8773

Formed by a merger of Olsten HealthCare, Kimberly Quality Care, and Upjohn HealthCare Services, this group has about six hundred offices throughout North America.

EMERGENCY RESPONSE SYSTEMS

Following are addresses and phone numbers for several of the largest national emergency response system (ERS) suppliers. An area hospital should be able to give you additional referrals to local ERS service providers.

American Medical Alert Corporation
3265 Lawson Boulevard
Oceanside, NY 11572
1–800–645–3244 or 516–536–5850
Fax: 516–536–5276

"BEEP-ALARM"
P.O. Box 9669
Marina Del Rey, CA 90295
1–800–359–4554

Lifeline Systems
640 Memorial Drive
Cambridge, MA 02139–4851
1–800–543–3546

Persys Medical Division
Amcest Corporation
1017 Walnut Street
Roselle, NJ 07203–9990
1–800–631–7370 or 201–241–6500

Other Helpful Free or Low-Cost Publications

"Community Services for Older People Living at Home." Free brochure. Send a self-addressed stamped envelope to: American Association of Homes and Services for the Aging, 901 E Street NW, Suite 500, Washington, DC 20004–2011.

"A Consumer Guide to Home Health Care." Guide describes the types, providers, and costs of home health services; includes consumer checklist. $4.00. Contact: National Consumers League, 1701 K Street NW, Suite 1200, Washington, DC 20006 (202–835–3323).

"The DoAble, Renewable Home: Making Your Home Fit Your Needs." Order #D12470. Free booklet. Contact: AARP

Fulfillment, 601 E Street NW, Washington, DC 20049 (1–800–424–3410).

"Increasing Your Safety: What We Have Learned About Falls in the Elderly." Free brochure on results of research into decreasing the risk of falls. Send a self-addressed stamped business-size envelope to: Center for Locomotion Studies, Room 10 IM Building, Pennsylvania State University, University Park, PA 16802.

"Safety for Older Consumers: Home Safety Checklist." Order #701 (in Spanish, #701S). Free 30-page booklet with room-by-room tips on eliminating potential safety hazards throughout the house. Send a postcard with name, address, and publication title and number to: U.S. Consumer Product Safety Commission Publication Request, Washington, DC 20207.

"Staying at Home: A Guide to Long-Term Care and Housing." Order #D14986. Free 48-page booklet. Contact: AARP Fulfillment, 601 E Street NW, Washington, DC 20049 (1–800–424–3410).

Chapter Three

Housing
Options

The doctor and the social worker from the hospital recommended this nursing home. It was a horrible place. The staff was not sufficient for the amount of people needing care. The people that you thought were nurses were not nurses, and they were administering medical care. Every day I went, there were about five things I had to do just to make her comfortable. She was in there for nine days and she hadn't had a shower; they hadn't changed the dressing on her wound. Right now she's in a different nursing home. Another social worker at the hospital gave me a whole list of places to go and I went around to all of them and put in a couple of applications, then the bed came up and I brought her there. It was very nice, cheerful and clean, and the aides seemed to be very helpful. They have a young lady that does the activities. They do a Jeopardy! *game, and they have people come in and play a piano or sing. She'll encourage them to talk about cooking or whatever; one day they made pizza. I mean, nothing's perfect. I don't expect to find perfect. But they do try.*

Moving On

The time may come when, even with extensive support services, your relative cannot or should not remain at home. Perhaps the neighborhood has deteriorated or the house has become too difficult or costly to maintain.

Community resources may be inadequate. Your parent may feel isolated and tired of trying to cope alone or may be in need of extensive nursing care.

Many people assume the only alternatives for an older person who is no longer able to live at home are moving in with an adult child or finding a nursing home. In fact, there are many other housing choices. Each provides a different level of support. Each has its pros and cons.

It is important not to wait for a crisis before investigating your parent's options. Finding, evaluating, and comparing alternative housing takes time, and the most attractive places often have long waiting lists. Giving up home, with its privacy, familiarity, nearby friends, and precious memories, is a painful decision. Discussing alternatives, preferences, and priorities early, before an immediate need arises, can give your parent time to prepare emotionally for the move.

You may want to use Checklist #7 as a conversation starter. The chart offers a capsule glance at the advantages and disadvantages of different housing options. To explore an option thoroughly, review the descriptions under "Alternative Living Arrangements." Then see this chapter's Directory of Resources for organizations providing detailed information, guidance, and local referrals.

Alternative Living Arrangements

The housing market for older adults is complex and constantly developing. Even the terms used to describe various housing options may be confusing. One area's "adult foster home" is another's "home for the aged." Assisted living facilities may be called "board and care homes," "adult care homes," or "residential care facilities." In the following overview of different types of adult housing facilities, we have used commonly accepted terms and also listed frequently used variations.

Joint Living with Adult Children

Don't jump to the conclusion that Mom or Dad would be happiest living with you. For some families, joining households may be the best possible arrangement, but for others, that same "solution" can turn into a nightmare.

"This is not the time to think positively," cautions former nurse Jill Watt. "Don't wait until after the move to consider any possible

54

problems." For you as caregiver, those problems might include intrusions on your privacy and personal space, loss of free time and spontaneity, excessive demands on time and energy, incompatible habits and lifestyles, the reawakening of old parent-child issues, conflicts between your parent and your spouse or children, and unanticipated financial burdens. Your parent may regret the loss of privacy and independence, miss friends and neighbors, and feel uncomfortable with your household's noise level, lifestyle, and habits. For all involved, a joint living arrangement requires major adjustments.

Before inviting your loved one to move in, carefully consider whether you have the space to ensure adequate privacy for all family members. When an extra room or other suitable living quarters are unavailable, some families add a room or an attached apartment, and some pool their resources to move into a larger home together. Perhaps it would be more sensible for you or a brother or sister to move in with your parent. Perhaps your parent could take turns living with you and your siblings.

If you do decide to join households, it is essential that all involved in the arrangement, including your parent and your spouse and children, join in a frank and thorough discussion of potential problems and solutions. Issues to explore include who will be responsible for your parent's care and transportation needs, how household tasks and expenses will be divided, and household rules and accommodations in shared living areas. As you explore these issues, be honest with yourself about your feelings and motivations. For a joint living arrangement to work—for all sides to feel the benefits—it must be something you want to do, not something you feel you should do out of duty, guilt, or sentiment.

Staying Home by Scaling Down

One sensible course for an older person who is relatively healthy and independent but can no longer manage a large home may be moving to a smaller house, rental apartment, or condominium or cooperative apartment. Having your parent close by but not under the same roof allows you to help out and spend time together while both households maintain their privacy and independence. If your relative is considering such a move, here are some questions to ask when deciding on a new home and community:

- Is the neighborhood safe?

- Is the new home close enough to family for convenience without being so close that either parent or child feels intruded upon?

- Will your parent be close to old friends or among people who might offer new friendships?

- Is transportation available to medical facilities, favorite stores, recreational activities, a place of worship, and other important sites?

- Will the new home accommodate cherished pets and belongings?

- Are bathroom and bedroom easily accessible?

- Is housing available and affordable?

- Are rent subsidies, fuel assistance, property tax breaks, or other housing assistance available? Check with the Area Agency on Aging (see Appendix B) for information on eligibility requirements in the new locale.

ECHO Housing

Elder Cottage Housing Opportunity, or ECHO housing, involves the placement of a prebuilt, self-contained cottage in the back or side yard of a single-family home. Called "granny flats" in Australia, where the idea originated, ECHO housing allows parents to live close to adult children while retaining privacy for all. Housing units include barrier-free features for older or disabled people, and they can be designed to fit in with local building styles and to match the siding, roofing, and other features of the home already on the property. Some units can be rented and removed when no longer needed. Costs for ECHO housing vary but are less than those involved in building a new home. According to the American Association of Retired Persons, many manufacturers offer completely installed, five-hundred-square-foot, one-bedroom units for less than $25,000. Zoning laws prohibit ECHO housing in some areas. Contact your State Unit on Aging (see Appendix B) and local zoning board for information on zoning requirements and housing manufacturers.

Homesharing

With homesharing, either your relative moves in with someone other than you or your siblings, or someone moves in to share your relative's house or apartment. That "someone" might be a college student, a young family, another healthy and independent older person, or a relative such as your parent's brother or sister. Housemates may share household chores and expenses, or your parent may offer free or reduced rent in exchange for housework, yard work, repairs, shopping, errands, and other chores. This living arrangement can allow an older person to remain independent in a home setting, with services, companionship, and possibly extra-income needs satisfied.

Many senior centers, community social service agencies, and private agencies run shared housing programs that screen and match housemates according to needs and mutual preferences. To find these programs, check with the Area Agency on Aging (see Appendix B), look in the local phone directory, or scan for ads in your parent's local newspaper. First matches don't always work out, but with persistence and a willingness to make some compromises, your parent may find a compatible, life-enriching partnership. You can help by ensuring that all responsibilities and financial arrangements are spelled out in writing in a contract or lease agreement. Also check local zoning laws to make sure this type of multifamily living arrangement is permitted.

Accessory Apartments

In this variation on homesharing, your parent's house is remodeled to include a self-contained apartment with separate entrance. The apartment can be rented out to generate extra income or the tenant may exchange services for free or reduced rent. Construction costs vary. Some homes may need expensive remodeling to add an accessory unit, while others may require only minor changes. Check local zoning laws before planning renovations, and make sure details of the living arrangement are spelled out in the rental agreement.

Adult Foster Care

For older adults who are frail but in reasonably good health, adult foster care homes provide lodging, meals, supervision, and some nonmedical personal care such as help with bathing, dressing, and taking medications. Most homes are privately owned and operated, housing from one to twenty people. Adult foster care often is offered by a family that owns a large house and needs the income provided by the monthly fee. If the home is listed with a social service organization, state law may require that a licensed social worker or other professional working as a geriatric care manager monitor care.

Medicare does not cover this type of care, but Medicaid may pay partial costs. Contact your Area Agency on Aging (see Appendix B) or department of social services for information and listings of nearby facilities.

Congregate Housing

Congregate or senior housing includes retirement hotels and retirement apartments. A residence in a retirement hotel usually consists of a bedroom, a bathroom, and sometimes a small living area. Retirement apartments may be studio, one-bedroom, or two-bedroom units, often with a small kitchenette, in high-rises or garden complexes. One or more daily meals are served in a central dining area. Housekeeping services, recreational programs, group transportation, counseling, and security services usually are available. In most cases residents are expected to get around unassisted and handle their own personal care, but most facilities are equipped with bathroom grab bars, handrails, and other design features for older residents. Many also are set up with twenty-four-hour emergency call service.

Congregate housing facilities may be sponsored by nonprofit or for-profit agencies. Rental rates vary considerably. Some facilities are federally subsidized, with specific low-income requirements; rent in these units is set at about one-third of income. Long waiting lists are typical for subsidized housing, so if you anticipate a need, it's wise to get your relative's name on the list early.

To locate congregate housing, check with your State Unit on Aging or Area Agency on Aging (see Appendix B), long-term care ombudsman (Appendix C), local senior center, or local housing authority. When helping your parent select this type of housing, visit facilities and ask residents for their impressions. Look for convenient transportation, meal accommodations for special diets, stimulating recreational and social activities, and adequate security.

Retirement Communities

These housing complexes developed exclusively for older adults may include apartment buildings, condominiums, cooperatives, townhouses, mobile homes, or single-family dwellings. Many retirement communities offer a communal dining hall, maid and linen service, group transportation, recreational activities, and security services. Some are campuslike mini-villages, with shops, health spas, health care facilities, and other amenities all on the grounds. Costs for buying or renting housing in retirement communities vary according to location and the quality of housing and services. Some complexes require an initial investment, which may or may not be refundable, in addition to monthly rent.

Assisted Living Facilities

This relatively new form of supportive housing goes by many names, including "board and care homes," "personal care homes," "residential care facilities," "domiciliary care," "sheltered care," "adult care homes," and "adult congregate living facilities." In general, these are places for older adults who need some assistance with daily living activities but do not require skilled nursing care. Many facilities will admit only residents who are mentally alert and able to deal with any bladder or bowel control problems on their own. Some do not accept people who use wheelchairs or walkers.

Services offered by assisted living facilities vary greatly, but many provide physical assistance, supervision, or reminders with bathing, dressing, grooming, eating, getting in and out of bed, and taking medications. Meals, housekeeping, and laundry services usually are included, and facilities often offer transportation, twenty-four-hour security and staff availability, emergency call systems in residents' units, and some social and recreational activities. Accommodations vary from single rooms to full apartments; personal living quarters often are furnished by the residents themselves. Small, familylike homes may have fewer than ten residents, while large ones may have one hundred or more.

Assisted living facilities are operated by both for-profit and nonprofit organizations. They may be part of senior housing facilities, retirement communities, or nursing homes, or they may stand alone. Monthly costs range all the way from a few hundred dollars to more than three thousand dollars. Medicare does not cover assisted living facility costs, but in some states Medicaid will pay for some services, or funding may be available for low-income seniors.

Most assisted living facilities are regulated and licensed by the state. However, inspections and quality assurance measures often are not strictly enforced. In some areas and under some circumstances, homes may be operated without any government scrutiny at all. To make sure your relative will be treated well, carefully inspect several different homes. Always include at least one unscheduled visit to each place you are considering. Checklist #8 can help you evaluate and compare facilities. Once you have made a selection, be sure to ask for a copy of the facility's resident contract and have it reviewed by a lawyer before signing. After your relative has moved in, try to visit frequently, scheduling your visits for different times of the day and week, to monitor the quality of care.

Continuing Care Retirement Communities

The continuing care retirement community (CCRC), or life care community, is a special kind of retirement community that offers several levels of care. Like other retirement communities, CCRCs often are campuslike settings with amenities such as dining rooms, shops, libraries, postal services, exercise and game rooms, and recreational facilities. Most people joining the community move into an independent living unit, which may be a cottage, a townhouse, a single-family dwelling, or a studio, one-, or two-bedroom apartment in a high-rise or garden complex. Supportive services typically available to these healthy, active residents include housekeeping, laundry, some meals, scheduled transportation, counseling and social services, security services, twenty-four-hour emergency assistance, and recreational, cultural, and educational programs. Health care services commonly are available through on-site primary and specialty physicians, nurses, therapists, dentists, and pharmacies, sometimes housed in one central health clinic. There are no restrictions on lifestyle; residents who are able to live independently often continue to travel and remain active outside the community.

If and when their care needs increase, CCRC residents may move to an assisted living unit, which may be located in a separate building or wing of a building within the community. Personal care staff in the assisted living unit provide assistance with daily living activities such as bathing, dressing, eating, grooming, toileting, and taking medications. If the need arises for short-term or long-term skilled nursing care, residents move to an infirmary or nursing facility located within the CCRC or close by. Some CCRCs also have special assisted living or nursing units for people with Alzheimer's disease or other dementing illnesses.

The unique appeal of the CCRC is that, as residents grow older, their long-term health care needs are met in a single, familiar setting. There's no need to go through the emotional turmoil of selecting and moving to a new care facility. Older couples are comforted by the knowledge that both wife and husband can continue to live in the same community, even if one remains independent and the other needs nursing home care.

Most CCRCs require a substantial entry or endowment fee, which may or may not be refundable, plus monthly payments. According to the American Association of Retired Persons, entry fees range from $50,000 to $250,000, depending on the quality of housing and the extent of services and health care covered. Some communities operate under rental arrangements, with no entry fee. Under these plans the rental payments cover housing plus certain specified services; these monthly fees are likely to be higher than those paid under the entry-fee-plus-monthly-fee arrangement. A few CCRCs offer ownership arrangements, in which residents purchase a membership or share in the community. The fee arrangement that is best for your relative will depend on her or his individual financial situation; an attorney or financial adviser can help make that determination. CCRCs often have long waiting lists and restrictions on eligibility. Many require a review of prospective residents' medical and financial records.

To join a CCRC, your relative must sign a contract or resident agreement that secures living accommodations and services. The three most common types of contracts are:

1. **Extensive contracts.** These include housing, residential services, and unlimited long-term nursing care, which is provided for little or no increase in monthly payments.

2. **Modified contracts.** This type of contract includes housing, residential services, and a specified amount of long-term nursing care, beyond which residents pay for care on a daily basis.

3. **Fee-for-service contracts.** Under this arrangement only housing and residential services are included. Residents pay daily rates for all health care, including assisted living services and long-term nursing care.

CCRC contracts are complicated documents involving a major long-term financial commitment. They should be reviewed by an attorney or financial adviser familiar with elder law issues. Also ask your relative's attorney to investigate the CCRC's financial statements and cash reserves. Some communities have gone bankrupt, taking residents' up-front fees with them.

To evaluate and compare CCRCs, you and your relative should visit several different communities, touring all facilities, including health care centers. Ask staff and residents for their opinions on lifestyle, services, and quality of care. Your parent may want to spend a few days in rented guest quarters to get a sense of daily life in the community. Checklist #9 includes additional points to consider and questions to ask. Also check the facility's complaint record and reputation with the state or local long-term care ombudsman (see Appendix C), local consumer affairs offices, and local Better Business Bureau (see Directory of Resources).

Nursing Homes

The decision to seek nursing home care for a loved one can be agonizing. You may feel like a failure for "putting Mom or Dad away." Perhaps you've promised your loved one (or yourself) that such a time would never come. The fact is, though, that for some older people, especially those who need twenty-four-hour care, a nursing home may be the best, safest, even the only choice.

That choice may be thrust on you, as when your parent is transferred from a hospital to a nursing home to convalesce after a sudden illness, accident, or operation. Or it may come gradually, with the slow deterioration of your parent's condition and your capacity to give proper care. In either case try to involve others in the decision. Include your loved one to the fullest extent possible, as well as other family members. Enlist a doctor, social worker, and/or geriatric care manager to help you decide when nursing home care is warranted. Also ask yourself these questions:

- Does my loved one need twenty-four-hour care and supervision?
- Is he or she chronically ill yet not sick enough to require the intensive care a hospital provides?
- Is help needed with daily living activities such as bathing, dressing, toileting, eating, and walking?
- Am I unable or no longer able to provide care and attention that improves my loved one's quality of life without threatening my own physical or mental health or family life?
- Is there no one else in the family who can take over the job of providing proper at-home care?

If you answered yes to most of these questions, you and your relative most likely have reached the point when nursing home care should be considered.

LEVELS OF CARE
Nursing homes provide two different levels of care:

1. Skilled nursing care
This is for people who need twenty-four-hour care by registered nurses, licensed practical nurses, and nurse's aides. Patients receiving skilled nursing care often are recovering from an operation or an illness previously treated in a hospital. Medicare pays for short-term skilled nursing care under certain conditions. Private long-term care insurance may cover some additional costs.

2. Intermediate custodial care

Also called "health-related care," this is for people who are not in need of skilled nursing care but cannot live independently, due to a disability or severe chronic illness. These patients require some personal nursing attention, medical aid, and a protective environment. Medicare and private health insurance rarely cover health-related care. Residents often enter a nursing home paying for care from their own income and savings, then apply for Medicaid to cover costs once their financial resources have been depleted. Most private nursing homes give private-pay residents preference over Medicaid recipients. That practice is illegal in some states. Even so, you could have difficulty finding a nursing home if your parent already is on Medicaid. For a further discussion of nursing home costs and payment options, see Chapter 4, "Planning to Pay for Care."

SEARCH AND SELECTION

Finding a good nursing home can be extremely difficult. No nursing home is perfect, and far too many provide substandard care. A 1995 *Consumer Reports* investigation found that "facilities allow life-threatening bedsores to develop, violate residents' dignity, fail to produce required care plans, [and] improperly use physical restraints." The report concluded, "The quality of care at thousands of the nation's nursing homes is poor or questionable at best."

Your parent is less likely to end up in a bad nursing home if you begin investigating options early. If future nursing home care seems likely, don't let an emergency force a hurried selection. Begin your search now, to get your parent's name on the long waiting lists typically found at the best facilities. A good way to start is to ask for recommendations from your parent's doctor, hospital staff, a social worker, a geriatric care manager, clergy, and friends. Your Area Agency on Aging (see Appendix B), state or local long-term care ombudsman (Appendix C), state or local health department, and some professional and consumer service organizations (see Directory of Resources) can provide lists of facilities in a specific area. Nursing homes may be owned and operated by government agencies, nonprofit organizations such as religious or community groups, or for-profit corporations. The form of ownership is no indicator of quality. You will have to judge each facility on its own merits.

Use the phone to eliminate some of the names from your list. Ask about vacancies, admission requirements, levels of care provided, and participation in Medicare and Medicaid programs. Make appointments to visit the places still under consideration, with your relative if possible. Then visit again, unannounced, several times. The U.S. Department of Health and Human Services recommends visiting at different times of the day, scheduling "one visit . . . during late morning or midday so you can observe whether people are out of bed, and, if possible, whether the noon meal is being served. You should also plan to visit during the afternoon to observe activities, as well as during and after the evening meal and evening hours." Ask residents for their opinion of the nursing home, and look for signs of neglect. Evaluate the quality of care and concern shown by staff. Use Checklist #10 to guide your observations and record information. Some questions on the list can be answered through your interviews with staff, others through your own observations.

After you have made your inspections, ask the facilities you are considering for a list of references, and speak to residents' families about their satisfaction with the care their loved one is receiving. Review contracts carefully, and consult a lawyer or your long-term care ombudsman if any elements seem unclear or questionable.

Once your loved one is settled in a nursing home, try to visit regularly, and ask other family members and friends to visit, too. Your visits not only reassure and cheer your parent, they also tell the home's staff that you are monitoring the quality of care. You can help the staff see your parent as an individual by sharing personal information. Post a copy of your "Parent Profile" (Appendix A), and talk to staff members about what your loved one likes—music, gardening, reading, sports, and so on. Get involved in the development of the home's plan of care for your relative, and, if possible, join or form a family council—a group of family members who meet periodically with nursing home staff to discuss mutual concerns and problems. In these ways you may be able to make an impact on the facility's policies and day-to-day practices, ensuring that your loved one enjoys a better quality of life.

When Problems Develop with Nursing Home Care

If you are dissatisfied with the quality of care your loved one is receiving in a nursing home, the New York–based association Friends and Relatives of Institutionalized Aged recommends these steps:

1. **Define and document the problem.** Try to be concrete when describing incidents. Give the date, time, place, and staff members involved. Note what action you took as well as actions taken by the staff

2. **Work out a solution.** Keep records of what corrective measures were promised and by whom. Make a detailed list of the actions planned to correct the problem. Set up a timetable for changes, and document results, both positive and negative.

3. **Get support from appropriate sources.** If changes are not made in a timely fashion, bring up the issue with the family council. Other sources of assistance include your state or local long-term care ombudsman (see Appendix C) and state or local department of health.

 CHECKLIST #7: PROS & CONS OF ALTERNATIVE HOUSING OPTIONS FOR OLDER ADULTS

OPTION	ADVANTAGES	DISADVANTAGES
Living with adult children	Most or all daily needs are met	Loss of privacy & independence
	Companionship; opportunity to be close to grandchildren	Isolation from friends & familiar places
	Safety & security	Potential conflicts with children & grandchildren
	Shared household chores & expenses (may benefit both parent & child)	House may be crowded, too hot or cold, or otherwise uncomfortable

OPTION	ADVANTAGES	DISADVANTAGES
		Children may expect parent to serve as built-in babysitter
ECHO housing	Privacy & independence Companionship; proximity to family Greater safety & security than completely independent living	Cost of building or renting unit is less than building a new home but greater than some other housing options May increase taxes on existing home Zoning laws may prohibit in some areas Space limitations & lack of utility connections prohibit in some areas
Homesharing (shared housing)/ Accessory apartment	Semi-independence, with shared household chores and/ or expenses; possibly additional income Companionship; new relationships Greater safety & security than completely independent living	Some loss of privacy Possible conflicts with mismatched housemates Remodeling to add accessory apartment can be expensive Zoning laws prohibit in some areas
Congregate housing/ Senior housing (retirement hotels, retirement apartments, retirement homes, rest homes)	Independence, with meal & housekeeping assistance Companionship; social & recreational activities Group transportation often available Security services often available Rent subsidies may be available	Some facilities may not accommodate special dietary needs Some facilities have restrictions on bringing own furniture, pets, or on ages of visitors or visitor hours Long waiting lists at many subsidized facilities Rents at nonsubsidized facilities may be high

OPTION	ADVANTAGES	DISADVANTAGES
Retirement communities	Independence, with services such as group dining, housekeeping often available Companionship; social & recreational activities Group transportation often available Security offices often available	Possible age restrictions on residents or long-term visitors Costs can be high In some cases initial investment fee is not refundable if resident leaves
Assisted living facilities (board & care homes/ personal care homes/ residential care facilities/ adult care homes/ adult homes/ domiciliary care homes/ adult congregate living facilities/ sheltered care)	Semi-independence, with medical & personal care assistance Companionship; social & recreational activities Transportation may be available Safety & security 24-hour emergency assistance usually available	Costs often are high Often poorly regulated; some facilities are unlicensed & unregulated
Adult foster care homes	Meals & some personal care provided Companionship Safety & security	Transportation & recreational activities generally not available May be little supervision of quality of care
Continuing care retirement communities	Privacy & independence with health care & needed services available Companionship; social & recreational activites Scheduled transportation often available	Entry & monthly fees can be very expensive May require substantial up-front investment, which may be nonrefundable Long waiting lists at many facilities

Option	Advantages	Disadvantages
	24-hour emergency assistance often available	Financial & health restrictions
Nursing home	Health & personal care needs met	Loss of privacy & independence
	Companionship; social & recreational activities	Isolation from friends & familiar places
	Safety & security	Possible conflicts with mismatched roommates
	24-hour emergency assistance	Long waiting lists at best facilities
		Care in many facilities is poor or questionable
		Can be very expensive

 CHECKLIST #8: EVALUATING ASSISTED LIVING FACILITIES

Look for these quality considerations as you and your relative check out assisted living facilities:

❏ *Is the facility licensed by the state?*
Check with your state long-term care ombudsman (see Appendix C) for information on a facility's license status, services, and reputation. You should also ask the facility for a copy of its latest state inspection report, if your state requires inspections.

❏ *What are the staff's qualifications and training?*
Ask about minimum staffing requirements and whether staff members are trained to handle medical emergencies.

❏ *What services are provided?*
The contract should spell out exactly what services will be provided and

how often. Make sure the facility accommodates special dietary needs, and ask when meals and snacks are served.

❏ What are the accommodations?

Look over the room your relative might occupy, and ask whether furniture and other personal belongings may be brought from home. Would the same room or a similar one be available if your parent had to leave temporarily, such as for a short hospital stay? Also make sure arrangements for sharing bathrooms are acceptable.

❏ Will your parent have privacy?

In some facilities staff have the right to walk into individual living quarters at any time to check on residents or perform room inspections or maintenance.

❏ Is the facility clean, attractive, and safe?

Look for inviting general living and activity areas, open space for roaming, and adequate space for private talks with visitors. Safety features should include handrails, bathroom grab bars, nonskid floors, clearly marked exits, and well-lighted stairs and hallways. If your parent uses a wheelchair or walker, make certain doorways, hallways, and rooms are accessible.

❏ What kinds of activities are available and how often?

Recreational opportunities should match your parent's needs and interests. Observe and speak with residents to judge whether they seem to be appropriate companions for your loved one.

❏ Is transportation available to doctors' offices, shopping, the hairdresser or barber, a house of worship?

If there is no convenient public transportation, make sure you understand what transportation the facility will provide, when, and how much advance notice is required.

❏ What is the cost?

Find out what services are covered by the rent and what costs extra. The resident contract should specify how much advance notice is given before rate increases.

❑ *What happens if your relative's care needs increase?*
Can the facility accommodate the need for additional services? Ask about the terms and conditions under which residents can be required to leave the facility if their condition deteriorates, how much advance notice is given, and refund policies.

 CHECKLIST #9: EVALUATING CONTINUING CARE RETIREMENT COMMUNITIES

Here are questions to ask as you inspect and compare continuing care retirement communities:

❑ *Does the facility suit your relative's lifestyle?*
CCRCs may be homey and quiet or large and busy; dress for dinner may be formal or casual.

❑ *What facilities, activities, and non-health-related services are available?*
Ask about chore and maintenance services as well as security and emergency systems. Review a schedule of activities and entertainment to see if they match your relative's interests. Remember that a swimming pool, health club, or golf course is a plus only if your relative is likely to use it.

❑ *What health care services are available within the CCRC or nearby?*
You'll want to know what degree of health care and personal care are provided to residents in independent living units, how the decision is made to transfer residents to assisted living or nursing units, and what happens when health care services are required outside the community.

❑ *What is the meal plan?*
Ask how many daily meals are included, and look into hours, seating arrangements, serving style, and menu choices.

❑ *Is transportation available to needed services?*
Check out transportation schedules, restrictions, and costs.

❏ **What are the rules and regulations of the community?**

You should be able to review a copy of the resident handbook, which can tell you whether rules are reasonable as well as flexible.

❏ **Is there an active resident association?**

A well-organized association that meets periodically with management can ensure that residents' views are reflected in the way the community is run.

❏ **What living accommodations and non-health-related services are covered by the contract and what costs extra?**

Make sure you understand any limitations or restrictions in covered services.

❏ **What health care services are covered by the contract and what costs extra?**

Ask about fee arrangements when required care is not available in community facilities.

❏ **Are entry fees refundable?**

In some cases entry fees are fully refundable if a resident decides to leave within a specified trial period; in others fees may be refundable in part or on a declining scale over time, or completely nonrefundable.

❏ **What is the procedure for adjusting monthly fees?**

Find out if adjustments would be made if your parent transferred to other accommodations within the community. Also ask about the history of increases in monthly fees.

❏ **What insurance coverage will your relative be required to maintain or purchase when entering the community?**

Ask how existing insurance such as a long-term care policy would affect the agreement.

❏ **Is the community accredited?**

The American Association of Homes and Services for the Aging's

Continuing Care Accreditation Committee (see Directory of Resources) accredits CCRCs that voluntarily agree to meet its program and financial standards.

 ## Checklist #10: Evaluating Nursing Homes

You may want to make several copies of this checklist, to record and compare your findings at different homes. Tailor the list to your needs by penciling in any additional questions relevant to your loved one's physical condition, interests, and concerns.

General

❏ *Is the home licensed by the state?*

❏ *Is it Medicare- and Medicaid-certified?*
Medicare and Medicaid will only cover costs incurred in certified facilities. If your parent is likely to need Medicaid assistance at some future point, consider only Medicaid-certified facilities. (Also see Chapter 4, "Insurance: Government Programs.")

❏ *Can you see a copy of the most recent state inspection report?*
Nursing homes are required to make these surveys available to residents and the public, but many do not. Based on yearly inspections by state licensing agencies, inspection reports detail all deficiencies and violations of federal law involving health, safety, and quality of life. If a current report is unavailable through the facility, see Appendix D for the state agency to contact for a copy.

❏ *Is a statement of residents' rights displayed?*
This is required in many states. Compare the written statement with your own observations as you tour the facility.

Staff

❏ **Does the full-time staff include an administrator, a director of nursing, a social worker, and an activities director?**

The administrator must have a current license to run the facility. Ask about staff membership in professional associations; for example, the National Association of Activity Professionals promotes high-quality, life-enhancing activities for residents in long-term care facilities.

❏ **What is the ratio of nurses to residents? Nurse's aides to residents?**

Use staff-to-resident ratios to compare facilities; the more staff per patient, the better the quality of care is likely to be. Skilled nursing facilities should have at least one registered nurse or licensed practical nurse on duty at all times.

❏ **Is a doctor available or on call twenty-four hours a day?**

❏ **Are nurses' aides trained before hiring?**

Also find out if the facility provides or requires continuing education for nurses' aides.

Policies

❏ **Is there a policy limiting the use of physical restraints?**

Federal and, in many cases, state laws require nursing homes to assess each resident's condition, try all possible alternatives to restraints, and create a realistic plan to ensure safety when restraints are not used. If you see a high proportion of residents tied into wheelchairs or beds, take that as a warning flag, and ask what percentage of residents are generally restrained and why.

❏ **Are residents permitted to use their own personal physicians?**

❏ **How long will the home hold a bed for a resident who is hospitalized?**

❏ *What is the policy regarding involuntary discharges and transfers?*

❏ *How does the home match roommates and deal with problems of incompatibility?*

❏ *What are the visiting hours?*
Consider whether hours are convenient for residents and family, and whether they are flexible to suit special needs. Ask whether children are permitted to visit.

❏ *What procedures are followed when a resident's property is lost or stolen?*
Also ask about theft prevention measures.

❏ *Is there a resident council and, if so, does it influence decisions about resident life?*
A resident council may be organized by nursing home residents, family members, or staff to meet periodically to discuss concerns and recommend changes within the home. Ask about the last time the resident council requested that a problem be addressed and how the facility responded.

❏ *Is there a family council and, if so, does the nursing home respond to its concerns?*

Resident Care

❏ *Do residents appear well groomed and appropriately dressed?*
Observe if hair, nails, and clothes look clean and if the men are shaved.

❏ *Do staff appear to treat residents as individuals?*
Note if staff members address residents by name, knock before entering residents' rooms, and attend to personal needs, such as toileting or grooming, with respect for privacy. Do they treat residents with patience and courtesy, and offer comfort and affection?

❏ **Do staff respond promptly to residents' calls for assistance?**

Activities

❏ **Do posted activities seem interesting, varied, and appropriate?**
Check out the space and supplies available for activity programs. Ask if activities are sometimes scheduled outdoors and away from the home. Contact with community-based volunteer groups may add social stimulation to in-home and outside activities.

❏ **Are residents encouraged but not forced to participate in activities and offered assistance, if needed, in getting to the activity area?**
If you are able to observe an activity session, note whether most of the residents present are actually participating.

❏ **Are activities tailored to individual needs and interests?**
Look for activities suitable for residents who are mobile as well as for those who are relatively inactive or confined to their rooms.

❏ **Is there a library for resident use, an accessible public library, or a visiting bookmobile?**
If your relative is visually impaired, find out if publications are available in large print or on audiocassette.

❏ **Do residents have an opportunity to attend religious services?**

Services—Medical

❏ **Will you and your relative be invited to participate in developing the plan of care?**
Nursing homes are required by law to perform a comprehensive assessment of each resident's medical condition, abilities, limitations, and rehabilitation potential, which should serve as the basis for an individualized care plan. It is important that you (and your loved one, if possible)

attend the initial care planning meeting as well as periodic reviews, which should be held at least once every three months. You are entitled to voice your disagreement with any aspect of the plan. You also should be promptly notified of any changes in the plan of care or in your relative's condition.

❏ *Are there programs to restore lost physical functioning?*
These might include physical, occupational, or speech therapy and other special services. Even residents who do not require therapy should have daily exercise to stem physical and psychological decline.

❏ *Are there arrangements through outside services or on-staff medical consultants for dental, eye, and foot care?*

❏ *What medical situations are beyond the staff's capabilities, and what is the procedure for handling them?*
Ask for an explanation of the policy on hospital transfers and how medical emergencies are handled. Is emergency transportation readily available to a nearby hospital?

❏ *Is psychiatric or psychological counseling available?*

❏ *Are pharmaceutical services provided by a qualified pharmacist?*

Services—Nonmedical

❏ *Are meals nutritious and appetizing?*
Meals should be planned by a trained dietitian. Find out when meals and snacks are served and whether accommodations are made for special diets, religious dictates, and food likes and dislikes. Look at a posted menu, and visit at mealtime to see if meals match the menu. Observe if food looks and smells appetizing and if serving sizes are adequate. Ask to sample a meal for taste and temperature.

❏ *Are aides available to help residents who have trouble feeding themselves?*

Observe how this service is performed. Do aides seem patient or rushed?

❑ *Are meals delivered to the room for residents who cannot or do not come to the dining room?*

❑ *Is the dining room attractive and comfortable?*
Small tables provide a more homelike setting than large cafeteria-style tables. Ask if residents may choose their own seats at mealtime.

❑ *Is fresh drinking water always within reach?*

❑ *Are hairdresser and barber services available?*

❑ *Is transportation to doctors' offices and other outside sites available?*

Physical Environment

❑ *Is the facility clean, orderly, and free of strong odors?*
Unpleasant or overly perfumed or antiseptic odors can mean that the staff is inattentive to residents' toileting needs or that cleanup is inadequate.

❑ *Are safety features adequate?*
Look for handrails on both sides of hallways, grab bars in bathrooms, nonslip footing in bathtubs and showers, dry floors, and clutter-free halls and staircases. There should be easy-to-reach light switches and call buttons in bedrooms and bathrooms. Smoke detectors and fire extinguishers should be in place throughout the building. Exits should be clearly marked, exit doors unobstructed and easy to open.

❑ *Are all areas accessible to residents who are in wheelchairs or use walkers?*
Hallways should be wide enough to allow two wheelchairs to pass.

❑ *Are all rooms well lighted, well ventilated, and a comfortable temperature?*

❑ *Is furniture comfortable and practical?*

An overstuffed sofa or armless chair may look attractive but make it hard for an older person to rise.

❑ *Is there a comfortable lounge and/or activity room for reading, craft work, TV viewing, and social activities such as card games?*

Also look for private areas where residents can visit with family and friends.

❑ *Are residents' rooms pleasant and an adequate size?*

All bedrooms should open onto a hallway and have a window to the outside. Look for accessible storage areas for personal items. Ask if residents are permitted to bring personal belongings such as furniture, a TV, a radio, bedding, or plants to make their rooms more homelike. If bedrooms are shared, does a curtain or screen provide privacy? Are there telephones in residents' rooms or an accessible telephone in shared living areas?

❑ *Are bathrooms easy to get to?*

❑ *Are outdoor areas accessible for resident use?*

Costs and Payments

❑ *What are the basic rates and what services and supplies are included?*

Ask for a list of fees for services not covered in the basic rates.

❑ *Have fees increased significantly over the past few years?*

Ask whether residents and family are notified before fee increases.

❑ *What is the refund policy if a resident leaves in the middle of a month that has been paid in advance?*

Directory of Resources

Many of the agencies and organizations listed below provide referrals to and guidelines for selecting alternative housing options for older adults. Some groups also work to safeguard the rights of long-term care facility residents and to assist residents and families in resolving grievances.

NATIONAL

Organizations on this list offer their services nationwide or over a significant area of the country.

American Association of Homes and Services for the Aging (AAHSA)
901 E Street NW, Suite 500
Washington, DC 20004–2011
202–783–2242
Fax: 202–783–2255

A national association of some five thousand not-for-profit nursing homes, health-related facilities, and community service organizations for the elderly, AAHSA accredits continuing care retirement communities and will send a free list of facilities that meet its standards. Send a self-addressed stamped envelope to AAHSA Continuing Care Accreditation Commission at the address above.

Helpful Publications:
Send a self-addressed stamped envelope for each copy requested of these free brochures.

"Assisted Living: Offering Supportive Care for the Older Adult"

"Choosing a Nursing Home: A Guide to Quality Care"

"The Continuing Care Retirement Community: A Life Style Offering Security and Independence"

"Living Independently: Housing Choices for Older People"

80

American College of Health Care Administrators
325 South Patrick Street
Alexandria, VA 22314–3571
703–549–5822
Fax: 703–739–7901

For an unevaluated list of nursing homes in your older relative's or friend's area, contact this membership society of long-term care administrators.

American Health Care Association (AHCA)
1201 L Street NW
Washington, DC 20005–4014
202–842–4444
Fax: 202–842–3860

AHCA is a federation of fifty-one state health care organizations, whose members include more than eleven thousand licensed nursing homes and other long-term care facilities. About 85 percent of members are for-profit organizations. Contact the national office to locate your state association, which will provide unevaluated lists of long-term care facilities by county or other specified region, along with guidelines for choosing a nursing home.

Helpful Publications:
Contact the national office for single copies of these free booklets.

"Thinking About an Assisted Living or Residential Care Facility? A Consumer's Guide to Selection"

"Thinking About a Nursing Home? A Consumer's Guide to Long Term Care"

Assisted Living Facilities Association of America (ALFAA)
10300 Eaton Place, Suite 400
Fairfax, VA 22030
703–691–8100
Fax: 703–691–8106

A trade association of assisted living and board and care

facilities, ALFAA will send you an unevaluated list of facilities in your area.

Helpful Publication:
    "Assisted Living." Brochure includes overview of assisted living facilities plus comprehensive consumer checklist. $1.00.

B'nai Brith Center for Senior Housing and Services
1640 Rhode Island Avenue NW
Washington, DC 20036–3278
202–857–6581
Fax: 202–857–0980

B'nai Brith sponsors nonsectarian housing for low-income seniors in twenty-one communities. These large federally subsidized rental apartment complexes are planned and constructed by local B'nai Brith lodges. Group projects and activities encourage self-reliance and a sense of community. Contact the center for information on locations, services, and eligibility. In the near future B'nai Brith plans to expand its services to include assisted living facilities.

Council of Better Business Bureaus (CBBB)
4200 Wilson Boulevard
Arlington, VA 22003
703–276–0100
Fax: 703–525–8277

Your local Better Business Bureau can give you information on nursing homes and other long-term care facilities in the area, including whether consumers have reported problems and how any problems were resolved. Phone the CBBB to locate your local office.

Helpful Publications:
    "Tips on Continuing Care Retirement Communities." Order #07–24–287. $2.00.
    "Tips on Long-Term Nursing Home Care." Order #07–24–248. $2.00.

Department of Housing and Urban Development (HUD)

HUD Building, 451 Seventh Street SW
Room 6130
Washington, DC 20410
202–708–1422 or 202–708–2866

HUD provides funding for the development of supportive housing for older adults. Contact your nearest HUD field office for information on federally sponsored housing and federal rent subsidies. The national office can refer you to your local field office, or look in the phone directory under "United States Government, Department of Housing and Urban Development."

Eldercare Locator

1–800–677–1116

An operator at this nationwide directory assistance service operated by the National Association of Area Agencies on Aging will discuss housing alternatives and provide phone numbers for agencies that can supply lists of specific types of facilities in your area. When you phone, have ready the county and city or zip code of the area you're interested in.

Episcopal Society for Ministry on Aging

323 Wyandotte Street
Bethlehem, PA 18015–1527
610–868–5400

Phone for referrals to housing facilities for the aged, including nursing homes, assisted living facilities, retirement homes, and facilities for independent living. These facilities are associated with individual Episcopal churches but are open to all older adults, regardless of religious affiliation.

Joint Commission on Accreditation of Health Care Organizations

One Renaissance Boulevard
Oakbrook Terrace, IL 60181
630–916–5800

The Joint Commission evaluates and accredits U.S. health care organizations, including more than one thousand nursing homes and other long-term care facilities. Phone the number above for information about a facility's accreditation history and current accreditation status, which includes levels reflecting the degree to which the facility meets the commission's performance standards. To register a complaint regarding an accredited facility, phone 630–916–5642.

Helpful Publication:
"Helping You Choose Quality Long Term Care." Free leaflet.

National Accessible Apartment Clearinghouse (NAAC)
201 North Union Street, Suite 200
Alexandria, VA 22314
1–800–421–1221 or 703–518–6141
Fax: 703–518–6191

When a disabled person in need of an accessible apartment phones NAAC's toll-free number, the staff discusses what accessibility features the caller needs and in what metropolitan area, then conducts a search of NAAC's database for suitable apartments. The caller receives a list of all accessible apartments in the specified geographic area, with information on apartment features and local transportation. This service is free and covers more than one hundred major metropolitan areas in forty states.

National Caucus and Center of Black Aged (NCBA)
1424 K Street NW, Suite 500
Washington, DC 20005
202–637–8400
Fax: 202–347–0895

NCBA, a nonprofit interracial membership organization, develops and/or manages safe, affordable housing, including assisted living facilities, for low-income seniors in a number of states and the District of Columbia. Phone the main office for referrals to NCBA housing facilities in your area.

National Citizen's Coalition for Nursing Home Reform (NCCNHR)

1424 Sixteenth Street NW, Suite 202
Washington, DC 20036-2211
202-332-2275
Fax: 202-332-2949

Representing three hundred grassroots advocacy organizations across the country, this group lobbies to protect the rights and improve the quality of life of long-term care facility residents. Under a federal grant, the group also operates the National Long Term Care Ombudsman Resource Center, providing services to the state and regional ombudsmen who resolve complaints and advocate for nursing home residents. Contact NCCNHR to find local groups working to safeguard residents' rights or to order a packet on how to start and operate a resident council, written for nursing home residents and their families (cost: $15.00).

Nursing Home Information Service (NHIS)
National Council of Senior Citizens

8403 Colesville Road, 12th floor
Silver Spring, MD 20910
301-578-8938 or 301-578-8993
Fax: 301-578-8999

A nonprofit information and referral service for consumers of long-term care, their families, and their friends, NHIS will send listings of local nursing homes, retirement homes, and adult residential facilities.

Helpful Publications:
Phone for copies of these free brochures.
"How to Choose a Good Nursing Home." Also available in Spanish.
"Nursing Home Patients' Bill of Rights"

United Methodist Communications InfoServe
P.O. Box 320
Nashville, TN 37202–0320
1–800–251–8140

This information and referral service of the United Methodist Church will help you locate local churches, clergy, and United Methodist retirement homes.

REGIONAL

Organizations on this list provide services in limited geographic areas. You may be able to find groups offering similar services in your relative's community.

Advocates for Nursing Home Reform (ANHR)
16908 South Ridge Lane
Austin, TX 78734–1235
512–266–1961

This advocacy group will give you names and descriptions of nursing homes throughout Texas and tell you about any serious problems cited in state inspection reports. ANHR also helps residents and their families start support groups to work for improved conditions.

Aging in America
1500 Pelham Parkway South
Bronx, NY 10461
718–824–4004

For Bronx victims of fire, crime, and abuse, Aging in America offers comfortable, secure, temporary housing until permanent housing can be found. Residents must be age sixty or older and able to function independently.

California Advocates for Nursing Home Reform (CANHR)
1610 Bush Street
San Francisco, CA 94109
1–800–474–1116 or 415–474–5171
Fax: 415–474–2904

CANHR is a nonprofit association working to improve conditions in California long-term care facilities. Phone for information on the state's 1,400 nursing homes, plus facts and advice on residents' rights and preplacement issues. The association will provide a county-by-county list of all California nursing homes (cost: $2.00) and regional lists for mental health, intermediate care, respite care, ventilator, multiple sclerosis, and AIDS services (cost: $2.00). It also will help relatives and friends of nursing home residents form family councils. CANHR members receive a quarterly newsletter listing all citations issued against nursing homes statewide. Annual membership fee: $25.00.

Helpful Publications:
"Getting Involved in the Care Plan: A Guide for Family Members/Legal Representatives of Nursing Home Residents." Available in English, Spanish, and Chinese. $1.00.
"Organizing Family Councils in Long Term Care Facilities." $2.00.

CARIE (Coalition of Advocates for the Rights of the Infirm Elderly)
1315 Walnut Street, Suite 1000
Philadelphia, PA 19107
215–545–5728
Fax: 215–545–5372
Telephone consultants at CARIE will provide information about Philadelphia-area housing alternatives and nursing homes. The organization also sends volunteers as once-a-week friendly visitors to Philadelphia nursing home residents. For residents with complaints about quality of care, CARIE's Long-Term Care Ombudsman Program, sponsored by the Philadelphia Area Agency on Aging, offers dispute investigation and mediation.

Citizen Advocates for Nursing Home Residents
4565 North 126th Street
P.O. Box 104
Butler, WI 53007–0104

414–783–7161
Fax: 414–781–6565

Wisconsin residents may contact this nonprofit organization for advice on choosing a nursing home, ensuring quality care, and forming a family council. The organization also provides information on relevant state laws, residents' rights, and state agencies responsible for handling complaints.

Citizens for Better Care
4750 Woodward Avenue, Suite 410
Detroit, MI 48201–1308
1–800–833–9548 or 313–832–6387

A statewide nonprofit consumer advocacy group for individuals who need long-term care, Citizens for Better Care will provide lists of nursing homes, adult foster care homes, homes for the aged, assisted living facilities, subsidized housing, and senior apartments in any Michigan county. The group also can refer you to adult day care programs, provide copies of the state licensing reports for specific nursing homes, and help resolve complaints from long-term care facility residents and their families and friends.

Helpful Publications:
Phone the 800 number for a complete listing of publications, plus ordering information for the following booklets and fact sheets.

"Guide to Admission Procedures and Contracts in Michigan Nursing Homes." Order #12. $2.00.

"A Guide to Filing Complaints with the Michigan Department of Public Health." 25¢.

"Staffing Requirements in Michigan Nursing Homes." 25¢.

"Your Rights as a Nursing Home Resident in Michigan." Order #06. $1.50.

Citizens for Quality Nursing Home Care
P.O. Box 56041
New Orleans, LA 70156
504–586–1627

If you are looking for a nursing home in the metropolitan New Orleans area, this all-volunteer advocacy organization offers advice and referrals to area facilities. While the group does not rate or recommend specific homes, it will give indications of conditions and problems.

Helpful Publication:
"Guide to Selecting a Nursing Home in Louisiana."
Free 26-page handbook.

Coalition of Institutionalized Aged and Disabled (CIAD)
Hunter-Brookdale Center on Aging
425 East Twenty-fifth Street
New York, NY 10010
212–481–4348
Fax: 212–481–5069

This nonprofit organization helps organize, guide, and support adult home and nursing home resident councils. Residents who call CIAD with complaints about the quality of care or services at specific institutions receive information about their rights and referrals to agencies that can help resolve grievances. CIAD also provides referrals to adult homes in New York City's five boroughs.

Council for Jewish Elderly (CJE)
3003 West Touhy Avenue
Chicago, IL 60645
312–508–1000
Fax: 312–508–1028

This private not-for-profit agency offers a variety of housing-related services to older adults in the Chicago area. Staff members will provide information about local alternative housing options, screen and match clients for homesharing, and supply lists of affordable homes and apartments. CJE also owns and operates senior apartments, assisted living residences, and a long-term care nursing facility.

Friends and Relatives of Institutionalized Aged (FRIA)
11 John Street, Suite 601
New York, NY 10038
212–732–4455
Fax: 212–732–6945

Contact this nonprofit consumer organization, which serves New York State nursing home residents and their friends and families, for advice about long-term care options and financing, nursing home selection and admission, and identifying and resolving care problems. FRIA will provide statewide referrals to nursing homes and intervene on your behalf if you have a complaint about services. Staff members also help form and sustain effective family councils. Assistance for Spanish-speaking callers is available two days a week.

Helpful Publications:

"Comprehensive Care Planning: A Family Guide to Effective Participation." Available in English and Spanish. Free booklet.

Free four-page brochures on nursing home care problems are available on these topics: "Food," "Mobility," "Pressure Sores," "Recognizing Overmedication," "Removing Restraints."

Friends of Residents in Long Term Care
3301 Woman's Club Drive, Suite 103
Raleigh, NC 27612
919–782–1530

Serving older people and their families in North Carolina, this nonprofit consumer advocacy organization provides information and referrals regarding long-term care facilities throughout the state. The organization offers support to family councils and works with the state ombudsman program to monitor quality and solve problems with resident care. Annual membership fee: $20.00 (long-term care residents: $5.00).

Kansas Advocates for Better Care

913 Tennessee Street, Suite 2
Lawrence, KS 66044–6904
913–842–3088
Fax: 913–832–2813

A clearinghouse of information about Kansas long-term care facilities and related care issues, this group will provide copies of state inspection reports for individual facilities, a listing of enforcement actions (penalties for inadequate care), a listing of facilities that have received a state exemplary care award for having no deficiencies during an inspection, and a copy of Kansas's nursing home regulations. The organization also provides FIND fact sheets on individual homes in nine Kansas counties. These periodically updated reports give details on a facility's occupancy, staffing ratios, licensed nurse coverage, enforcement action history, and more. There is a $1.00 charge per report.

Helpful Publication:
"Consumer's Guide to Kansas Nursing Homes." 64-page guide to selecting a nursing home, paying for care, exercising residents' rights, and contacting Kansas agencies involved with nursing homes. $2.00.

Living Is for the Elderly (LIFE)

27 Maple Street
Arlington, MA 02174
617–646–1000, ext. 4733
Fax: 617–646–1000, ext. 4735

This nonprofit organization develops intergenerational programs, information-sharing and group decision-making meetings, educational seminars, and Olympics-style LIFE Games for Massachusetts nursing home and rest home residents. Contact LIFE to inquire about bringing its programs to the facility where your relative or friend resides.

Minnesota Alliance for Health Care Consumers
2626 East Eighty-second Street, Suite 220
Bloomington, MN 55425–1381
612–854–7304
Fax: 612–854–8535

Operating statewide, this nonprofit agency helps organize and support nursing home and boarding home resident or family councils as well as area-wide councils composed of members of individual councils in a given area. The agency also offers educational workshops on topics of interest to long-term care consumers. Members receive a newsletter, special bulletins, and discounts on publications and workshops. Annual membership fee: $25.00.

Helpful Publications:
"Discussion Topics for Family Councils." $3.00.
"Discussion Topics for Resident Councils." $3.00.
"Making Visits Meaningful." $3.50.

Nursing Home Hotline Patrol
6429 Gulfport Boulevard South
St. Petersburg, FL 33707–3015
813–347–0953

Phone for referrals to Florida nursing homes and answers to your questions about evaluating facilities, correcting problems, clearing up billing errors, and related matters. If you live out of state, this service will phone the Florida-only 800 number for the state's Agency for Health Care Administration and ask the agency to send you county listings of nursing homes, which detail size, charges, Medicare and insurance acceptance, and other facts.

Richmond Friends and Relatives
1426 Claremont Avenue
Richmond, VA 23227
804–264–2730

Assisting Richmond-area nursing home residents and their families, this grassroots organization provides guidelines for evaluating nursing home services, helps resolve problems and concerns, and gives referrals to other local resources.

Texas Advocates for Nursing Home Residents (TANHR)
P.O. Box 763143
Dallas, TX 75376
214–371–6330

Working to improve the quality of care and quality of life for Texas nursing home residents, this volunteer group organizes family councils and provides information and educational programs for friends and family on all facets of long-term care and complaint resolution. Phone TANHR before selecting a nursing home for advice and information on the quality of care at specific facilities.

United Senior Action
1211 South Hiatt Street
Indianapolis, IN 46221
317–634–0872
Fax: 317–687–3661

A statewide membership organization, United Senior Action advocates on behalf of older Hoosiers. Members receive a monthly newspaper focusing on Indianapolis public policy issues. Contact the organization for referrals to local resources that can help you resolve problems with long-term care facilities.

Helpful Publication:
"Your Indiana Guide to Long Term Care." Free 20-page newspaper supplement.

Other Helpful Free or Low-Cost Publications

"Age Page: When You Need a Nursing Home." Free fact sheet and consumer checklist. Contact: National Institute on Aging, P.O. Box 8057, Gaithersburg, MD 20898–8057 (1–800–222–2225).

"A Consumer Guide to Life-Care Communities." Information on the benefits and disadvantages of continuing care retirement communities, with consumer checklist and resource guide. $4.00. Contact: National Consumers League, 1701 K Street NW, Suite 1200, Washington, DC 20006 (202–835–3323).

"Family Guide for Alzheimer Care in Residential Settings." Order #PF108Z. 40-page booklet on choosing a residential health care facility for a person with Alzheimer's disease. $1.50. Contact: Alzheimer's Association, 919 North Michigan Avenue, Chicago, IL 60611–1676 (1–800–272–3900).

"Loss and Theft in Nursing Homes." Free booklet. Contact: National Committee to Preserve Social Security and Medicare, 2000 K Street NW, Suite 800, Washington, DC 20006 (202–822–9459).

To order the following free brochures, send a self-addressed stamped envelope to: Nursing Home Community Coalition of New York State, 11 John Street, Suite 601, New York, NY 10038 (212–385–0355).

"Case Mix Reimbursement and Resource Utilization Groups (RUGS): What Consumers Should Know." Describes New York State's reimbursement system, detailing consumer concerns.

"Consumers' Guide to Improved Nursing Home Care: The Use of Restraints in New York State."

"Nursing Home Life: A Guide for Residents and Families." Order #D13063. Free 52-page booklet. Contact: AARP Fulfillment, 601 E Street NW, Washington, DC 20049 (1–800–424–3410).

Chapter Four

Financial & Legal Concerns

I recommended to my mother at one time that she should have some sort of a Medigap policy. She was smart enough to take one out, so that when this happened—she was diagnosed with pancreatic cancer—it really saved her quite a bit of money. She had surgery to try to correct the condition. In the last two or three months she had round-the-clock care, family during the day and nursing care after dinner up until nine or ten o'clock the next morning. Toward the end it was twenty-four hours a day. Most of the providers billed Medicare direct and they would be paid. A lot of the providers just agreed to the Medicare amount, but the ones that were in excess of Medicare would send us a bill and then we would send that to the Medigap insurance. I found that in a great many cases the Medigap covered probably a good 70 to 90 percent of the remaining bills. She said to me, on a couple of occasions, "I'm really thankful I have this policy."

Time to Talk

Many families wait too long to face the future. It's easy to postpone a discussion of the financial and legal issues associated with potential chronic illness, disability, mental incapacity, and death. Unfortunately, the consequences of procrastination can be severe. If your loved one suddenly becomes seriously ill or dies without essential financial and legal documents in place, you may be forced to make hasty decisions in difficult times, and you may face expensive and time-consuming court proceedings. Planning for worst-case scenarios won't solve all problems. But it can help protect your parent's assets, reduce the chance of sibling squabbles, and ensure that your loved one's wishes are observed.

There are three major areas to consider in helping your parent put affairs in order:

1. Information gathering
2. Planning to pay for care
3. Legal arrangements

Information Gathering

Whether you are seeking in-home help from community resources, evaluating alternative living arrangements, helping to pay for long-term care, or handling affairs for a loved one who is incapacitated, you will need to understand your parent's financial situation and have key information and records on hand. Checklist #11, "Financial Inventory," will help you assess your parent's financial resources. Checklist #12, "Personal and Financial Records," will guide you in assembling essential facts and documents. Review both lists with your relative, if possible, filling in the details and the location of important papers. You'll want to collect most of these from their scattered nests in desks, attic, dresser drawers, and shoe boxes, and store them in one safe, convenient spot.

While reviewing the records checklist, mark an X beside items that your parent has but cannot locate. Later you can help search for the missing documents or track them down through appropriate sources—present or former lawyers or accountants, government agencies, and so on. Star any items on the list that your parent should have but does not, such as a durable power of attorney or living will. You'll find discussions of these documents below under "Legal Arrangements" and in Chapter 7 under "Advance Directives." Once you've organized your parent's existing records, your next challenge will be to ensure that these other important legal instruments are prepared.

96

Planning to Pay for Care

The bill for long-term home care services can top $30,000 a year. Nursing home care averages $36,000 yearly and in some parts of the country may cost $60,000 or more. Unless your relative has very substantial assets, paying for medical care during a long-term illness or disability could easily wipe out a lifetime of savings.

Preparing financially for the later years can minimize those threats. Wise planning involves making the best use of available financial resources, knowing how to get the most from government programs, and understanding alternatives for private payment. This section presents an overview of income sources and insurance options. Not included here are aspects of financial planning such as investment strategies or estate planning. Decisions in these complex matters depend on your parent's unique financial situation and priorities and should be made with the assistance of a financial planner, banker, accountant, or attorney who is experienced in elder law issues. The Directory of Resources includes organizations providing guidance to help you select and work with these professionals.

Income: Public Benefits

According to the American Association of Retired Persons, at least half of all low-income Americans who are eligible for public benefits do not receive them. Public benefits may be an important source of relief for your older relative if long-term illness or disability threatens resources. You can help conserve your parent's assets by finding out about the benefits she or he is entitled to as a taxpayer and a consumer.

Social Security

Social Security retirement benefits are available at age sixty-two for those who retire early and at sixty-five for all others who meet eligibility requirements. Eligibility is based on the number of years a person worked. Most older adults who worked for at least ten years are entitled to benefits. Spouses age sixty-two or older and widows or widowers of individuals eligible for retirement benefits are also entitled to receive benefits.

The amount of benefits paid is based on average lifetime earnings. The average monthly retirement benefit paid to a single worker retiring in 1996 was $720; the maximum monthly benefit was $1,248. If your parent is not already collecting Social Security, you can request an estimate of future benefits by phoning the Social Security Administration (see Directory of Resources). Keep in mind that the government's calculations are not foolproof. In fact, one in six Americans receives incorrect Social Security benefits. To make sure the system is paying all the benefits your parent is entitled to, check Social Security's estimate of earnings against copies of old W–2 forms. If you find a discrepancy, you are entitled to provide evidence and request that the error be corrected.

Supplemental Security Income (SSI)

SSI is a financial safety net providing a monthly cash payment to people who have limited income and resources and are disabled, blind, or over age sixty-five. Unlike Social Security, SSI has no work history requirements. However, there are strict limits on income and assets. Though amounts vary, the basic federal payment to a single person in 1996 was $470 a month. Generally, individuals who are eligible for Medicaid benefits (see "Medicaid," below) may also be eligible for SSI. Your local Social Security office can help you determine if your relative qualifies.

Food Stamps and Home Energy Assistance

These government programs provide assistance with paying food bills and home heating costs to individuals with limited income and resources. Contact your local public assistance office or department of social services to determine if your relative is eligible.

Veterans' Benefits

The Veterans Administration offers a wide variety of services for older and/or disabled veterans, though recent budgetary constraints have forced some cutbacks. Your relative may be eligible for free or low-cost medical care at a Department of Veterans Affairs (VA) medical center, care at a VA nursing home or veterans' home, or VA programs such as adult day care, mental health clinic services, or special benefits for home care. To find out what programs are available in your area and if your parent qualifies, contact the Department of Veterans Affairs, Paralyzed Veterans of America, and/or Blinded Veterans Association (see the Directory of Resources at the end of this chapter and at the end of Chapter 5).

Note: If your parent becomes physically or mentally incompetent and unable to endorse and cash Social Security, SSI, veterans' benefits, or civil service retirement checks, you can apply to the appropriate government agency to be named a representative payee. Becoming a representative payee gives you the right and responsibility to manage those funds on your relative's behalf.

Income: Private Sources

Your relative may have income from a number of private sources, including savings and investments, retirement accounts, and survivors' benefits. Following are a few other potential sources of income that call for special consideration.

Annuities

Offered by many insurance companies, annuities are investment contracts that provide a guaranteed income over time. The purchaser either pays a single lump sum or makes a series of contributions over a number of years. In exchange, the insurance company agrees to make a series of fixed payments later to the purchaser or other beneficiary. These payments must begin at a predetermined time, called the maturity date, and they extend for either a fixed length of time or for a lifetime, depending on the terms of the contract. The rate of payment may be fixed, or it may vary according to the success of investments.

The IRS's tax treatment of annuities has changed several times, and the terms are complex. Urge your parent to consult an experienced financial adviser before investing or withdrawing annuity funds. Since annuities are not federally insured, it also is crucial to check on the financial soundness of the issuing insurance company (see "Rating the Insurance Companies," below). Finally, consider these advantages and disadvantages of annuities, as outlined by California's Advocates for Nursing Home Reform.

ADVANTAGES	DISADVANTAGES
Provides a guaranteed amount of income at some future point for a chosen period of time.	Money is tied up for a long period of time. Once a contract begins making payments, it cannot be cashed in.
Interest and, in some cases, capital gains are generally not taxed until withdrawal.	There may be substantial penalties for early withdrawal.
There are no restrictions on the size of annuities that can be bought.	Payments usually are not adjusted for inflation; the income stream that looks attractive at age 65 may seem like very little at 70 or 80.
	Annuities have more limited investment options and may be more vulnerable to loss than some other retirement plans.

Home Equity Conversion Mortgages/Reverse Mortgages

A large portion of the assets of many retirees is tied up in a house. Home equity conversion allows individuals age sixty-two and older who are "house-rich but cash-poor" to turn their home into a source of income. In the most popular form of home equity conversion, the reverse mortgage, a lender advances an amount of money based on the value of the home, either through regular monthly payments, one lump sum payment, or as a line of credit on which the borrower may draw as needed. A lien is placed on the house, but the homeowner continues to own it and live in it. When the homeowner dies or moves permanently, the loan principal and accumulated interest are repaid, usually through the sale of the house.

To be eligible for a reverse mortgage loan, the borrower must own a single-family home free and clear or have a very low outstanding mortgage balance. The amount of money available under a reverse mortgage depends on the value of the home, the age of the borrower, the type of loan selected, and other factors. In general, the older the homeowner, the greater the amount that can be borrowed. People in their seventies usually are considered the best candidates for this type of loan. Term loans, in which monthly payments continue for a specified number of years, usually pay more than tenure loans, in which payments continue as long as the owner lives in the home. Reverse mortgages also are affected by changes in the interest rate. These changes do not affect the monthly payments but are reflected in the amount owed when the loan comes due.

Most reverse mortgages are insured by the U.S. Department of Housing and Urban Development (HUD) and have additional built-in borrower protections. For example, there are limits to the amount the interest rate can increase over the life of the loan. Further, if the home's value drops below what it was at the time the loan was made, the borrower or the borrower's estate owes no more than the home's assessed value. No additional claims can be made against the heirs or estate.

Reverse mortgages are a fairly recent option, with complex and widely varying terms. Your parent should consult an attorney experienced in property law before entering into any agreement. The Area Agency on Aging (see Appendix B), HUD field office (see Directory of Resources), and your state's department of taxation can provide information on qualified lenders and the types of reverse mortgages locally available.

Home Equity Loans

Home equity loans allow homeowners of any age to borrow against the value of their house. Unlike a reverse mortgage, a home equity loan must be repaid in monthly installments. If the borrower cannot make the payments, the home may be put at risk.

A home equity loan can provide a source of ready money for paying bills, and the interest may be tax deductible if the loan finances medical expenses. It is essential, however, that your parent gather information, shop around for the best rates, and ask advice from an experienced lawyer, accountant, or financial adviser before making a commitment. The Internal Revenue Service can advise on tax aspects.

Tax Facts

One way to maximize financial resources is to take advantage of all appropriate tax credits and deductions. The Internal Revenue Service, your state revenue department, or an attorney, accountant, or financial planner can help you learn about health-care-related income tax deductions. In many cases these may include:

- Medical and dental expenses (including the cost of home renovations to accommodate disabilities)
- Hospital expenses
- Home care expenses
- Home care workers' meals
- Lodging expenses incurred while away from home to receive medical care
- Ambulance service or mileage for transportation to a medical facility
- Health insurance premiums
- Special medical equipment and items such as a motorized wheelchair, oxygen equipment, false teeth, hearing aids, etc.

Other tax deductions, credits, and exclusions that may apply either to your relative or to yourself as a caregiver include:

- Special tax credits for the elderly or disabled
- Special tax treatments for widows and widowers

- Special tax deductions and exclusions for homeowners
- Income tax exclusions for sickness or injury benefits, veterans' benefits, public assistance payments, and reimbursements related to volunteer work
- Special state tax exclusions and state, county, or city tax relief programs for older taxpayers
- Income tax exemptions for caregivers who claim care-receivers as dependents (generally available if you provide more than half of a parent's support and that person's income is less than a specified exemption amount)

Your parent also may be able to take advantage of free tax assistance and counseling programs, widely available through the IRS and other agencies and organizations. Volunteer Income Tax Assistance (VITA) provides free tax assistance to people with low or fixed incomes, the disabled, the elderly, and others with special needs. Volunteers at VITA sites, which usually are located at community centers, libraries, schools, shopping malls, and other convenient locations, help prepare basic tax returns and some basic schedules. Tax Counseling for the Elderly and Tax-Aide are volunteer programs that provide free tax help to people age sixty and older. Volunteers with these programs often are retirees associated with nonprofit organizations working under an IRS grant. They offer tax counseling at locations such as retirement homes and senior centers, and will schedule home visits to homebound seniors. Contact your local IRS office for information and the locations of tax counseling sites in your parent's area.

Pensions and Profit-Sharing Plans

Don't assume that your relative is receiving all applicable benefits from employer-sponsored pensions and profit-sharing plans. It might be a wise precaution to contact all former employers for a record of earnings and pension benefits. Compare these with your parent's work history and personal earnings records. Also remember that past or present membership in a union or the clergy may carry benefits.

Insurance: Government Programs

Medicare
Medicare is a federal health insurance program for people age

sixty-five and older and for certain disabled people under sixty-five. Anyone who is receiving Social Security or Railroad Retirement Board benefits when he or she turns sixty-five is enrolled in Medicare automatically. Others must contact their local Social Security Administration office to enroll.

The Medicare program has two parts. Part A, Medicare Hospital Insurance, covers inpatient hospital and skilled nursing facility care, skilled home health care, and hospice care. Part B, Medical Insurance, covers doctors' services, including medical and surgical services, diagnostic tests, and some treatment of mental illness; outpatient hospital care; durable medical equipment such as wheelchairs or oxygen equipment used at home; and a number of other medical services and supplies not covered by Part A. In general, individuals qualify for premium-free Medicare Part A if they or a spouse worked for at least ten years. Those qualifying for Part A also may choose to enroll in Part B by paying the monthly Part B premiums. In 1996 the premium was $42.50 for most beneficiaries. That's a good deal—because Medicare is federally sponsored, enrollees generally get more benefits for their dollar than with any form of private insurance.

Even so, on average Medicare pays less than half of older Americans' health care expenses. Among Medicare's exclusions—the items *not* covered—are most routine and preventive health care, most outpatient prescription drugs, and nonskilled, or custodial, care (services that help with daily living activities or personal needs). Medicare pays for only about 4 percent of all nursing home costs. Home care costs are covered only if the patient is homebound and requires intermittent (not twenty-four-hour) skilled nursing and therapy, which are provided by a Medicare-certified home health agency. Besides Medicare's exclusions, other "gaps" in coverage include deductibles and copayments. In 1996, for example, a Medicare beneficiary who was hospitalized paid a deductible of $736 for each benefit period and a coinsurance amount of $184 per day for hospital stays longer than sixty days. To fill Medicare's gaps, many older adults buy additional insurance from private carriers. That may include Medicare supplemental (Medigap) insurance, long-term care insurance, or employer-sponsored policies (see "Private Insurance," below).

Medicare regulations are complicated and constantly changing. Even your relative's doctor or home health care agency may not fully understand the extent of the program's coverage. Whenever home health care services are prescribed, it's a good idea to contact the local Area Agency on Aging (see Appendix B) or a Medicare advocacy group (see Directory of Resources) to make certain your parent gets full benefits. Your local Social Security office also can provide information and comprehensive publications.

Medicaid

Medicaid is a joint federal-state health insurance program for people with very limited financial resources, including those whose resources have been exhausted by long-term care expenses. To qualify for coverage, individuals must meet strict financial requirements, which vary from state to state. In 1996 the typical annual income limit for a single adult was $6,700; the typical assets limit, excluding the value of a home and certain personal effects, was $3,350. States also have varying medical requirements. Some have tightened those restrictions in recent years so that, for example, Alzheimer's disease patients who are otherwise healthy may no longer qualify for Medicaid-paid nursing home care.

Individuals whose financial resources exceed Medicaid limits must "spend down," or use up, their assets in order to qualify for the program. (Many states also have a spend-down calculation that allows higher-income individuals to become eligible for aid if they have considerable uncovered medical expenses.) There are strict rules on how assets can be spent down. In general, money must go to the patient's own medical and personal needs or those of a spouse or disabled child. Transferring assets through gifts to adult children usually is not allowed. However, money that was transferred as a gift three years or more before application for Medicaid is no longer counted as part of the applicant's assets. Medicaid trusts—irrevocable living trusts that transfer assets to a child or other named trustee—have been used to qualify for assistance, but recent changes in federal law sharply restrict that practice.

Once a person qualifies for Medicaid, most or all of the costs of long-term care are covered. Medicaid pays for home health care, though the eligibility criteria and covered services vary greatly among the states. The program also pays nursing home costs, regardless of whether the resident requires skilled or custodial care.

Nursing home residents receiving Medicaid assistance must pay all of their income (except a $30 monthly personal allowance) directly to the home. Medicaid then covers the balance of the cost of care. Because Medicaid reimburses for care at a lower rate than residents who pay privately, nursing homes prefer to admit individuals who are able to pay with their own resources for at least some period of time. In most states, even if a facility is Medicaid-certified, it is not required to accept every Medicaid patient. In fact, many nursing homes have informal limits on the number or percentage of Medicaid residents they will accept.

Federal law requires that Medicaid patients in nursing homes receive the same quality of care and services as private pay residents. Further, it is against the law for a Medicaid-certified facility to discharge a private pay resident who becomes eligible for Medicaid or to require residents to sign a contract guaranteeing private payment for a specified period of time. If you have questions about the treatment your parent is receiving at a Medicaid-certified facility or about the rules regarding eligibility or coverage, contact your local Area Agency on Aging (see Appendix B), local department of social services, or state Medicaid agency. To locate your Medicaid agency, look in your phone directory or call the Medicare Hotline at 1–800–638–6833. Contact these resources early—before Medicaid becomes a necessity—to learn about your relative's rights and options. Many families use up more of their assets than necessary to qualify for assistance.

QMB and SLMB

Besides Medicaid, two other programs are available through

state Medicaid offices to help low-income Medicare beneficiaries meet health care costs.

The Qualified Medicare Beneficiary (QMB) program pays Medicare premiums, deductibles, and coinsurance amounts for people who are entitled to Medicare Part A and meet strict income and asset requirements. In 1996 the limit on assets was $7,980 for a single person and $10,608 for a couple, not including the value of a home and certain personal effects. Monthly income must be at or below the national poverty level.

The Specified Low-Income Medicare Beneficiary (SLMB) program is for people entitled to Medicare Part A whose assets meet the same limits as required for QMB and whose income does not exceed the national poverty level by more than 20 percent. Under this program the state pays the monthly Medicare Part B premium, but recipients are responsible for Medicare deductibles and coinsurance.

To apply for QMB or SLMB assistance, your parent must file an application at a state, county, or local medical assistance office. To locate your nearest office, call the Medicare Hotline at 1–800–638–6833.

Private Insurance

Medicare Supplemental (Medigap) Insurance

About three-quarters of all Medicare beneficiaries rely on private supplemental insurance to cover the costs of Medicare's deductibles, coinsurance, and exclusions. In the past, shopping for Medicare supplemental (or Medigap) insurance was a headache, with insurance companies offering a bewildering variety of options. The Medigap Fraud and Abuse Prevention Act of 1990 addressed that problem, instituting reforms that resulted in ten standard Medigap insurance packages, which are identical from company to company. The packages, labeled A through J, each offer a specific level of benefits, from the most basic level of coverage to the highest. Standardization has made it easier to shop around and compare policies offered by different companies.

Checklist #13 outlines the benefits contained in each Medigap package and includes space for noting the premiums charged by different insurance companies for the same package. To select a policy, your relative must begin by deciding which benefits are most important. A person who never travels outside the United States, for example, doesn't need a policy that covers foreign travel emergencies, while someone who uses only doctors who accept Medicare assignment may not need to look for coverage of fees that exceed Medicare-approved amounts. Next compare the prices quoted by different insurance companies for the package with the benefits your relative wants. According to United Seniors Health Cooperative, prices from different companies for identical coverage may vary by as much as 100 percent.

Here are some additional points to consider when shopping for Medigap insurance:

- If your relative is likely to need Medigap coverage, it pays to act early. Medigap insurers cannot deny coverage on the basis of illness, injury, or existing medical problems to anyone who applies within six months of enrolling in Medicare Part B. After that, many companies require a medical screening, and applicants may be rejected for having certain health problems.

- If your relative owns a Medigap policy purchased before standardization, the insurance company may offer the option of converting to one of the ten standard policies. Before switching, carefully evaluate the older policy. It may include desirable coverage no longer available in the new packages.

- Medigap insurers use three different methods to calculate annual premiums: issue age, no age rating, and attained age. If a company uses the issue age method, the premium is set according to the age at which your relative buys the policy and will always remain the same as the premium paid by individuals of that age. For example, if your parent buys a policy at age sixty-five, the premium will always be the same as that paid by a sixty-five-year-old. If the company uses the no age rating method, everyone pays the same premium, regardless of age; these policies often are the least costly for individuals under age seventy-five. Under both the issue age and no age rating methods, annual premiums may rise to reflect inflation. Under the third method of calculating premiums, the attained age method, the premium is based on current age and rises automatically as the policyholder grows older. Attained age plans typically are less expensive at younger ages but become considerably more expensive—even unaffordable—in later years.

- Scrutinize policies for other factors that may lead to premium hikes. Ask if premiums can be increased due to changes in health or the number of claims made.

- Carefully consider the additional cost of each benefit beyond the price of a basic policy. For example, the extra premium charged to cover the annual Medicare Part B deductible sometimes costs more than the deductible itself.

- Check for preexisting condition exclusions. Many policies do not immediately cover health problems existing at the time of purchase. All Medigap policies, however, are now required to cover preexisting conditions after the policy has been in effect for six months.

- Check policy exclusions. Most Medigap policies do not cover items such as the cost of routine examinations, dental or foot care, eyeglasses, hearing aids, or cosmetic surgery. Neither Medicare nor Medigap covers custodial nursing home care.

- Your state insurance department or Health Insurance Counseling and Advocacy Program (see Directory of Resources) can provide free information, counseling, and publications to help you and your relative consider insurance options.

Information also may be available from the State Unit on Aging or Area Agency on Aging (see Appendix B).

- Check with your state insurance department to make sure the company you are considering is licensed in the state. Also look into the insurer's financial stability (see "Rating the Insurance Companies," below), and check the company's complaint record with the local Better Business Bureau (see Directory of Resources).

Long-Term Care Insurance

Because Medicare and Medigap insurance cover only a fraction of the costs of long-term care, many people have sought protection in a relatively new form of coverage, long-term care insurance. This type of policy pays a fixed dollar amount, usually $50 to $250 a day, for each day the policyholder is in a nursing home. Some policies also provide benefits for long-term care services in the home, often at an amount one-half of that paid for nursing home care. Long-term care insurance is not a substitute for either Medicare or Medigap insurance. Instead, it offers separate coverage that neither of these provides.

Most long-term care policies have a waiting period before benefits kick in, which may range from twenty to one hundred days after the start of a nursing home stay. Benefit periods also vary. Benefits may last for only one or two years or for longer periods, up to a lifetime. The shorter the waiting period and the longer the benefit period, the higher the premium. Also adding to the cost of premiums are inflation protection features. Because the per-day benefit bought today is unlikely to cover higher costs in the future, most policies offer some option for inflation adjustment. Benefits may automatically increase at a fixed percentage over a certain number of years, or the policy may offer the holder the option of purchasing additional coverage every few years, with an increase in premiums.

Long-term care policies offered by different companies may vary in dozens of other ways, including what services are covered in what types of facilities, the amount of daily benefits paid, restrictions on eligibility for benefits, coverage for preexisting conditions, and, of course, cost. With so many different options, it can be extremely difficult to shop around and compare policies.

Long-term care insurance is not only complex, it is also controversial. Premiums are extremely high for people who wait until later years to buy. The annual cost for nursing home plus home care coverage ranges from $300 to $1,500 at age fifty-five, $600 to $2,600 at age sixty-five, and $1,700 to $5,000 at age seventy-five. Most policies pay back only between 60 and 65 percent of total premiums in benefits, much less than other types of health insurance. Limits on coverage may mean that a policyholder who ends up in the "wrong" type of care facility—an assisted living facility instead of a nursing home, for example—receives no benefits. On the other hand, long-term care insurance can provide important financial protection against the high cost of needed care, especially for individuals who have substantial assets to protect. United Seniors Health Cooperative suggests that older adults should consider buying long-term care insurance only if they meet the following criteria:

1. More than $75,000 in assets per person in the household (not including the value of the primary residence)
2. Annual retirement income over $30,000 per person
3. Premium payments can be made comfortably, without the necessity for lifestyle changes
4. Policy could be afforded even if premiums were to increase by 20 to 30 percent

Checklist #14 can help you compare long-term care policies offered by different companies. Before deciding on a policy, your relative will need to look into local nursing home costs, to get an idea of how much coverage might be needed. You also must decide on the length of the benefit period. Most nursing home stays are short—three months or less—but some illnesses requiring nursing home care may last several years. United Seniors Health Cooperative advises that, for most people, a policy covering two or three years will be more cost-effective than one covering five years or longer.

Your state insurance department, state Health Insurance Counseling and Advocacy Program, Area Agency on Aging, and/or an elder law attorney or financial planner can help assess your relative's insurance needs and evaluate options. Also remember to check on the financial stability of the insurance companies you are considering (see "Rating the Insurance Companies," below) and to contact the local Better Business Bureau for insurers' complaint records.

Employer-Sponsored or Retirement Plan Health Insurance

Many people reaching age sixty-five still have private insurance through their own or their spouse's employer or union membership. Group health insurance that is continued after retirement may offer several advantages. Usually there are no waiting periods or exclusions for preexisting conditions. Coverage generally is based on group premium rates, which often are lower than the rates for individually purchased policies. Group health insurance also may offer benefits not included in a Medigap policy, such as prescription drug coverage or routine dental care.

If your relative has supplemental coverage through a former employer, check the benefits to make sure the plan fills the major gaps in Medicare. If it does, there probably is no need to buy additional coverage. Be aware, though, that retirement plans provided by employers or unions are not subject to the rules that apply to the standardized Medigap policies. Private retirement plans have their own rules and might not fill key Medicare gaps. If you have questions on how the retirement plan works in conjunction with Medicare, get a copy of the benefits booklet or contact the plan's benefits office. If you find that your parent's group insurance is inadequate or too expensive, it may be better to drop it and buy a Medigap policy instead.

Also keep the following tips in mind:

- Even with good comprehensive health coverage, there still will be gaps. No single insurance policy will cover all contingencies.
- Retirement plans may not pay medical expenses during any period in which your parent was eligible for Medicare but did not sign up for it.

112

- Until recently, it was illegal for an insurer to sell a Medigap policy if it would duplicate benefits available under another policy such as a retiree health plan. Under new rulings, however, your parent now may be sold a Medigap plan even if it duplicates existing coverage. If the retiree plan contains a coordination-of-benefits clause, it will not pay benefits for services covered by the Medigap policy. Before purchasing a Medigap policy that duplicates any retiree plan benefits, your parent should ask for advice from the state Health Insurance Counseling and Advocacy Program (see Directory of Resources).

Other Private Insurance

Hospital indemnity insurance pays a fixed cash amount for each day the policyholder is hospitalized, up to a designated maximum number of days. This is not a substitute for a comprehensive Medicare supplemental policy, especially since the way in which Medicare reimburses hospitals tends to minimize the length of hospital stays.

Specified disease, or "dread disease," insurance provides benefits for treatment of a single disease such as cancer. The value of the coverage depends on the chance that the policyholder will contract the disease covered. Remember that Medicare and any Medigap policy your relative owns very likely would cover costs associated with any of these policies' specified diseases.

Disability income insurance replaces earned income, typically at a rate of 70 to 80 percent, when the policyholder becomes sick or injured and unable to work. When the policyholder retires, eligibility for benefits ends. This type of policy does not pay for medical, personal, or long-term care.

Life insurance policies sometimes offer accelerated, or living benefits, provisions. These pay a portion (typically 50 percent or more) of the policy's death benefits to the policyholder if that person is diagnosed with a terminal illness, requires a major organ transplant, or meets other specified criteria. The payments can be used to

Rating the Insurance Companies

Benefits and costs aren't the only factors to consider when helping your relative choose insurance coverage. The National Association of Insurance Commissioners also recommends that consumers check on the reliability and financial stability of insurance companies. The following private rating agencies can help. These firms conduct financial analyses of insurers and issue ratings that reflect their analysts' views of the companies' financial health. Some offer their ratings free, while others charge for the service (note that there will be an extra charge on your telephone bill for calls to a 900 number). You also might check the reference section at your local library for insurance ratings.

Best Company
900-555-2378

Moody's Investor Service
212-553-1653

Demotech
614-761-8602

Standard & Poor's
212-208-8000

Duff & Phelps
312-368-3157

Weiss Research
800-289-9222

Fitch Investors Service
212-908-0500

Another good resource is *Insurance Forum,* a monthly periodical covering the insurance industry. *Insurance Forum* publishes a yearly special ratings issue. The September 1996 special issue listed about 1,500 life and health insurance companies, with the financial strength ratings assigned to them by four rating firms: Standard & Poor's, Moody's, Duff & Phelps, and Weiss. Cost of the issue: $15.00. For information on current issue contents and cost, contact: *Insurance Forum,* P.O. Box 245, Ellettsville, IN 47429 (812-876-6502).

finance long-term care or for any other purpose the policyholder chooses. However, unless the life insurance policy includes significant death benefits, say $100,000 or $200,000, a living benefits provision won't go far toward covering long-term care costs.

Managed Care Plans

Managed care plans may be thought of as a combination insurance policy and health care delivery system. Like insurance, these plans cover health care costs in exchange for a monthly premium or membership fee; like a doctor or hospital, they provide health care services.

The most familiar form of managed care is the health maintenance organization (HMO). Typically, HMOs operate in a group setting. Patients visit one or more centralized health facilities, where the doctors and nurses who work for the plan provide medical care. The HMO network also may include hospitals, skilled nursing facilities, home health care agencies, pharmacies, and other health care providers. In variations on this standard plan, HMO members may be treated in the private practice offices of professionals affiliated with the plan or, in some cases, may choose providers outside the network for an additional fee.

In addition to the monthly premium, managed care plans commonly charge a small copayment each time a service is used; for example, $10 for every office visit or each prescription filled in the plan's pharmacy. Usually there are no additional charges, no matter how often a member visits the doctor, is hospitalized, or accesses other covered services.

Most Medicare beneficiaries who are enrolled in Medicare Part B are eligible to join the Medicare managed care plan serving their area. Once enrolled in an HMO, Medicare beneficiaries generally do not need Medigap or other supplemental health insurance.

There are arguments on both sides of the HMO debate. The chart below lists some of the pros and cons of managed care plan membership for older adults. If your parent is tilting toward the "pro" column, contact the state Health Insurance Counseling and Advocacy Program or the Medicare Hotline (see Directory of Resources) for referrals to local Medicare HMOs. Also see Checklist #15, which can help you evaluate the quality of care and services provided by different HMOs.

Managed Care Health Plans

ADVANTAGES	DISADVANTAGES
Out-of-pocket expenses usually are less than under the standard fee-for-service system.	Members are not free to go to any physician, hospital, or nursing facility they choose. Except in emergencies, they must use the HMO's providers and facilities.
Some plans offer benefits beyond those covered by Medicare, such as physicals, dental care, prescription drugs, hearing aids, and eyeglasses.	Members must have the prior approval of their HMO primary care physician to see a specialist or receive institutional care, medical equipment, or other medical services.
Medicare beneficiaries (excluding those with end-stage renal disease) cannot be denied membership because of poor health or disability.	It can take up to 30 days to disenroll from an HMO. Members must continue to use the plan during that time.
Paperwork is reduced or eliminated.	Individuals who drop Medigap insurance to join an HMO and later disenroll may find it difficult or impossible to get their formal Medigap cover age at the same price.

Legal Arrangements

Legal issues to be addressed in planning for the later years include arrangements to protect survivors and to enable someone else to manage care and resources in the event of incapacity. The key to putting these affairs in order is working with an attorney who is knowledgeable about lifetime planning and the special concerns of the elderly. A small but growing number of attorneys specialize in these elder law concerns. To find an elder law attorney, contact the Area Agency on Aging (see Appendix B), state branch of the American Bar Association, National Academy of Elder Law Attorneys, or local branches of agencies and organizations that work for the legal rights of the elderly (see Directory of Resources).

The National Academy of Elder Law Attorneys suggests asking the following questions in initial phone calls to the attorneys you and your relative are considering:

1. How long have you been in practice?
2. Does your practice emphasize a particular area of the law? (Elder law encompasses many fields—disability planning, transfer of assets, estate planning, conservatorship and guardianship, etc.—and most attorneys do not regularly handle matters in every one of these areas.)
3. How long have you been in this field?
4. What percentage of your practice is devoted to elder law?
5. Is there a fee for the initial consultation? If so, how much?
6. What information should we bring to the initial consultation?

When you select an attorney, ask for an explanation of how fees are computed and an estimate of the time and cost that would be involved in handling your parent's particular problem. If fees are out of reach, ask if the attorney offers reduced rates for clients with limited resources. Most communities have some type of legal aid program to help older adults and their families handle legal problems and make basic legal arrangements. There often are age or income requirements determining eligibility for these programs. Your State Unit on Aging or Area Agency on Aging (see Appendix B), local social services department, or a local social worker can help you locate community legal aid programs. Also see the Directory of Resources for organizations providing legal assistance, publications, and referrals.

Wills

A will describes how an individual's assets and property are to be distributed after death and designates a person or persons to be responsible for distributing the property and paying estate taxes and other expenses. If your relative dies intestate—without having drawn up a will—state law will determine who gets what, and heirs will pay considerably higher estate taxes. Problems also may arise if a will is not drawn up exactly according to law or if it is confusing or contradictory, as is often the case with informal documents created with legal "kits," without the help of an attorney.

If both of your parents are living, each should have a separate will. Also remind your parents to review their wills every three to five years or whenever they go through a major life change such as the death of a named beneficiary or a move to another state.

Living Trusts

A living trust is an agreement between your relative and another individual or entity that determines how assets placed in a trust fund will be managed and distributed. The trust contains special instructions for distribution of those assets after death and so may ensure that the estate avoids probate—the court process of validating a will and supervising the administration of an estate. Avoiding probate saves the costs of estate administration and the time it takes the court to complete its proceedings.

Living trusts also can be set up to reduce the costs of long-term health care, to provide for the management of assets if your relative becomes incapacitated, to transfer assets to a person receiving public benefits, and to serve other specific needs. In general, living trusts make sense only when there is a large estate to protect. Like a will, a living trust should be prepared by an experienced elder law attorney and reviewed regularly to reflect changes in the law and in family or financial circumstances.

Letter of Instruction

A letter of instruction prepared for beneficiaries of a will or trust can make it easier for the family to close out affairs. Your relative's letter of instruction should include the names of individuals to be notified upon death and cover funeral arrangements, disposal of personal property, and other final wishes. A letter of instruction is not a legal instrument—it may be drawn up without an attorney—but it should be in agreement with the will.

118

General Power of Attorney

A power of attorney is a legal document that gives one person the right to conduct another's financial affairs. If your parent signs over power of attorney to you, you can act as a surrogate in paying bills, buying and selling property, and handling other financial matters. The power of attorney specifies how much authority you have, from the limited power to write checks from a simple checking account to broad powers such as running a business. Your authority remains in effect only as long as your relative is alive and mentally competent.

Durable Power of Attorney

More effective than the general power of attorney is the durable power of attorney. Both documents give you or another designated individual the authority to handle specific aspects of your relative's financial affairs, but the durable power of attorney remains in effect even if your loved one becomes physically or mentally incompetent. Some states allow the option of creating a "springing" power of attorney, which confers authority only in the event of incapacity or under other specified circumstances. Again, this important legal document should be drawn up by an experienced elder law attorney. Be aware that some banks, insurance companies, and other financial institutions require the use of their own durable power of attorney forms.

Durable Power of Attorney for Health Care

This document allows your parent to designate you or another trusted relative or friend to make decisions regarding medical care if he or she becomes unable to do so. For a discussion of this and other forms of advance directives, see Chapter 7, "Advance Directives."

Conservatorship and Guardianship

Conservatorship is similar to a durable power of attorney except that a court appoints the conservator who handles another person's financial affairs. The court may bestow limited powers, such as the right to cash checks, or wide-ranging authority to invest and manage the protected person's assets.

A guardian is appointed by a court to make financial, personal, and health care decisions for someone who is incapacitated because of physical or mental disability. Guardians have the same rights, powers, and responsibilities over their wards as parents have over their minor children. They determine where the ward will live, what medical treatments will be received, and all other aspects of the ward's life. In some cases, where no family member or close friend is available or there is disagreement among the family members over the older person's welfare, the court may appoint a public servant or a volunteer as guardian.

Guardianship is an expensive and time-consuming legal process that strips an older adult of the right to choose and limit the power of a surrogate decision maker. The durable power of attorney and advance directives can be used to avoid the possibility of guardianship.

Joint Ownership Accounts

Older people often place some or all of their assets in joint accounts with a trusted son or daughter. The purpose of joint ownership usually is to make it easier for the adult child to pay bills if the parent becomes incapacitated. Joint ownership also is used as a technique to avoid probate, since the surviving joint owner automatically owns shared assets after the other's death.

Joint ownership arrangements have potential drawbacks. If assets are mingled in a shared account, the parent may be unable to qualify for public benefits when needed. The joint account also may be vulnerable to the debts or liabilities of either party. For example, if one joint owner is responsible for damages from an auto accident, the other's share in the account may go to pay those expenses. Also, since jointly owned assets are transferred directly to the survivor when one owner dies, a parent may unintentionally leave assets to one child that were intended to be distributed equally among family members.

If you and your relative are setting up a joint account to give you easy access to bill-paying funds, make sure only your parent's funds enter the account. Be cautious about setting up a joint ownership account if there is a possibility that at some point your loved one may need to apply for Medicaid or may require long-term nursing home care. Before setting up the account, discuss implications and alternatives with an attorney knowledgeable about public assistance program regulations.

CHECKLIST #11: FINANCIAL INVENTORY

Date: _____

ASSETS (PRINCIPAL AMOUNTS)   VALUE

Certificates of deposit $ _____
Checking accounts $ _____
"Hard" assets (auto, jewelry, art, antiques,
    other valuable personal property) $ _____
Money market accounts $ _____
Mutual funds $ _____
Real estate $ _____
Savings accounts $ _____
Stocks and bonds $ _____
Other: $ _____

MONTHLY INCOME
(including nonreinvested interest and dividends from assets)

SOURCE   AMOUNT
Annuities $ _____
Employment income $ _____
IRAs/401-K/Keogh plan $ _____
Money market accounts $ _____
Mortgage income $ _____
Mutual income funds $ _____
Pensions $ _____
Rental income $ _____
Savings accounts $ _____
Social Security $ _____
Stocks and bonds $ _____
Other: $ _____

MONTHLY EXPENSES

EXPENSE   AMOUNT
Automobile payments $ _____
Building and grounds maintenance $ _____

Cable television $ _____
Charitable contributions $ _____
Clothing $ _____
Credit card payments $ _____
Electric $ _____
Entertainment $ _____
Food $ _____
Heating/air-conditioning $ _____
Housekeeping services $ _____
Insurance premiums $ _____
Loans $ _____
Medical/dental (unreimbursed) $ _____
Mortgage $ _____
Personal grooming $ _____
Refuse removal $ _____
Rent $ _____
Taxes—property/school $ _____
Taxes—quarterly estimated income $ _____
Telephone $ _____
Transportation $ _____
Water and sewer $ _____
Other: $ _____

✔ ## CHECKLIST #12: PERSONAL & FINANCIAL RECORDS

Date: _____

Full legal name: _____

Social Security number: _____

Date and place of birth: _____

Legal residence: _____

IMPORTANT NAMES, ADDRESSES, AND PHONE NUMBERS

Attorney:

_____

_____

_____

_____

( ) _____

Accountant:

_____

_____

_____

_____

( ) _____

Stockbroker:

_____

_____

_____

( ) _____

Financial Planner:

_____

_____

_____

( ) _____

Insurance agent(s):

_____

_____

_____

( ) _____

Bank officer(s):

_____

_____

_____

( ) _____

Doctor(s):

_____

_____

_____

( ) _____

Clergy:

_____

_____

_____

( ) _____

IMPORTANT NAMES, ADDRESSES, AND PHONE NUMBERS

Other:
_____
_____
_____
_____
(   ) _____

Other:
_____
_____
_____
_____
(   ) _____

Other:
_____
_____
_____
(   ) _____

Other:
_____
_____
_____
(   ) _____

IMPORTANT RECORDS/DOCUMENTS
Important papers may be stored in these locations:

Safe deposit box

Number: _____

Location: _____
_____

Home safe

Location: _____

Combination: _____

Authorized users:

(   ) _____
_____
(   ) _____
_____

Keys (to desk, file cabinets, safe deposit boxes, etc.)

Location: _____
_____

PERSONAL AND FAMILY RECORDS	
	Location
Address books	
Adoption papers	
Birth certificate	
Diplomas/educational records	
Divorce/separation papers	
Marriage certificate	
Military records	
Naturalization (citizenship) papers	
Organizational memberships	
Passport	
Other:	

FINANCIAL RECORDS

Bank, investment, and other financial accounts

	Financial institution/ address/phone #/ contact	Account #	Location of records (statements/ canceled checks/ checkbooks/ passbooks/ bonds, etc.)
Annuity contracts			
Bank checking accounts			
Bank savings accounts			
Brokerage accounts			
Certificates of deposit			
Credit union			
401-K			

	Financial institution/ address/phone #/ contact	Account #	Location of records (statements/ canceled checks/ checkbooks/ passbooks/ bonds, etc.)
IRA			
Keogh plan			
Money market accounts			
Mutual funds			
Partnership agreements			
Pension			
Savings bonds			
Social Security (card & records)			
Stock certificates			

	Financial institution/ address/phone #/ contact	Account #	Location of records (statements/ canceled checks/ checkbooks/ passbooks/ bonds, etc.)
Stock options			
Trust agreements			
Other:			

CREDIT CARDS/ CHARGE ACCOUNTS		
Credit card company/address phone number	Account number	Location of card/ statements

INSURANCE RECORDS			
	Agent/ company/ address/ phone #	Policy number	Location of policy/records
Automobile			
Death benefits			
Dental			
Disability			
Health			
Homeowners			
Liability			
Life—group			
Life—individual			
Long-term care			
Medicare (note location of card and records)			

INSURANCE RECORDS

	Agent/ company/ address/ phone #	Policy number	Location of policy/records
Medigap			
Property & casualty			
Other:			

PERSONAL PROPERTY/REAL ESTATE/TAX RECORDS

	Description of property	Location of records/documents
Auto ownership title		
Bills of sale		
Boat ownership title		
Deeds		
Guarantees/ warranties		
Income tax records		
Mortgages		

	Description of property	Location of records/documents
Personal property appraisals		
Personal property inventory		
Property tax receipts		
Rental property records		
Title insurance		
Other:		

ESTATE/END-OF-LIFE RECORDS	
Document	Location
Burial instructions	
Cemetery plot deed	
Durable power of attorney —health care	
Durable power of attorney —regular	
Letter of instruction for beneficiaries	

Document	Location
Living will	
Special bequests	
Trusts	
Will	

 ## CHECKLIST #13: CHOOSING A MEDIGAP POLICY

The benefits offered by Medigap's ten standard plans (A through J) are outlined in the chart on page 133. Some plans may not be available in your parent's area. Your state insurance department or Health Insurance Counseling and Advocacy Program can tell you which packages are for sale in your state, which companies sell Medigap, and what premiums they may charge.

1. BASIC BENEFITS: Included in all ten packages are:

HOSPITALIZATION:
- Part A coinsurance for days 61 to 90 in each benefit period
- Part A coinsurance for each of Medicare's 60 lifetime reserve days
- 100 percent of Part A eligible expenses after Medicare coverage ends, for a lifetime maximum of 365 days

BLOOD:
- First three pints per calendar year

MEDICAL EXPENSES:
- Part B coinsurance (generally 20 percent of eligible expenses), after $100 annual deductible

2. PART A DEDUCTIBLE:
- Covers the annual Part A hospital deductible

132

✔ CHECKLIST #13: CHOOSING A MEDIGAP POLICY

	A	B	C	D	E	F	G	H	I	J
1. Basic Benefits	✔	✔	✔	✔	✔	✔	✔	✔	✔	✔
2. Part A Deductible		✔	✔	✔	✔	✔	✔	✔	✔	✔
3. Skilled Nursing Coinsurance			✔	✔	✔	✔	✔	✔	✔	✔
4. Part B Deductible			✔			✔				
5. Part B Excess						100%	80%		100%	100%
6. Foreign Travel Emergency			✔	✔	✔	✔	✔	✔	✔	✔
7. At Home Recovery				✔			✔		✔	✔
8. Prescription Drugs								*	*	**
9. Preventive Care					✔					✔
Company #1										
Company #2										
Company #3										

* Basic $1,250 limit   ** Extended $3,000 limit

3. SKILLED NURSING COINSURANCE:
- Covers the coinsurance for days 21 to 100 of skilled nursing facility care

4. PART B DEDUCTIBLE:
- Covers the annual Part B deductible

5. PART B EXCESS:
- Covers either 80 percent or 100 percent of the difference between doctors' charges and Medicare-approved Part B charges

6. FOREIGN TRAVEL EMERGENCY:
- Covers 80 percent of medically necessary emergency care in a foreign country, after a $250 deductible

7. AT HOME RECOVERY:
- Covers up to $40 per visit and $1,600 per year for short-term home health care services after an illness, injury, or surgery

8. PRESCRIPTION DRUGS:
- Covers 50 percent of prescription drug costs, up to either $1,250 or $3,000 annually, after a $250 deductible

9. PREVENTIVE CARE:
- Covers up to $120 per year for health exams, tests, and screenings

 ### CHECKLIST #14: CHOOSING A LONG-TERM CARE POLICY

Because there are no standardized long-term care policies, it is difficult to compare coverage and costs. Use this checklist to zero in on the benefits your relative considers important and to make sure policies include essential features.

	POLICY #1	POLICY #2	POLICY #3

1. Levels of care
Does the policy cover:

Skilled nursing care?	Yes/No	Yes/No	Yes/No
Intermediate care?	Yes/No	Yes/No	Yes/No
Custodial care?	Yes/No	Yes/No	Yes/No

2. Where care is covered
Does the policy cover:

Care in any licensed facility?	Yes/No	Yes/No	Yes/No
(If no, list restrictions)	_____	_____	_____
Home care?	Yes/No	Yes/No	Yes/No
(If yes, list restrictions—Skilled care only? Home health aides? Homemakers?)	_____	_____	_____
Adult day care?	Yes/No	Yes/No	Yes/No
Other care settings?	Yes/No	Yes/No	Yes/No
(If yes, list)	_____	_____	_____

3. Amount of benefits
What is the daily benefit for:

Nursing home care?	$ _____	$ _____	$ _____
Home health care?	$ _____	$ _____	$ _____
Adult day care?	$ _____	$ _____	$ _____
Other? (specify)	$ _____	$ _____	$ _____

What are maximum lifetime benefits for:

Nursing home care?	$ _____	$ _____	$ _____
Home health care?	$ _____	$ _____	$ _____
Total lifetime limit?	$ _____	$ _____	$ _____

4. Length of coverage

What is the benefit period
you are considering? _____ days _____ days _____ days

Does the policy limit the number of days or visits per year for:

Nursing home care?	Yes/No	Yes/No	Yes/No
	_____ days	_____ days	_____ days
Home health care?	Yes/No	Yes/No	Yes/No
	_____ days	_____ days	_____ days

5. Waiting/elimination period

What is the waiting period before benefits begin for:

Nursing home care?	_____ days	_____ days	_____ days
Home health care?	_____ days	_____ days	_____ days

6. Preexisting conditions

How long before preexisting
conditions are covered? _____months _____months _____months

How far does the company
look back at medical history
for preexisting conditions? _____months _____months _____months

7. Inflation protection

Are benefits increased
automatically? Yes/No Yes/No Yes/No

If yes, at what rate? _____% _____% _____%

How often? _____/__ _____/__ _____/__

For how long? _____years _____years _____years

At what age does it stop?	_____years	_____years	_____years
Can additional increments of coverage be bought?	Yes/No	Yes/No	Yes/No
If yes, when?	_____	_____	_____
How much?	_____	_____	_____
At what age does the option end?	_____years	_____years	_____years

If inflation coverage is bought, what daily benefit would be received for:

Nursing home care?	$ _____	$ _____	$ _____
In 5 years?	$ _____	$ _____	$ _____
In 10 years?	$ _____	$ _____	$ _____
Home health care?	$ _____	$ _____	$ _____
In 5 years?	$ _____	$ _____	$ _____
In 10 years?	$ _____	$ _____	$ _____

8. Eligibility for benefits

Which of these is required to determine eligibility?

Doctor certification?	Yes/No	Yes/No	Yes/No
"Medical necessity"?	Yes/No	Yes/No	Yes/No
Assessment of daily living activities?	Yes/No	Yes/No	Yes/No
Prior hospital stay?	Yes/No	Yes/No	Yes/No
Prior nursing home stay (for home health coverage)?	Yes/No	Yes/No	Yes/No
Other? (Specify)	_____	_____	_____

Are there separate requirements for benefits covering Alzheimer's and other cognitive impairments?	Yes/No	Yes/No	Yes/No
Does the policy clearly spell out eligibility requirements and restrictions?	Yes/No	Yes/No	Yes/No

9. Other provisions

Is there a waiver-of-premium provision? (premiums stop while benefits are received)	Yes/No	Yes/No	Yes/No
Is there a death benefit?	Yes/No	Yes/No	Yes/No
If yes, what are the restrictions?	_____	_____	_____
Is there a nonforfeiture or return-of-premiums benefit (returns portion of premium if coverage is dropped)?	Yes/No	Yes/No	Yes/No
Is the policy guaranteed renewable?	Yes/No	Yes/No	Yes/No
Is there a grace period for late payment?	Yes/No	Yes/No	Yes/No

10. Cost

What is the annual premium *excluding* all riders?	$ _____	$_____	$_____

What is the cost of the inflation rider?	$ _____	$ _____	$ _____
What is the cost of the nonforfeiture benefit?	$ _____	$ _____	$ _____
What is the annual premium *including* all riders?	$ _____	$ _____	$ _____

 ## CHECKLIST #15: EVALUATING MANAGED CARE PLANS

Use these questions to evaluate the suitability and quality of HMO services.

❏ *Does the plan have a "risk" or "cost" contract with Medicare?*

Risk contracts lock members into receiving all covered care (excluding emergency services) through the plan's network or through referrals by the plan to outside providers. If your parent goes outside the plan for services, neither the plan nor Medicare may pick up the bill.

❏ *How flexible is the plan?*

Ask what happens if your relative disagrees with the HMO's refusal to pay for certain treatments and services. What is the process for appealing the plan's decision and requesting a second opinion? Will the plan pay for a second opinion from a doctor outside its network? Also ask whether it is possible to switch doctors within the plan if your parent is unhappy with the first primary care physician chosen.

❏ *Does the plan carefully review the qualifications of doctors before letting them into its network?*

Other quality considerations include how often the plan checks on doctors' performance, what percentage of doctors are board certified (meaning they have had extra training and passed a difficult exam), what percentage leave the plan each year, and how satisfied plan members are with care and service. For answers to these questions, contact the

National Committee for Quality Assurance; your state's Health Insurance Counseling and Advocacy Program (see Directory of Resources); your local public health or consumer affairs office; the plan's customer service representative; and friends or neighbors who belong to the plan.

❑ *What are the guidelines regarding skilled nursing care, physical therapy, and home health care?*
Some HMOs may balk at paying for costly long-term care. Ask local nursing facilities and other caregivers how the HMO handles these cases, and contact the Area Agency on Aging (see Appendix B) for information on the plan's complaint record.

❑ *How easy is it to get an appointment?*
Ask the plan's customer service representative and HMO members how long your relative can expect to spend in the doctor's waiting room and whether doctors are available for phone consultations.

❑ *Are the plan's providers conveniently located?*
Look into the transportation available to doctors, specialists, hospitals, and other health care facilities in the network.

❑ *What happens if your relative needs health care services out of state?*
HMOs offer varying coverage for services provided outside their area. Make sure coverage would be adequate if your relative travels frequently or spends part of the year in another state.

❑ *Is your relative's area served by more than one managed care plan?*
If so, compare quality features, benefits, premiums, and copayments to select the plan that offers the most suitable coverage at the best rates.

✔ *CHECKLIST #16: MORE MONEY-SAVING OPTIONS*

Not all of the following tips will be relevant to your parent's unique situation, but you may find information here that can help you cut costs or discover financial assistance in unexpected places.

140

❏ If your relative is referred to a medical specialist, ask if the physician accepts assignment of Medicare benefits. If so, the doctor cannot charge more than Medicare's allowable rates, which in the long run can mean substantial savings. Your local Social Security office or Medicare carrier can provide a directory of doctors participating in the Medicare program. Also be aware that some nonparticipating physicians will accept assignment on a case-by-case basis. Even doctors who do not accept assignment are subject to a "limiting charge"—their fees cannot be more than 15 percent above Medicare's approved amounts.

❏ If your parent's doctor prescribes in-home skilled nursing or therapy services, ask for a letter documenting the need. This can help persuade a home health care agency to accept your relative as a patient and convince Medicare to pay for the care.

❏ Medicaid usually does not cover over-the-counter (OTC) drugs such as aspirin. However, if your relative is on Medicaid and has sound medical reasons for taking an OTC drug, the doctor can fill out forms requesting a special dispensation to pay for the medication.

❏ Taking advantage of community resources can add up to big savings. Be sure to review all the in-home care resources discussed in Chapter 2 and to explore local services thoroughly. You may find that the same service offered by a private company for a fee is available free or at low cost through the Area Agency on Aging or a religious, civic, or other community organization.

❏ Many fraternal and religious groups have special funds to assist members who are in need of long-term care. Social, medical, and housing services may be available free of charge or for a fee based on income. Ask for information from the group's membership office or local clergy.

❏ Your community may have special funds earmarked for

charitable purposes such as helping people pay extraordinary medical expenses or purchase special medical equipment. Talk to a local social worker or social service agency.

❑ If your relative is about to turn sixty-five, prompt enrollment in Medicare could reduce monthly premiums. Premiums are lowest for individuals who enroll from three months before to four months after their sixty-fifth birthday. After that, premiums rise by about 10 percent for each year until enrollment. If your parent is covered under an employer-sponsored health plan, the seven-month window of opportunity does not take effect until that plan is terminated.

❑ Scrutinize your relative's insurance policies for duplicate or unnecessary coverage or overcoverage. You may be able to cut premiums by dropping certain benefits, such as comprehensive coverage on an older automobile, or by eliminating policies with strictly limited coverage, such as travel or dread disease insurance.

❑ If your relative is shopping for long-term care insurance, check with your own employer too. Many companies allow employees to buy long-term coverage for their parents, and that coverage often offers advantages an older person won't find when buying a policy independently.

Directory of Resources

The following resources either provide direct financial or legal information and services or will refer you to local financial and legal professionals and programs. Also listed are membership organizations that offer financial benefits such as insurance plans and discounts on products and services. If your parent has a physical impairment or disability, see the Directory of Resources in Chapter 5 as well. There you will find listings of organizations offering free or low-cost benefits and services to people with hearing or visual impairments and other specific disabilities.

NATIONAL

Organizations on this list offer their services nationwide or over a significant area of the country.

American Association of Retired Persons (AARP)
601 E Street NW
Washington, DC 20049
1–800–424–3410 or 202–434–2300
TTY: 202–434–6561

The nation's largest organization for people age fifty and older, AARP offers members a number of financial benefits, including travel, lodging, and auto rental discounts; life, group health, auto, homeowners, and mobile home insurance; a motorists' plan; discounts on mail-order drugs and health care products; retirement, investment, and financial planning services; and a financial skills-building program for midlife adults with limited income. Annual membership fee: $8.00.

Helpful Publications:
To order these free booklets and handbooks or to request a complete catalog, write to AARP Fulfillment at the address above.

"Before You Buy: A Guide to Long-Term Care Insurance." Order #D12893.

"Medicare: What It Covers, What It Doesn't." Order #D13133.

"Medigap: Medicare Supplement Insurance, A Consumer's Guide." Order #D14042.

"Product Report: Life Insurance for Older Adults." Order #D14139.

"Tomorrow's Choices: Preparing Now for Future Legal, Financial, and Health Care Decisions." Order #D13479.

American Bar Association
750 North Lake Shore Drive
Chicago, IL 60611–4497
312–988–5000

Contact this national organization of the legal profession for the address and phone number of your state bar association, which can provide referrals to attorneys in your area.

Helpful Publications:
Phone 1–800–285–2221 for ordering information.
"The American Lawyer: When and How to Use One." 36-page booklet on selecting and working with a lawyer and understanding fees. $2.50.
"Buying and Selling Your Home: A Consumer's Guide to Residential Real Estate Transactions." 32-page booklet on issues involved in real estate transactions. $2.00.
"Employment and Education Rights over Age 50." Leaflet on older person's rights and remedies for rights violations. 50¢.
"Health and Financial Decisions: Legal Tools for Preserving Personal Autonomy." Free brochure on powers of attorney, trusts, advance directives, and other planning tools.
"Planning for Life and Death." Free 20-page booklet on probate, wills, and estate planning.
"Wills: Why You Should Have One and the Lawyer's Role in Its Preparation." Free pamphlet on wills and probate.

American Red Cross
2025 E Street NW
Washington, DC 20006
703–206–7090
Red Cross workers will assist veterans in the preparation of claims for financial benefits through the Board of Veterans Appeals. Contact the national headquarters for referral to your local chapter.

Bankcard Holders of America (BHA)
524 Branch Drive
Salem, VA 24153
540–389–5445
Fax: 540–389–3020

BHA offers lists of issuers of low-rate and secured credit cards, plus a newsletter and a variety of other publications related to credit, debt, and money management. All publications plus access to an 800 line providing information and assistance with consumer credit questions and problems are free to members. Annual membership fee: $24.00.

B'nai Brith

1640 Rhode Island Avenue NW
Washington, DC 20036–3278
1–800–723-BNAI (1–800–723–2624) or 202–857–6625
via Internet: http:\\bnaibrith.org

B'nai Brith offers members of the Jewish faith comprehensive major medical and long-term care insurance, as well as reduced rates on long-distance phone service, group and individual tour packages, and discounts on hotels, car rentals, and at local businesses. Annual membership fee varies among local lodges, from $35.00 to $167.00.

Brookdale Center on Aging

425 East Twenty-fifth Street
New York, NY 10010–2590
212–481–4433
Fax: 212–481–5069

Based in the City University of New York, this academic gerontology center operates the Institute on Law and Rights of Older Adults. The institute offers free, speedy advice to older adults and their families who have questions regarding the laws regulating Medicare, Medicaid, Supplemental Security Income, Social Security Disability, and New York State's Adult Protective Services.

Helpful Publications:
Phone for a complete catalog.

H.E.L.P. for Seniors is a monthly newsletter for older people, with information on public benefits. Issues cost $3.00 each and include:

"Explanation of Medicare Benefits." Order #LAW–019B.

"Explanation of Medigap Insurance." Order #LAW–019C.

"Long Term Care Financing." Order #LAW–019G.

"SSI May Mean Cash for You." Order #LAW–019A.

"Understanding the Medicaid Program." Order #LAW–019F.

Catholic Golden Age (CGA)
430 Penn Avenue
Scranton, PA 18503
1–800–836–5699 or 717–342–3294
Fax: 717–963–0149

Money-saving benefits for Catholics age fifty and older who join CGA include discounts on long-distance phone rates, pharmaceuticals, eye exams and eyeglasses, hotels, travel, car rentals, and some mail-order and retail merchandise, plus group rate insurance plans. Annual membership fee: $8.00.

Communicating for Seniors
P.O. Box 677
Fergus Falls, MN 56538
1–800–432–3276

A national organization for older rural Americans, Communicating for Seniors offers members low-cost Medigap insurance, a free accidental death benefit, a mail-order prescription drug plan, airfare discounts, and a bimonthly newsletter and other publications. Annual membership fee: $30.00.

Council of Better Business Bureaus (CBBB)
4200 Wilson Boulevard
Arlington, VA 22003
703–276–0100
Fax: 703–525–8277

Phone the CBBB to locate your local Better Business Bureau, which will give you information on the complaint records of local businesses providing financial and legal services.

Helpful Publications:

"Tips on Consumer Problems of the Elderly." Order #07–24–171. $2.00.

"Tips on Financial Planners." Order #07–24–225. $2.00.

"Tips on Insurance: Medicare and Medigap." Order #07–24–200LG. $2.00.

"Tips on Tax Preparers." Order #07–24–226. $2.00.

Department of Housing and Urban Development (HUD)

HUD Building, 451 Seventh Street SW, Room 6130
Washington, DC 20410
202–708–1422 or 202–708–2866

Contact your local HUD field office for information on the types of home equity conversion mortgages available in your area and referrals to qualified lenders.

Department of Veterans Affairs (VA)

Office of Public Affairs
810 Vermont Avenue NW
Washington, DC 20420
1–800–827–1000
TTY: 1–800–829–4833

Veterans and their families can call the VA's 800 number to be connected with their regional office, which will provide information about veterans' and survivors' benefits and send benefits applications and other forms.

Direct Marketing Association

Mail Preference Service
P.O. Box 9008
Farmingdale, NY 11735–9008
202–955–5030

Telephone Preference Service
P.O. Box 9014
Farmingdale, NY 11735–9014
202–955–5030

If your parent is bothered by unsolicited mail offers or telephone sales calls, the Direct Marketing Association can help cut those solicitations by 65 to 70 percent. Contact the association's free Mail Preference Service or Telephone Preference Service. You will receive forms to complete and return. Marketers that subscribe to DMA's services will then be notified to remove your parent's name from mail and/or phone sales lists.

Helpful Publications:
For copies of these free brochures, write: Direct Marketing Association, 11 West Forty-second Street, P.O. Box 3861, New York, NY 10163–3861.

"Make Knowledge Your Partner in Mail or Telephone Order Shopping"

"Sweepstakes Advertising: A Consumer's Guide"

"Tips for Telephone Shopping: How to Enjoy a Convenient, Easy Way to Shop, and Avoid Possible Problems"

Eldercare Locator
1–800–677–1116

This nationwide directory assistance service of the National Association of Area Agencies on Aging will put you in touch with community resources providing legal services and financial planning assistance to seniors. You must give the operator your relative's county and city name or zip code.

Families USA Foundation
1334 G Street NW, Suite 300
Washington, DC 20005
202–628–3030
Fax: 202–347–2417

This grassroots lobbying network for health care reform offers its members newsletters, special alerts, and tips on communicating their views to legislators. The group's Medicaid Advocacy Network keeps members posted on changes in Medicaid and shares strategies and tactics for influencing lawmakers.

Fannie Mae Public Information Office
3900 Wisconsin Avenue NW
Washington, DC 20016–2899
1–800–7-FANNIE (1–800–732–6643) or 202–752–7000

Fannie Mae (Federal National Mortgage Association) is a private company that provides mortgage funds to banks, savings and loans, credit unions, and mortgage companies. Contact for a free packet of information on home equity conversion mortgages, which includes a list of participating lenders.

Health Insurance Counseling and Advocacy Program (HICAP)

Every state has a health insurance counseling program providing free information and assistance to older adults who have questions about Medicare, Medicaid, Medigap, long-term care, and other forms of health insurance. The program usually is called HICAP but in some states may go by a different name. Services also vary from state to state. Typically, counselors at local offices will help file Medicare and private insurance claims, challenge claims denials, review insurance options, plan for financing long-term care, and develop a system for organizing doctor and hospital bills. To locate your state program, phone the Medicare Hotline at 1–800–638–6833.

Institute of Certified Financial Planners
3801 East Florida Avenue, Suite 708
Denver, CO 80210
1–800–282-PLAN (1–800–282–7526) or 303–759–4900

Phone the toll-free referral line for a list of certified financial planners in your area and a free copy of the brochure "Selecting a Qualified Financial Planning Professional: Twelve Questions to Consider."

Helpful Publications:
Order these brochures by mail.

"Avoiding Investment and Financial Scams: Seeking Full Disclosure Is the Key." Free brochure.

"Considerations for a Comfortable Retirement." 15-page booklet. $2.00.

"How to Manage Your Financial Resources: Creating a Spending Plan You Can Control." Free brochure.

Internal Revenue Service
1–800-TAX-FORM (1–800–829–3676)
TTY: 1–800–829–4059

Phone for the location of your state's toll-free TeleTax line, which provides recorded tax information on about 140 topics. This is also the number to call for copies of free IRS forms and publications (or write your nearest IRS Forms Distribution Center; check your income tax package for that address).

Helpful Publications:

"Credit for the Elderly or the Disabled." Order #524.

"Guide to Free Tax Services." Order #910.

"Large-print Form 1040 and Schedules A, B, D, E, E1C, R." Order #1614.

"Large-print Form 1040A and Schedules 1, 3, E1C." Order #1615.

"Survivors, Executors, and Administrators." Order #559.

"Tax Information for Older Americans." Order #554.

International Association for Financial Planning (IAFP)
5775 Glenridge Drive NE, Suite B-300
Atlanta, GA 30328
1–800–945-IAFP (1–800–945–4237) or 404–845–0011

Phone the toll-free number of this international professional association for the names of up to five financial planners in your area. You will also receive the "Financial Adviser Disclosure Form," with tips on selecting a financial planner.

Helpful Publications:

"How Financial Advisers Are Paid." Free brochure answers common questions about fees and commissions.

"How to Protect Yourself against Fraud." Free

brochure includes ten steps to ensure financial planners are looking out for their clients' best interests.

Legal Counsel for the Elderly (LCE)
American Association of Retired Persons (AARP)
601 E Street NW
Washington, DC 20049
202–434–2120
TTY: 202–434–6562
This AARP program maintains telephone hotlines that offer free legal consultation for callers age sixty and older. Hotlines currently are operating in Arizona, the District of Columbia, Florida, Maine, Michigan, New Mexico, Ohio, Pennsylvania, Texas, and Puerto Rico. Phone the main office for hotline numbers.

Medical Business Associates
P.O. Box 1479
Etowah, NC 28729
1–800–659–3171 or 704–891–5524
This claims management service will file a client's medical insurance claims, maintain copies and records, check benefit statements for correct payment, follow up on problems, initiate appeals when necessary, and send quarterly reports detailing all insurance activity. Cost per individual: $10.00 per month. The service also will organize and file claims relating to past illness or an estate, at $45.00 per hour.

Medicare Hotline
1–800–638–6833
TTY: 1–800–820–1202
This federally operated hotline provides information on Medicare, Medicaid, Medigap, income guidelines for special benefits, and advice on following up on specific claims. Also phone to request insurance-related publications or to report suspicious health insurance sales practices. The hotline can give you referrals to your area's Medicare carrier (for information on specific claims, payments, and appeals), Medicare-certified

151

HMOs, state Health Insurance Counseling and Advocacy Program, and state Peer Review Organization Hotline or Home Health Hotline (for registering complaints about the quality of care provided by Medicare-certified hospitals, nursing homes, and home health agencies).

National Academy of Elder Law Attorneys (NAELA)
1604 North Country Club Road
Tucson, AZ 85716
602–881–4005
Fax: 602–325–7925

Contact this professional association when you need referrals to elder law attorneys—lawyers who specialize in legal problems affecting the elderly and their families. NAELA gives referrals by geographic area and expertise.

Helpful Publications:
Send a self-addressed stamped business-size envelope for this free brochure.

"Questions and Answers When Looking for an Elder Law Attorney."

National Association of Insurance Commissioners (NAIC)
444 North Capitol Street NW, Suite 701
Washington, DC 20001–1512
202–624–7790
Fax: 202–624–8579
via Internet: http://www.naic.org

NAIC's members are insurance regulators from the fifty states, the District of Columbia, and the U.S. territories. Contact for referrals to your state insurance department, which can provide information on many insurance-related topics, and to your state's Health Insurance Counseling and Advocacy Program for seniors.

Helpful Publications:
Contact NAIC or your state insurance department for these free publications.

"Consumer's Guide to Home Insurance." Brochure.

"A Shopper's Guide to Cancer Insurance." Brochure.

"A Shopper's Guide to Long-Term Care Insurance." 52-page booklet includes worksheets for estimating needs and comparing policies.

National Association of Retired Federal Employees (NARFE)

1533 New Hampshire Avenue NW
Washington, DC 20036–1279
1-800-NARFE-94 (1–800–627–3394) (member line) or 202–234–0832
Fax: 202–797–9698

Dedicated to protecting the retirement benefits of federal employees and retirees, this organization provides members with advice and assistance in resolving problems with federal retirement and health benefits. Members also receive a monthly magazine and discounts on a variety of products and services, including health, life, auto, and homeowners insurance; a credit card program; travel packages; and group tours. Annual membership fee varies among local chapters, from no fee to $15.00.

National Committee to Preserve Social Security and Medicare

2000 K Street NW, Suite 800
Washington, DC 20006
1–800–998–0180 (Senior Flash Hotline—recorded weekly legislative updates) or 202–822–9459
Fax: 202–822–9612

Contact this education and advocacy organization, which lobbies for senior programs, when you need referrals to government or social service agencies that can help resolve problems with Social Security, Medicare, and other benefits and entitlements. Member benefits include periodic legislative updates, a bimonthly newsletter, and direct responses to inquiries. Annual membership fee: $10.00.

Helpful Publications:
Phone for a complete catalog or to request these free brochures.

"Buying Your Medigap Policy." Also available in Spanish.

"Entitlements: What You Need to Know."

"Fast Facts for Seniors." Covers Social Security and Medicare.

"Qualified Medicare Beneficiary Program." Also available in Spanish.

"Social Security Disability Benefits." Also available in Spanish.

"Supplemental Security Income: Questions and Answers About a Program to Help Seniors." Also available in Spanish.

National Committee for Quality Assurance (NCQA)
2000 L Street NW, Suite 500
Washington, DC 20036
1–800–839–6487 or 202–955–3515
via Internet: http:\\www.ncqa.org

When selecting an HMO or other managed care plan, phone this not-for-profit accrediting organization for its free Accreditation Status List, which gives the results of the organization's evaluation of the plan's quality of service. The list will tell you whether the plan was accredited for three years, one year, provisionally, or failed altogether.

Helpful Publication:
"Choosing Quality: Finding the Health Plan That's Right for You." Free brochure.

National Council of Senior Citizens (NCSC)
8403 Colesville Road, 12th floor
Silver Spring, MD 20910
301–578–8800
Fax: 301–578–8999

An advocacy organization for older Americans, NCSC offers members low-cost health, Medigap, and long-term care insurance; a mail-order prescription drug service; group travel and tour discounts; discounts on hotels, motels, and rental cars; and a monthly newsletter and other publications related to legislative issues and senior programs. Annual membership fee: $12.00.

National Foundation for Consumer Credit
8611 Second Avenue, Suite 100
Silver Spring, MD 20910
1–800–388-CCCS (1–800–388–2227) or 301–589–5600
Spanish language assistance: 1–800–682–9832
Fax: 301–495–5623

When you phone this nonprofit organization's toll-free number using a touch-tone phone, an automated response system will give you the phone number and location of one or more local financial counseling offices. More than 1,160 member offices in the United States, Puerto Rico, and Canada provide free or low-cost professional money management counseling to help consumers solve personal financial problems. A counselor will help you or your relative analyze personal finances, budget for future spending, and, if credit problems are severe, work with creditors to set up a plan to pay off debts. Many member offices operate under the name Consumer Credit Counseling Service (CCCS); if you don't have a touch-tone phone, look in your phone directory under that listing to find your nearest office.

National Insurance Consumer Helpline
1–800–942–4242

Trained operators and licensed agents with this toll-free information service, sponsored by the American Council of Life Insurance, Health Insurance Association of America, and Insurance Information Institute, will answer general questions and send consumer guides about life, health, auto, homeowners, and business insurance. Also phone for referrals to appropriate agencies for help in registering and resolving insurance-related complaints.

National Legal Aid and Defender Association (NLADA)
1625 K Street NW, Suite 800
Washington, DC 20006
202–452–0620

The nation's oldest and largest organization of legal service providers to the poor and underprivileged, NLADA may be able to refer you to a local program specializing in free legal aid to indigent senior citizens.

Older Women's League (OWL)
666 Eleventh Street NW, Suite 700
Washington, DC 20001
202–783–6686 or 202–783–6689 (OWL Powerline)

A national grassroots membership organization, OWL works to achieve economic, political, and social equity for midlife and older women. Member benefits include access to long-term care insurance, discounts on OWL publications, and a bimonthly newspaper. The OWL Powerline is a taped weekly update on congressional activities affecting women. Annual membership fee: $15.00.

Pension Rights Center
918 Sixteenth Street NW, Suite 704
Washington, DC 20006–2902
202–296–3776
Fax: 202–833–2472

Contact this public interest group for referrals to a national network of pension attorneys, some of whom will represent retirees on a pro bono or reduced-fee basis.

Helpful Publication:
"Where to Look for Help with a Pension Problem." Also available in Spanish. Free booklet lists government agencies, private organizations, and legal referral programs providing assistance in pension cases.

Railroad Retirement Board
1301 Clay Street, Suite 392N
Oakland, CA 94612–5220
510–637–2973
  Contact for information on benefits available to retired railroad workers under the Railroad Retirement System.

Retired Officers Association (TROA)
201 North Washington Street
Alexandria, VA 22314–2539
1–800–245–8762 or 703–549–2311
E-mail: troa@troa.org
via Internet: http://www.troa.org
  A membership organization for retired officers and warrant officers of the seven uniformed services, their families, and their survivors, TROA offers its members counseling and assistance with benefits; various insurance plans; investment programs; a credit card program; discounts on legal services, travel, hotels, rental cars, prescription drugs, and eyewear; and a monthly magazine. The Survivor Assistance Service helps surviving family members apply for benefits and entitlements. Annual membership fee: $20.00.

Retirement Office Information
U.S. Office of Personnel Management
1900 East Street NW, Room 1323B
Washington, DC 20415
202–606–0500
Fax: 202–606–0145
  Phone this automated caller assistance line for information on benefits available under the Federal Civil Service Retirement System, covering most civilian employees of the U.S. government hired before 1984.

Sears Mature Outlook
P.O. Box 10448
Des Moines, IA 50306–0448
1–800–336–6330
  This membership organization for people age fifty and older

offers travel, hotel, restaurant, and car rental discounts plus discounts at Sears optical departments and coupons for savings on Sears store and catalog purchases. Membership includes a bimonthly travel and lifestyle magazine. Annual membership fee: $14.95.

September Days Clubs
P.O. Box 10108
Knoxville, TN 37939–0108
1–800–241–5050
Fax: 404–728–4460

Adults age fifty and older may join this membership organization, sponsored by Days Inn, to receive discounts on car rentals, airline tickets, group tours, admission to participating theme parks and other attractions, plus room rates and meals at Days Inns. Annual membership fee: $14.00.

Social Security Administration
1–800–772–1213 or 1–800–537–7005
TTY: 1–800–325–0778

Phone 1–800–772–1213 for Medicare and Social Security information, to apply for benefits, to request proof of benefit payment or a new Medicare card, to report missing Social Security checks, or to locate your nearest Social Security office. Phone 1–800–537–7005 to receive a form for requesting your record of personal earnings and benefit estimate statement. Also available are copies of free government publications on Medicare, Social Security, SSI, and supplemental insurance. Lines often are busy; try phoning early in the morning or late in the afternoon, and late in the week or in the month.

Helpful Publications:
Phone for a complete list of publications or to request these free booklets.

"Disability." Order #05–10029. Explains Social Security retirement benefits.

"SSI." Order #05–11000. Explains the Supplemental Security Income program.

"Survivors." Order #05–10084. Explains Social Security survivors' benefits.

"Understanding Social Security." Order #05–10024. Comprehensive explanation of all Social Security programs.

United Seniors Health Cooperative (USHC)
1331 H Street NW, Suite 500
Washington, DC 20005–4706
202–393–6222
Fax: 202–783–0588

A nonprofit health care cooperative for older adults, USHC offers its members a bimonthly newsletter plus discounts on publications related to health insurance, financial planning, Medicare and Medicaid, and other health care issues and financial issues. Medical Bill Minder is a health insurance claims service. Members forward their medical bills and the service sorts them out, files insurance claims, and sends an easy-to-read analysis of insurance payments and amounts owed. Annual USHC membership fee: $25.00. Medical Bill Minder: $10.00 per month.

Helpful Publications:
Phone for ordering information and a complete catalog.

"How to Be an Informed Consumer of Health Insurance: Medigap Update and Medicare Summary." 8 pages. $3.50.

"Medicare HMOs: Some Tips for Consumers." 4 pages. $2.00.

"Private Long Term Care Insurance: To Buy or Not to Buy." 4 pages. $2.00.

United Way of America
701 North Fairfax Street
Alexandria, VA 22314–2045
703–836–7100

Your local United Way may be able to refer you to community resources offering emergency food and shelter or assistance with rent and utilities payments to older and disabled individuals. Phone the national office or look in your phone directory to locate your local United Way.

REGIONAL

Organizations on this list provide services in limited geographic areas. You may be able to find groups offering similar services in your relative's community.

AgeWell Resource Center
Westgate Mall
2341-M Schoenersville Road
Bethlehem, PA 18017
610–954–3999
Fax: 610–954–3525

AgeWell's volunteer counselors provide older adults in the Lehigh Valley area of Pennsylvania with free assistance in resolving health insurance billing problems and completing application forms for health benefit programs. Counselors also will advise on health insurance options.

Aging in America
1500 Pelham Parkway South
Bronx, NY 10461
718–824–4004

Aging in America's seven senior centers in the Bronx offer older adults free information and referrals for dealing with legal and financial problems.

California Advocates for Nursing Home Reform (CANHR)
1610 Bush Street
San Francisco, CA 94109
1–800–474–1116 or 415–474–5171
Fax: 415–474–2904

For referrals to elder law attorneys in California, phone CANHR's Lawyer Referral Service. A staff member will ask about your needs and match you with an appropriate prescreened attorney.

Helpful Publications:

Phone or write for these free publications.

"Long Term Care Insurance: A Consumer's Checklist

"Pension Rights Fact Sheets." 8 fact sheets on pension issues cover company pensions; personal retirement plans; annuities; Social Security; issues for divorced and widowed spouses; and civil service, railroad, and military retirement plans.

CARIE (Coalition of Advocates for the Rights of the Infirm Elderly)

1315 Walnut Street, Suite 1000
Philadelphia, PA 19107
215–545–5728
Fax: 215–545–5372

Older people and their caregivers in the Philadelphia area may call CARIE's free telephone consultation line for information and assistance in these areas: discounts for seniors, entitlements, insurance options, legal resources, and utilities assistance. Operators speak English and Spanish.

Citizens for Better Care

4750 Woodward Avenue, Suite 410
Detroit, MI 48201–1308
1–800–833–9548 or 313–832–6387

This nonprofit advocacy group will answer Michiganers' questions about Medicare and Medicaid coverage and other financial issues.

Helpful Publications:

Phone the 800 number for a complete list of publications and ordering information.

"Authority to Act for Others: Guardianship and Other Options." Order #10. $2.00.

"Financial Assistance for Residents of Adult Foster Care Homes and Homes for the Aged." Order #09. $2.00.

"Hospital Care under Medicare." 25¢.

"Nursing Home Resident Trust Funds." 25¢.

Council for Jewish Elderly (CJE)
3003 West Touhy Avenue
Chicago, IL 60645
312–508–1000
Fax: 312–508–1028

This private agency operates two Resource Service Centers in Chicago, where seniors can receive free information and counseling in areas including Medicare, Social Security, insurance claims processing, and legal, medical, and landlord-tenant issues.

HMO Hotline
1–800–400–0815

If your parent lives in California and has a complaint against an HMO that cannot be resolved through the HMO's mandatory grievance procedure, this hotline established by the California Department of Corporations will intervene.

Jewish Association for Services for the Aged (JASA)
40 West Sixty-eighth Street
New York, NY 10023
212–724–3200

JASA helps New York City adults age fifty-five and older of all faiths apply for and obtain benefits, including Social Security, Medicare, Medicaid, and rent exemptions. The organization also provides referrals to local legal and financial resources. Staff speaks English, Spanish, and Yiddish.

Legal Assistance for Seniors (LAS)
614 Grand Avenue, Suite 400
Oakland, CA 94610
510–832–3040

Alameda County, California, residents age sixty and older can obtain free legal advice, information, representation, and community referrals through this nonprofit agency. Legal areas in which LAS provides assistance include income maintenance, housing, incapacity, guardianship, elder abuse, and health care.

North Carolina Senior Citizens Association (NCSCA)
P.O. Box 34
Fayetteville, NC 28302–0034
910–323–3641

A nonprofit membership organization, NCSCA offers insurance plans and discounted services to North Carolina adults age sixty and older. Member benefits include a prescription drug program, travel and rental car discounts, and access to health, long-term care, homeowners, renters, and auto insurance.

Senior Health Insurance Information Program (SHIIP)
Indiana Department of Insurance
311 West Washington Street, Suite 300
Indianapolis, IN 46204–2787
1–800–452–4800

Trained volunteers answer Hoosiers' phone inquiries about Medicare, Medicaid, Medigap, long-term care insurance, and the Indiana Long Term Care Program. Counselors in a statewide network of SHIIP sites offer free assistance in filing insurance claims, organizing Medicare records, and appealing Medicare decisions.

Other Helpful Free or Low-Cost Publications

"Age Page: Getting Your Affairs in Order." Free fact sheet. Contact: National Institute on Aging, P.O. Box 8057, Gaithersburg, MD 20898–8057 (1–800–222–2225).

To order the following publications on financial and legal issues for people with Alzheimer's disease and their families, contact: Alzheimer's Association, 919 North Michigan Avenue, Suite 1000, Chicago, IL 60611–1676 (1–800–272–3900).

"Financial and Health Care Benefits You May Need." Order #ED222Z. Free brochure.

"Legal Considerations for Alzheimer Patients." Order #ED208Z. Free brochure.

"Private Long-Term Care Insurance." Order #PP305Z. $2.00.

"Check Up on Health Insurance Choices." Order #AHCPR 93–0018. Free 20-page booklet on shopping for and comparing health insurance plans. Contact: Agency for Health Care Policy and Research, Publications Clearinghouse, P.O. Box 8547, Silver Spring, MD 20907–8547 (1–800–358–9295).

For a catalog of free and low-cost government publications on legal and financial concerns of the elderly, or to order the following publications, write: Consumer Information Center, P.O. Box 100, Pueblo, CO 81002:

"Facts About Financial Planners." Order #353C. 17 pages. 50¢.

"Fair Debt Collection." Order #346C. 7-page booklet on what debt collectors may and may not do, and how to register complaints. 50¢.

"Finding Legal Help." Order #366C. 20-page booklet on public and private legal resources for older people. 50¢.

"66 Ways to Save Money." Order #352C. 11-page booklet on practical ways to cut everyday costs. 50¢.

"What You Should Know About Your Pension Rights." Order #358C. 48 pages. 50¢.

"Where to Write for Vital Records." Order #143C. 32-page booklet on obtaining copies of birth, death, marriage, and other certificates. $2.25.

Consumer's Resource Handbook. Free 126-page handbook, updated and published annually by the U.S. Office of Consumer Affairs, offers advice on avoiding consumer fraud and resolving consumer complaints. Directory

164

section includes addresses and phone numbers for major consumer organizations, corporate consumer contacts, auto manufacturers, dispute resolution programs, state and local consumer protection offices, military commissary and exchange offices, and selected federal agencies, including agencies with TTY lines. Write: Handbook, Consumer Information Center–6A, Pueblo, CO 81009.

"Fact Sheet: The Medicare Program." Free 6-page fact sheet detailing Medicare coverage. Contact: Public Policy Institute, American Association of Retired Persons, 601 E Street NW, Washington, DC 20049 (1–800–424–3410).

The Health Care Financing Administration, the federal agency that administers Medicare and Medicaid funds, publishes numerous booklets and brochures on various aspects of coverage. The list of publications changes often, so phone or write to find out what topics are currently available and order copies. Health Care Financing Administration, 7500 Security Boulevard, Baltimore, MD 21244–1850 (410–786–7843).

"Health and Financial Decisions: Legal Tools for Preserving Personal Autonomy." Covers powers of attorney, trusts, advance directives, and other planning tools. Free brochure. Contact: American Bar Association Commission on Legal Problems of the Elderly, 740 Fifteenth Street NW, 8th floor, Washington, DC 20005 (202–662–8690).

To order these free consumer guides, contact: Health Insurance Association of America, 555 Thirteenth Street NW, Suite 600 East, Washington, DC 20004–1109 (202–824–1610).

"Consumer's Guide to Health Insurance"

"Guide to Long-Term Care Insurance"

"HIAA Guide to Disability Income (DI) Insurance"

"Guide to Hospital Bills"

"Guide to Medicare Supplement Insurance"

"Reverse Mortgage Locator." Names and phone numbers of FHA lenders providing reverse mortgages in each state. $1.00. Send self-addressed stamped envelope to: National Center for Home Equity Conversion, 7373 147th Street West, Suite 115, Apple Valley, MN 55124 (612–953–4474).

"What Cancer Survivors Need to Know About Health Insurance." Free brochure. Contact: National Coalition for Cancer Survivorship, 1010 Wayne Avenue, Suite 505, Silver Spring, MD 20910–9796 (301–650–8868).

"What You Should Know About Buying Life Insurance." Free brochure. Contact: American Council of Life Insurance, 1001 Pennsylvania Avenue NW, Washington, DC 20004-2599 (1–800–338–4471).

Women & Aging Letter. Bimonthly newsletter provides practical and useful information on medical and financial questions confronting midlife and older women. One-year subscription: $5.00. Write: American Society on Aging, 833 Market Street, Suite 511, San Francisco, CA 94103–1824.

"Your Medicare Handbook." Free 56-page handbook describes the Medicare program and coverage. Also available in Spanish. Order by phone through the Social Security Administration (1–800–772–1213), Health Care Financing Administration (410–786–7843), or Medicare Hotline (1–800–638–6833); or by mail from: Consumer Information Center, Department 33, Pueblo, CO 81009. You also can pick up a copy at your local Social Security office.

Chapter Five

Healthy Aging & Common Disorders

We have a mother-daughter house. My mother is diabetic, and she has macular degeneration. She's had laser surgery, which isn't solving it but is keeping it from getting worse. Even with her glasses on, she can't read, but she still sees well enough to enjoy TV. She can't read the labels so I help her with the grocery shopping. She can't clean anymore but we did get someone to come do that. She eats dinner with us—myself, my husband, and our daughter—every night. I work three days a week. My days off are pretty much spent with my mother, taking her shopping, to the eye doctor, and to all her various doctor appointments.

What's Normal, What's Not

You're well aware of the feelings and problems associated with caregiving, but what does life look like from the other side? How does your aging relative feel about being a care-receiver? What changes in physical and mental health is she or he experiencing? Understanding your loved one's emotional ups and downs can help you cope with your own, and knowing the natural physical changes of aging may enable you to distinguish between "normal" aging and illness.

There is no timetable for aches and pains, for slowing down or suffering illness. Some people show the signs of aging at a relatively young age, while others are blessed with a hearty constitution that keeps them going strong well into their seventies or eighties. A healthy lifestylegetting adequate exercise, eating a well-balanced diet, avoiding smoking and excessive alcohol consumption, and other good habits—also decreases the likelihood that normal body changes will become disabling. In general, though, certain predictable changes occur over time. The chart below outlines these, along with common health problems that are *not* a normal part of aging. Following the chart is an overview of the most common health disorders affecting older people. Finally, this chapter's Directory of Resources introduces the many organizations and associations that are devoted to educating and supporting individuals and families struggling with specific health problems.

One Note of Caution

None of the information given here is intended to substitute for expert medical advice. If you are concerned about your loved one's health, encourage a checkup with a trusted family physician, internist, or geriatrician.

PREDICTABLE AGE-RELATED BODY CHANGES

Remember, even so-called normal body changes should be reported to the doctor, who can rule them out as symptoms of disease and offer suggestions for adapting or for managing discomfort.

Brain/memory	Increased simple forgetfulness, especially in short-term (recent event) memory; tendency to slow down in performance of simple cognitive tasks; increased ability to perform some untimed tasks involving use of accumulated knowledge and management of practical information
Cardiovascular system	Slight increase in blood pressure; some thickening and loss of elasticity in blood vessels

Digestive system	Dry mouth common; may make swallowing difficult; increased likelihood of lactose intolerance (inability to digest milk products)
Emotions	Emotions commonly experienced by those facing chronic illness include fear of loss of control, fear of dependency, fear of abandonment, fear of isolation
Feet	Prolonged wearing of tight, narrow, and/or pointed-toe shoes may cause corns, calluses, and bunions; skin on feet may become dry, cracked, and susceptible to infection
Hearing	Some hearing loss, especially in high frequencies, such as high-pitched voices; difficulty distinguishing rapid sounds and similar-sounding words, and difficulty understanding speech in the presence of loud background noises
Muscles and bones	Some decrease in muscle mass, strength, and elasticity (may be due to factors other than aging, such as inactivity or nutritional deficiency); bone growth slows and bones become thinner and more porous; posture may slump or stoop; some loss of height.
Respiratory system	Some decrease in lung capacity (total airflow in and out of lungs), efficiency, and ability to fight disease; may take longer to recover from colds and the flu; increased susceptibility to pneumonia
Sense of smell	Declines rapidly after age fifty, affecting taste and enjoyment of food
Sight	Less able to focus on nearby and/or distant objects, and to shift focus from near to far/far

	to near; less able to see clearly in dim light or glaring light; dryness of eyes also common
Skin	Skin becomes drier, thinner, and less elastic; may sag, wrinkle, and form dark "age" spots; bruises easily and heals slowly; more susceptible to damage from sunlight and to allergic reactions
Nails	Nails become thicker and more brittle
Hair	Hair grays and becomes thinner and less oily
Touch	Response to painful stimuli such as extreme heat and cold diminishes
Urinary system	Bladder capacity diminishes and kidneys produce more urine, causing more frequent urination; increased susceptibility to urinary tract infections

These common complaints are not "normal" aspects of aging but symptoms requiring medical intervention: frequent dizziness or faintness; constant itching; constant aches and pains; blurred vision; labored breathing during moderate exertion (such as climbing stairs); incontinence (involuntary loss of urine); constant depression, anxiety, or apathy; frequent confusion.

Common Diseases of Aging

Arthritis

Arthritis is the nation's number-one cause of disability. It affects one in seven Americans, including 48 percent of all people age sixty-five and older, and hits women twice as often as men.

Arthritis actually is not one disease but a broad family of more than one hundred different diseases. In its many forms it causes pain, swelling, and limited movement in joints and connective tissues throughout the body. Some common forms of arthritis include:

- **Osteoarthritis**
  A degenerative joint disease in which cartilage covering the ends of bones in joints deteriorates, causing permanent stiffness in fingers, knees, feet, hips, and back.

- **Fibromyalgia**
  Affects muscles and their attachments to bone, causing widespread pain and tenderness.

- **Rheumatoid arthritis**
  A fault in the body's immune system causes painful inflammation in joint linings, limiting movement in hands, wrists, feet, knees, ankles, shoulders, and elbows.

- **Gout**
  Needlelike chemical crystals form in the joints, causing severe pain and swelling in the big toe, knees, and wrists.

In most cases arthritis is a chronic condition—it lasts for life. But much can be done to reduce its impact. Treatment programs include a combination of medication, exercise, use of heat or cold, pacing activities (alternating periods of activity with periods of rest), joint-protection techniques, self-help skills, and sometimes surgery. The key to successful treatment is early diagnosis and a treatment plan tailored to the individual needs of the patient.

Warning Signs of Arthritis
Symptoms may develop suddenly or gradually. If your relative

has any of these symptoms in or around a joint for more than two weeks, it's time to see a doctor.

- Pain
- Stiffness
- Swelling

Cancer

Cancer is a group of more than one hundred diseases in which abnormal body cells grow and spread without control. The cancerous cells usually form a malignant tumor, which grows and invades nearby tissues. (A benign tumor is a growth that does not spread.) If the spread of cancer is not controlled, it can result in death.

The incidence of cancer increases with age—more than half of all cancer patients are over age sixty-five. However, in recent years, impressive advances in methods of treatment and pain control have significantly prolonged life and relieved symptoms. In the 1940s only one in four people lived five years after being diagnosed with cancer. By the 1960s that number had increased to one in three. Today the five-year survival rate for all cancers is 52 percent.

Modern cancer treatment includes surgery, radiation therapy, chemotherapy (using chemicals to kill cancer cells), hormone therapy (preventing some types of cancers from using or accessing the hormones they need to grow), biological therapy (using drugs to boost the body's immune system), and combinations of these methods. Early detection is critical to the effectiveness of treatment, especially among older people.

Listed below are some of the early warning signs of cancer. Since early cancer rarely causes pain and older people often mistake their symptoms for signs of a chronic disease or aging itself, regular self-examination and diagnostic tests are critical to early detection. Women should perform monthly breast self-exams; men, monthly exams of the testicles. Both should examine their skin monthly for changes that might signal skin cancer. The National Cancer Institute also recommends that both men and women over age sixty-five have these regular diagnostic tests: digital rectal exam (every year or as part of regular health exams); skin exam (as part of regular health exams); guaiac stool test, or hemoccult test, to test for blood in stool samples (every year); and sigmoidoscopy, or "procto" (every three to five years). In addition, women should have a mammogram and clinical breast exam every one to two years and a pelvic exam and Pap smear every year (after three normal Pap tests the doctor may recommend a less frequent schedule).

Warning Signs of Cancer

These symptoms, described by the National Cancer Institute, may be caused by less serious conditions than cancer, but only a doctor can make that diagnosis.

- Changes in bowel and bladder habits
- A sore that does not heal
- Unusual bleeding or discharge
- Thickening or lump in the breast or any other part of the body
- Indigestion or difficulty swallowing
- Obvious change in a wart or mole
- Nagging cough or hoarseness

Diabetes

About one in eleven adults age sixty-five or older has diabetes; 95 percent of this group has the type II, or adult-onset, form. Diabetes is a disease characterized by the body's inability to control glucose, the blood sugar that fuels all activity, and to produce or correctly use insulin, the hormone that allows glucose to enter the cells. In type I, or juvenile diabetes, the body produces little or no insulin. Patients with juvenile diabetes must have daily insulin injections. In adult-onset diabetes the body produces insulin but does not properly respond to it. Some of these patients are able to control their resulting high blood sugar levels through diet and lifestyle changes, but many need drugs and some also must have insulin injections.

Uncontrolled diabetes can lead to blindness, heart disease, stroke, kidney disease, gangrene (requiring amputation), and nerve damage. Yet this serious disease often goes undiagnosed or improperly treated. Symptoms develop gradually and may be vague. Until recently doctors often sent newly diagnosed patients home with a diet sheet and the admonition to lose some weight. Today many doctors recommend a more aggressive five-pronged treatment approach, which includes blood glucose self-monitoring, weight loss for the overweight, a healthy diet, regular exercise, and, for about half of all adults with diabetes, medications.

The key to diabetes diagnosis is a blood glucose text, performed in a doctor's office. The key to successful treatment is working with an experienced diabetes care team that will develop and supervise a personalized care plan. Your relative's care team may include a physician who specializes in diabetes treatment and control, nurses, an eye doctor, a dietitian, and other specialists the primary doctor recommends. The Directory of Resources lists organizations providing referrals to local diabetes specialists and clinics.

Warning Signs of Diabetes

If your relative shows any of these symptoms, listed as warning signs by the American Diabetes Association, call for a doctor's appointment.

- Extreme thirst
- Occasional blurry vision
- Frequent urination
- Unusual tiredness or drowsiness
- Unexplained weight loss

Hearing Impairments

One in three adults over age sixty-five experiences some loss of hearing. Causes range all the way from impacted earwax to natural age-related degeneration of nerve and sensory cells to diseases affecting the ear. Hearing loss often comes on gradually and painlessly. Your aging relative may not even be aware of the loss or may be embarrassed to admit it. For these reasons it is essential that older people have an annual hearing evaluation.

Restoring hearing may be as simple as removing earwax or eliminating medications, such as some antibiotics or diuretics, that can cause temporary hearing loss. In other cases it may involve the proper fitting and use of a hearing aid.

Hearing aids differ in design, amount of power, and ease of handling. A hearing health care specialist will advise which style best suits your relative's needs. The five basic types of hearing aids include:

174

- *Canal aids*

  All parts of the aid are contained in a tiny case that fits inside the ear canal. These are the smallest aids available and so may be the most cosmetically appealing. Tiny controls may be hard to adjust.

- *All-in-the-ear aids*

  All parts of the aid are contained in a small case that fits in the outer part of the ear. All-in-the-ear aids are somewhat larger than canal aids, but controls still are very small.

- **Behind-the-ear aids**

  A small earmold worn inside the ear canal is connected to a plastic control box hooked behind the ear. Behind-the-ear aids are durable, easy to adjust, and easy to repair. They may be recommended for individuals with moderate to severe hearing loss.

- **Eyeglass aids**

  In this variation on the behind-the-ear aid, parts of the aid are contained inside the frames of the eyeglasses. Clear plastic tubing connects the hearing aid to an earmold. Eyeglass aids are no longer commonly prescribed.

- **Body aids**

  A rectangular, radiolike box worn in the shirt pocket or on the belt is attached by a cord to the earmold. Body aids are large, with easy-to-use controls. Though they may be recommended in cases of severe impairment, they are no longer commonly prescribed.

Your parent's doctor or one of the organizations listed in the Directory of Resources can provide referrals to local hearing health care specialists. It is important to buy a hearing aid only from a certified audiologist or comprehensive hearing aid center providing assessment, service, and rehabilitation. Be wary of mail-order or over-the-counter hearing aids—these often are both expensive and ineffective. All reputable suppliers will offer a trial period and money-back guarantee.

Many other helpful devices and services are available to help hearing-impaired individuals with daily living activities. Assistive living devices include vibrating or light signals for the telephone ringer and doorbell, telephone voice amplifiers, headset amplifiers and closed-captioned decoders for TV viewing, amplified smoke detectors and alarm clocks, and more. A TTY (TeleTypewriter), also called TT (Text Telephone) or TDD (telecommunication device for the deaf), is a communication device consisting of a keyboard and a display screen that allows people with hearing and/or speech impairments to communicate with one another over the phone lines. Telecommunications Relay Service (TRS) is a telephone service that allows TTY users to communicate with voice telephone users; a TRS communication assistant relays the TTY user's typed message to the voice telephone user, then types back the verbal response. See the Directory of Resources for organizations providing information and referrals related to assisted living devices and for listings of mail-order suppliers.

Warning Signs of Hearing Loss
Encourage your relative to have a hearing test if you notice any of these signs of possible hearing loss:

- Speaks very loudly or very softly
- Talks over others who have begun speaking
- Accuses others of not speaking clearly
- Asks speakers to repeat themselves
- Turns head toward whoever is speaking
- Cups hands to ears
- Fails to hear doorbell, telephone, or other sudden sounds
- Turns TV or radio volume too high

Now Hear This!

Hearing loss can isolate and alienate your older relative. The following suggestions are designed to help keep communication and contact flowing. Be sure to share these tips with family members, friends, and other visitors.

- Make certain you have your relative's attention before you begin speaking.

- Give your listener a good view of your face. Position your face at your relative's eye level, at a distance of about three to six feet. Keep hands, cigarettes, and other objects away from your face, and make sure adequate lighting falls on your face but not directly into the listener's eyes.

- Speak clearly and a little more slowly than usual, in a normal tone of voice or slightly louder. Allow slightly longer intervals between sentences. Do not shout, exaggerate lip movements, or speak directly into the ear.

- If your listener does not understand you, rephrase your message, using shorter sentences and simple words. Maintain eye contact while speaking, and use facial expressions and gestures to help get across your meaning.

- Reduce background noise as much as possible. Turn off the TV, radio, and appliances, and close doors and windows if outside noise is distracting.

- When conveying important information, ask the listener to repeat what you've said, to make sure it's been understood. Write down important instructions in addition to communicating them verbally.

Heart Disease

Heart disease is the number-one killer of people over age sixty-five. As many as one in three older Americans suffers from the disease in one of its several forms. Yet improvements in diet and lifestyle, along with advances in medical treatment, have dramatically reduced death rates from heart attack and stroke. Once it was believed that an increased risk of heart failure was a normal and unavoidable consequence of aging. Now we know that most declines in heart function are due to disease and that lifestyle factors are a major contributing cause.

Common forms of heart disease include:

- **Coronary artery disease**
  A progressive narrowing of the arteries supplying blood to the heart.

- **Cardiomyopathy**
  Damage to the heart muscle, caused by metabolic diseases such as diabetes or toxins such as alcohol or chemotherapy.

- **Valvular heart disease**
  Heart valve defects, including narrowing or leaking of a valve.

- **Abdominal aortic aneurysm**
  The widening or ballooning of the major blood vessel leading from the heart.

- **Peripheral arterial disease**
  Poor circulation in the blood vessels of the limbs.

- **Congestive heart failure.**
  The heart is unable to pump enough blood to supply the body's needs. Usually develops as a result of a previous problem such as high blood pressure or atherosclerosis—clogging or hardening of the arteries.

Untreated heart disease can lead to the reduction or cutoff of the heart's blood supply. The result may be angina (intermittent chest pain) or a heart attack (damage to the heart muscle). A stroke occurs when the blood supply to the brain is cut off, causing injury to brain tissue and affecting any number of body functions.

Major controllable risk factors contributing to the likelihood of heart disease include cigarette smoking, high blood pressure, high blood cholesterol, obesity, diabetes, lack of exercise, and stress. You can help your aging relative reduce the risk of heart disease by encouraging healthy habits, being aware of the warning signs of disease, and ensuring that symptoms—including changes in symptoms after treatment begins are promptly reported to the doctor. Treatments for heart disease include medication, surgery, angioplasty (opening clogged arteries through insertion of a tiny balloon), dietary changes, exercise, stress management, and other techniques. The earlier your parent starts treatment, the better the chances for controlling symptoms, maintaining energy, and preventing or halting damage to the heart.

Warning Signs of Heart Disease

Be on the lookout for these symptoms. A doctor or cardiologist must perform a thorough physical exam, health history, and diagnostic tests to determine if they indicate heart disease.

- Difficulty breathing, especially during exertion or when lying flat in bed
- Waking up breathless at night
- Frequent dry, hacking cough, especially when lying down
- Fatigue or weakness
- Dizziness or fainting
- Swollen feet, ankles, and legs
- Nausea, with abdominal swelling, pain, and tenderness
- Pain in chest, upper abdomen, neck, jaw, middle of back between shoulder blades, or down inner arm
- Pain in calf, leg, or buttock during exertion

Hypertension (High Blood Pressure)

Nearly half of all people older than age sixty-five have hypertension, or abnormally high blood pressure. Simply put, blood pressure is the measurement of the force the blood exerts against the sides of the blood vessels. In someone who has hypertension the system regulating blood flow malfunctions, and blood continually rushes forcefully through the blood vessels. That makes the heart pump harder and weakens the blood vessel walls. Over time high blood pressure can permanently damage the heart and the arteries (the vessels supplying blood to the heart) and lead to stroke, heart attack, heart failure, kidney failure, or severe visual impairment.

Hypertension usually causes no symptoms until it has done serious damage. To defeat this "silent killer," a simple blood pressure check should be performed at least once a year and during every medical exam. The measurement is expressed in two numbers: systolic pressure (the pressure when the heart is pumping) over diastolic pressure (the pressure when the heart is resting). In general, normal systolic pressure is considered to be about 120 to 130 mm Hg (millimeters of mercury), normal diastolic pressure about 70 to 80 mm Hg.

Mild hypertension often can be effectively treated with nondrug therapies, including weight loss for the overweight, reduction of salt intake, regular moderate exercise, reduction of alcohol intake, and stress management. If nondrug treatment fails, a variety of very effective medications may be used alone or in combination. Often, once a person's blood pressure has been controlled using nondrug treatments plus medication for six months, the drug dosage can be slowly tapered down. It is very important, though, that your relative stay on the medication the doctor prescribes. Too often older patients stop taking prescribed hypertension medication because of the expense and bother or because they are experiencing side effects. Hypertension drug side effects may include depression, confusion, fatigue, sleep disturbances, dizziness, constipation, nausea, dry mouth, leg cramps, incontinence, or impotence. Urge your parent to report any side effects to the doctor, who will minimize them by lowering the dosage or switching medications.

Because older people are particularly susceptible to drug side effects and because the benefits of treating mild hypertension in older patients are low, most doctors take a moderate approach to treatment. According to the American Geriatrics Society, "modest lowering of the diastolic blood pressure to about 85 to 90 mm Hg and lowering of systolic blood pressure to around 150 mm Hg appear to be the most appropriate targets for most elderly people."

Warning Signs of Hypertension
Hypertension usually causes no symptoms, but the National Hypertension Association notes that in some cases danger signs may include:

- Breathlessness
- Fatigue
- Unexplained nosebleeds
- Headaches
- Dizziness

Incontinence

One in every twenty-five Americans—about ten million people—have difficulty controlling their bladder. Some may leak urine when they laugh, sneeze, or exercise; others lose urine as soon as they feel the need to go to the bathroom; and still others lose urine day and night. Urinary incontinence can lead to embarrassment and social isolation. More than half of the people with the condition have never sought treatment. Many believe their condition cannot be helped. And unfortunately, says the Simon Foundation for Continence, most health care professionals fail to provide adequate diagnosis and treatment.

If you suspect your parent is suffering from incontinence—and perhaps keeping the problem a secret—you can help by breaking through your own and your loved one's embarrassment to urge medical treatment. Incontinence is *not* part of normal aging, and in almost *every* case the condition causing it can be cured or substantially improved. Conditions causing incontinence may be temporary, such as a urinary tract infection, or they may involve age-related body changes, such as weakness in the muscles of the bladder or the urethral sphincter muscles. Treatment may be as simple as changing the diet, reducing caffeine and alcohol intake, or adjusting the dosage of medications. Bladder training techniques may be effective in teaching ways to control the urge to urinate. Pelvic muscle exercises, called Kegel exercises, help to strengthen the muscles that control the flow of urine; sometimes the effectiveness of these exercises is reinforced through biofeedback. Some people are helped by medications to treat conditions such as urinary tract or vaginal infections or hormone imbalances. In the most serious cases implants or various surgical procedures are used to treat tissue blockage, severely weakened pelvic muscles, or other physical causes.

Products such as specially designed pads and catheters also can help manage incontinence. However, because they are heavily marketed and readily available without a prescription, incontinence pads often are used by people who have not sought medical attention for their problem. Don't let your loved one fall into that category. More pleasant, less expensive alternatives are available. Incontinence products should be used only to make other treatments more effective or as a last resort when all other treatments have failed.

In seeking treatment for incontinence, ask your parent's doctor to recommend a urologist, gynecologist, or other physician who provides specialized incontinence services. Another good resource might be an incontinence clinic at a nearby hospital or medical center. You also may want to contact organizations listed in the Directory of Resources for information, support, and local referrals.

Warning Signs of Urinary Incontinence

Your aging relative knows if she or he is incontinent, but you may have to be a bit of a sleuth to recognize the problem. If you observe any of these behaviors, you may suspect that your parent is keeping a urinary problem secret.

- Refusal to leave the house or join in family activities
- Towels over the bottom bedsheet
- Urine stains on clothing, sheets, furniture
- Acrid smell
- Boxes of incontinence pads or sanitary napkins hidden in bathroom or closet

Mental Health

According to the American Psychiatric Association, nearly 25 percent of people over age sixty-five suffer from significant symptoms of mental illness, yet the vast majority do not seek care. They may feel ashamed of their symptoms or view them as an inevitable part of aging. Their families and often their own doctors may fail to recognize the symptoms of treatable mental illness. Often older people and their families believe that nothing can be done to ease the problems associated with mental disorders.

Lingering sadness, apathy, memory loss, confusion, and major personality changes are *not* part of the normal aging process. In many cases they are signs of illnesses that can be accurately diagnosed and effectively treated. If you notice any of the warning signs listed below, a good first step is to make an appointment for your parent with the family doctor, who will look for physical causes such as illness or medication side effects. From that point the doctor, a mental health clinic, or one of the organizations listed in the Directory of Resources can refer you to an appropriate specialist—perhaps a geriatric psychiatrist or a doctor who specializes in treating patients with Alzheimer's disease and other dementing illnesses. Following is a closer look at the two most common mental health problems of later life, depression and dementia.

Depression

Clinical depression is more than the ordinary "down" moods everyone experiences now and then or the feeling of grief after the loss of a loved one. Clinical depression is an illness, a whole-body disorder that affects the way a person thinks and feels, both emotionally and physically. An estimated 5 to 10 percent of people age sixty-five and older suffer from depression. This illness nearly triples the risk of stroke, slows the rate of recovery from illness or infection, and leads to a higher rate of suicide in people over sixty-five than in any other age group.

Depression in older people often is a side effect of medications, especially those used to treat heart disease or arthritis. When the medications are changed, such depression typically disappears. Long-term or sudden physical illnesses and life events such as the death of a loved one or moving to a new place also can trigger or aggravate depression. Whatever the cause, studies show that up to 80 percent of depressed older people can be treated successfully, outside a hospital, with psychotherapy or behavior therapy used alone or in combination with antidepressant medications. Even serious depressions usually respond rapidly to the right treatment.

Warning Signs of Depression

If four or more of these symptoms last for more than two weeks, a doctor and/or a mental health specialist should be consulted.

- Sadness, anxiety, or a feeling of "emptiness"
- Fatigue; lack of energy
- Loss of interest or pleasure in ordinary activities, including sex
- Sleep problems, including insomnia, oversleeping, or waking too early in the morning
- Loss of appetite; significant weight loss or gain
- Difficulty concentrating, remembering, or making decisions
- Feelings of hopelessness or pessimism
- Feelings of guilt or worthlessness
- Irritability
- Excessive crying
- Persistent aches and pains
- Thoughts of death or suicide

Alzheimer's Disease and Other Dementias

About 15 percent of older Americans suffer from dementia—a medical condition that disrupts the way the brain works, causing confusion, memory loss, disorientation, and other intellectual impairments. Dementia may take several forms and have several different causes. Vascular (blood vessel) diseases can cause the condition through a series of small strokes that decrease the blood supply to parts of the brain. Some infections, including the HIV virus, can enter the brain and cause dementing illness. Thyroid disease, long-term alcoholism or exposure to other toxic substances, nutritional deficiencies, severely advanced Parkinson's disease or Huntington's disease, and other diseases and disorders also can cause dementia. Depending on the cause, these mentally debilitating illnesses may progress slowly or rapidly. Some are irreversible, while in other cases treatment offers improvement or even a complete cure.

Alzheimer's disease, the most common form of dementia among people age sixty-five and older, is incurable, and its cause is unknown. The disease typically begins in a part of the brain that controls memory and then spreads to other parts, killing some of the brain's nerve cells and breaking down communication channels among others. The first symptom of Alzheimer's disease usually is a loss of short-term memory. The affected person may forget to turn off the stove or have trouble remembering names of recent acquaintances. As the disease progresses, Alzheimer's patients begin to have problems understanding language, speaking, reading, or writing. They may forget how to perform simple tasks such as combing their hair or brushing their teeth, become increasingly irritable, quarrelsome, or agitated, and wander away from home. Eventually they become completely dependent on others for their care. The course the disease takes and how fast changes occur varies from person to person, but on average most Alzheimer's patients are severely disabled within eight to twelve years of the disease's onset.

Many older people worry that every incidence of forgetfulness or confusion is a sign of Alzheimer's disease. These fears usually are unfounded. Anyone, at any age, can have trouble finding the car keys or remembering a name. Further, there are many conditions whose symptoms look like dementia but are not. These reversible conditions, often called pseudodementias, may be caused by problems such as drug interactions, malnutrition resulting from poor eating habits, depression, or some diseases of the heart, lungs, or adrenal, thyroid, pituitary, or other glands. Though not dementia, these medical problems can be serious and should be promptly diagnosed and treated.

If your older relative is showing any of the warning signs of dementia, a thorough physical, neurological, and psychiatric evaluation is in order. Your parent's regular doctor might perform this evaluation, or you might ask the doctor or one of the organizations listed in the Directory of Resources for referrals to local professionals or medical centers specializing in dementia diagnosis and treatment. A complete evaluation includes a medical history; basic medical tests, including blood and urine tests; neuropsychological tests, which assess memory, problem solving, language, and other mental abilities; and a brain scan, to rule out curable brain disorders.

If the diagnosis is Alzheimer's disease, the doctor can give you an idea of what to expect, so that you can make plans and arrange future care. There also are many organizations offering educational materials, counseling, and support for people with Alzheimer's disease and their caregivers. Medications may alleviate symptoms for some people in the early and middle stages of the disease, and proper care can help a person with dementia maintain daily routines, physical activities, and social contacts for as long as possible. No care or treatment, however, can stop the disease's progress. Taking care of a loved one with Alzheimer's disease is a long-term, exhausting, emotionally draining job. For your own sake and your loved one's, start early to find out about local resources, and be sure to take advantage of every bit of help that's offered.

Warning Signs of Dementia

These symptoms in a loved one may indicate something more than simple forgetfulness or absentmindedness and should prompt you to seek a medical evaluation.

- Loss of memory, including recall of recent events and well-known information
- Loss of ability to find appropriate common words or phrases
- Uncharacteristic difficulty in working with numbers—balancing the checkbook, handling money, paying bills
- Difficulty in performing familiar tasks such as reading or knitting
- Disorientation; getting lost in familiar places
- Changes in personality or emotions, including increased apathy or indifference, agitation, irritability, suspiciousness, or social withdrawal

186

Osteoporosis

About half of all women over age sixty-five and one-fifth of men over age seventy have the bone-thinning disease known as osteoporosis. In this debilitating illness the bones become fragile and more likely to break. Osteoporosis often progresses silently and painlessly until some minor stress such as coughing or lifting a bag of groceries suddenly causes a bone to fracture, typically in the hip, spine, or wrist. Hip fractures often mean the permanent loss of mobility and independence. Fractures in the vertebrae may result in reduced height and stooped posture, often called "widow's hump" or "dowager's hump."

The causes of osteoporosis are unknown, but certain risk factors increase its likelihood. If your parent has any of the risk factors listed below, suggest an appointment to discuss concerns with a doctor. The doctor may recommend a bone density measurement test, which measures the amount of bone mass in the hip, spine, or wrist. If osteoporosis is present, early diagnosis and treatment can reduce the risk of fractures.

Treatment for osteoporosis begins with diet and lifestyle changes that promote bone health. These include consuming adequate amounts of calcium and vitamin D. Recommended dosages of calcium are 1,000 mg per day for most premenopausal women and for men under age sixty-five, and 1,500 mg per day for most postmenopausal women and men over age sixty-five. The recommended daily intake of vitamin D is 400 IU. Most people get that naturally, through exposure to sunlight, but some older people, especially those confined to home, may need to take supplements. Other recommended diet and lifestyle changes include avoiding excessive alcohol and caffeine consumption, quitting smoking, and getting regular weight-bearing exercise. (That's exercise that makes the body work against gravity; walking is a weight-bearing exercise, swimming is not.) These measures can be taken at any age to help prevent osteoporosis or to keep the disease from worsening. In addition, doctors often prescribe estrogen replacement therapy for women at menopause. Estrogen use helps protect against bone loss and may protect against heart disease, but there are health risks, too, including increased risk of uterine and breast cancer. Your relative will need to discuss benefits and drawbacks with the doctor. Other medications may be prescribed in addition to or in place of estrogen therapy to increase bone density and reduce the risk of fractures.

If your parent has osteoporosis, it is especially important to safeguard home surroundings to reduce the chance of falls. For tips on fall-proofing the house, see Chapter 2, "Home Safety and Security."

Risk Factors for Osteoporosis

There are no early warning signs for osteoporosis, but being aware of these risk factors can enable your parent to seek early diagnosis and treatment.

- Thin, small-boned frame
- Family history of osteoporosis (may be evidenced by broken bones or stooped posture in older family members, especially women)
- Early menopause (before age forty-five), occurring naturally or surgically induced through removal of ovaries
- Diet low in calcium
- Inactive lifestyle with little or no exercise
- Being white or Asian
- Cigarette smoking
- Excessive alcohol or caffeine consumption (more than two alcoholic drinks or several cups of coffee or caffeinated drinks a day)
- Prolonged use of certain medications, including glucocorticoids, excessive thyroid hormone, and some antiseizure medications

Visual Impairments

There is a significant link between aging and sight loss. About 70 percent of severely visually impaired people are age sixty-five or older. Half of this group is classified as legally blind. Most blindness among older Americans is caused by one of these four common diseases:

- ### Cataracts
  A clouding of the eye's lens causes blurred vision or double vision and hypersensitivity to glare. Surgery can restore vision 95 percent of the time. In some people cataracts may cause no severe vision loss. The only treatment needed

in these cases may be a change of glasses and avoiding problem activities such as driving at night.

- **Glaucoma**
  Fluids build up in the eye, damaging the optic nerve and causing a gradual loss of peripheral vision, blurred or foggy vision, and the inability to adjust the eyes to dim light. Vision lost to glaucoma cannot be restored. Treatment to stop the disease's progress usually involves the use of eyedrops and/or oral medications.

- **Diabetic retinopathy**
  Deterioration of blood vessels in the eye causes severe and progressive blurring of vision. People who have diabetes, especially if the disease is long-standing or poorly controlled, and people with uncontrolled high blood pressure are at high risk for this condition. Diabetic retinopathy may be treated successfully with surgery or laser therapy, particularly when the disease is detected early.

- **Macular degeneration**
  Age-related deterioration of the macula, a small area of the retina, causes blurry, faded, or distorted central vision. Peripheral vision is unaffected. Laser therapy or surgery may halt the disease, especially if it is caught early, but in most cases there is no effective cure.

These and most other diseases of the eye may cause no changes in vision in the early stages. By the time vision is affected, chances are the disease has progressed significantly, possibly causing some permanent vision loss. Every person age sixty-five or older should have an eye examination at least every other year to check for the onset of vision problems. Besides urging your parent to seek regular eye care, you can help by watching for the signs of vision loss outlined below. If you notice any of these warning signs, encourage your loved one to make an appointment for an eye exam with an ophthalmologist and a low-vision evaluation by a low-vision specialist—usually an optometrist who specializes in low-vision diagnosis and treatment.

If your relative has a visual impairment, the low-vision specialist will assess her or his abilities and offer counseling and training to make the most of remaining vision. You also may want to seek out vision-related rehabilitation services, offered through government and private agencies, which specialize in teaching visually impaired people adaptive techniques for daily living. Assistive devices for people with visual impairments include simple items such as talking watches, special telephones with large dials and buttons, self-threading sewing needles, and hand-held magnifiers. There also are high-tech aids such as talking computers; tactile display scanners, which allow the user to feel the shape of standard printed letters of the alphabet; and electronic reading devices, which use scanners and synthetic speech to read written documents. In the Directory of Resources you will find many helpful organizations that provide information on assistive devices, along with a listing of mail-order suppliers.

Warning Signs of Vision Loss

Be alert to these behaviors, which the American Foundation for the Blind warns may be signs that an older relative is experiencing vision loss.

- **Daily activities**

  Difficulty identifying faces, objects, or colors; difficulty locating personal objects, even in familiar surroundings; changes in the way the person reads, watches television, drives, walks, or performs hobbies; squinting or tilting the head to get an object into focus; reaching for objects in an uncertain manner

- **Reading and writing**

  Holding reading material close to the face or an angle; writing less clearly or precisely; complaining that lighting is inadequate for reading and other activities; no longer able to read mail or a newspaper

- **Moving**

  Brushing against the wall while walking; bumping into objects; difficulty walking on irregular or bumpy surfaces; going up and down stairs slowly and awkwardly (in the absence of other physical limitations)

190

Getting a Good Night's Sleep

Sleep problems—insomnia, restlessness, early-morning waking, and resulting daytime drowsiness—are a common complaint among older people. Sleep cycles change with age, with a decrease in continuous sleep, an increase in the number of awakenings during sleep, and a tendency for the deepest sleep to occur early in the night. While some sleep disturbance may be an unavoidable part of aging, your parent may get a better and more comfortable night's sleep by following these suggestions from the American Geriatrics Society:

- Go to bed only when sleepy.
- Get up at the same time each morning.
- Limit the time spent in bed each night to seven hours.
- Limit naps to no more than thirty to forty-five minutes a day.
- Avoid using the bedroom for activities not conducive to sleep.
- Reduce use of nicotine, alcohol, and caffeine.
- Avoid fluids just before bedtime.
- Exercise regularly.
- Ask the doctor about eliminating depressant or stimulant drugs.
- Discuss persistent sleep problems with a doctor.

- **Eating and drinking**
  Difficulty getting food on a fork, cutting food, or taking food from a serving platter; spilling off plate while eating; pouring liquids over the tops of cups; knocking over items on the table

 ## CHECKLIST #17: MANAGING MEDICATIONS

Older people may have a number of different health problems and may need to take several medications at once. That can mean double trouble. First, an older person's reaction to any single drug often is different from a younger person's, with increased risk for adverse side effects. Second, in any person, regardless of age, multiple medications can interact and cause a confusing array of symptoms.

Here are some precautions your parent can take to reduce the risks associated with multiple drug use:

❑ **One regular doctor—a family practitioner, internist, or geriatrician—should coordinate care.**
Though your parent may also see specialists from time to time, one doctor should be in charge of coordinating care and monitoring all medications.

❑ **Ask questions when a new drug is prescribed.**
Questions your parent should ask when the doctor writes a new prescription include:

- What is the drug called? Ask for both brand and generic names. Is there a less costly, approved generic version?
- What will it do for my problem?
- When should it be taken? (At what time of day? With food or between meals?)
- How long will it be needed?
- Will it interact with other medications?
- Should any foods or activities be avoided?
- What are the possible side effects?

❑ **Set up a system for organizing medications.**
You may want to make copies of the following Medications Record, or copy it out in large print as an easy-to-read reminder form to be tacked to the refrigerator or kitchen or bathroom wall. Also useful are the daily or weekly pill organizers sold in drugstores and through catalogs. These allow you to organize a day's or week's worth of pills in advance.

❑ **Do a periodic medications check.**
Your parent should bring an up-to-date copy of the current Medications

Medications Record
Prescription Drugs

Medication name & dosage	Description (color, form, shape)	Condition treated/ doctor who treated	How much/ how often	Special directions/ precautions	End date (date to stop taking)

Medications Record (continued)
Nonprescription Drugs & Drugs That Cause an Allergic Reaction

Over-the-Counter (Nonprescription Drugs)		Drugs that caused an allergic or adverse reaction:	
Medication name & dosage	When/how often taken	Medication name & dosage	Reaction

Record to every doctor's appointment, enabling the doctor to easily check for overmedication and possible drug interactions.

❑ *Phone the doctor if any unusual reactions occur to a new medication.*
Drugs to which your parent has had a bad reaction should be noted at the bottom of the Medications Record and pointed out to the doctor whenever a new medication is prescribed.

Directory of Resources

The following organizations provide information, advice, referrals, services, and printed materials related to health, illness, and disability. Many also can link you with self-help groups for older adults and/or their families. Discovering that others have similar problems can be comforting; these groups also can be a valuable source of information on coping strategies, local health professionals, and other resources. Appendix E lists phone numbers for clearinghouses set up to help you find additional self-help groups in your area. Also listed below are professional associations and other organizations that provide referrals to health care professionals such as geriatricians, orthopedists, optometrists, and mental health counselors. For groups providing referrals to home health care agencies, home care nurses, and home care aides, see the Directory of Resources in Chapter 2.

Following this chapter's directory are listings of specialty catalogs that sell products designed for people with hearing, visual, or other impairments. You'll also find information on publishers, lending libraries, and other groups to contact for accessible reading materials for the visually impaired. At the end of the chapter is a toll-free health directory, listing hotline numbers for a wide variety of organizations that offer information, counseling, and other services to people with specific health concerns.

NATIONAL

Organizations on this list offer their services nationwide or over a significant area of the country.

ABLEDATA/Information for Independence
8455 Colesville Road, Suite 935
Silver Spring, MD 20910
1–800–227–0216 (voice/TTY) or 301–588–9284
(voice/TTY)
Fax: 301–587–1967

An information specialist will search this organization's database of more than 21,000 assistive technology products, then give you detailed descriptions of each product, including price and manufacturer information. Searches can be tailored to a disability such as low vision or deafness, to a functional need such as eating or bathing, or to a specific device such as signaling systems or powered wheelchairs. Simple searches are free; a listing of fifty or fewer products costs $5.00. Lists are available in large print or Braille and on audiocassette or PC-compatible disk.

ABLE INFORM BBS provides direct access to the ABLEDATA database via modem. Phone 301–589–3563 (line settings of 1200 to 9600 baud, N=8=1).

Helpful Publications:
   "Assistive Devices for People with Arthritis." $1.00
   "Blindness/Low Vision Resource Packet." $5.00
   "Wheelchair Information Packet." $5.00

Adventures in Movement for the Handicapped (AIM)
945 Danbury Road
Dayton, OH 45420
513–294–4611
Fax: 513–294–3783

AIM is a specialized movement education program, taught to music, used as a recreational and rehabilitation tool in adult day care centers, nursing homes, and other adult residential settings. Family caregivers also may attend AIM training workshops to learn how to work with a disabled older adult at home. Workshops are presented to schools, colleges, universities, and sponsoring organizations throughout the country. Contact the

196

AIM national office for information on the AIM method and workshop schedules.

Al-Anon Family Group Headquarters
1600 Corporate Landing Parkway
Virginia Beach, VA 23454–5617
1–800–344–2666 or 804–563–1600

Al-Anon Family Groups are a network of support groups for relatives and friends of alcoholics. More than 32,000 groups around the world meet to share their experiences and work to solve their common problems. The program is nondenominational but relies on a spiritual foundation. For local meeting information, look in your phone directory for an Al-Anon listing, check the community calendar in your local newspaper, or contact the national headquarters.

Helpful Publications:
"Adult Children of Alcoholics: Newcomer Packet." 9-piece introduction to Al-Anon. $1.75.
"Al-Anon Is for Adult Children of Alcoholics." 24-page brochure. 60¢
"Al-Anon Sharings from Adult Children." 20-page brochure. 60¢

Alzheimer's Association
919 North Michigan Avenue, Suite 1000
Chicago, IL 60611–1676
1–800–272–3900
TTY: 312–335–8882
Fax: 312–335–1110
via Internet: http://www.alz.org/

Dedicated to research, education, and support for people with Alzheimer's disease and their caregivers, this voluntary organization has a nationwide network of more than two hundred local chapters. Your area's chapter will help you learn about the disease and care options, locate professional and community services, and access clinical drug trials. To receive free information on Alzheimer's and related disorders plus the address and phone number of your local chapter, phone the 800 number above. If you have specific questions about Alzheimer's disease or need referrals to other sources of assistance, phone the association's research library at 312–335–9602 (fax: 312–335–0214).

The association also sponsors a Safe Return program, which provides identification materials, including ID jewelry, clothing labels, and a wallet ID card, to help others identify a person with Alzheimer's disease who has wandered and gotten lost. When someone who finds the lost person phones the 800 number on the identification materials, family members are notified. One-time registration fee for Safe Return: $25.00.

Helpful Publications:
Phone for a complete catalog.

"Alzheimer's Disease: Services You May Need." Order #ED210Z. Free brochure.

"Caregiving at Home." Order #ED213Z. Free brochure.

"Communicating with the Alzheimer Patient." Order #ED220Z. Free brochure.

"Home Care with the Alzheimer Patient." Order #ED302Z. 26-page booklet. $1.50.

"If You Think Someone You Know Has Alzheimer's." Order #ED204Z. Free brochure.

"Steps to Choosing a Physician." Order #ED307Z (in Spanish, #ED307ZS). 15-page booklet. $1.00.

"Steps to Finding Home Health Care." Order #ED306Z (in Spanish, #ED306ZS). 15-page booklet. $1.00.

Alzheimer's Disease Education and Referral Center (ADEAR)
P.O. Box 8250
Silver Spring, MD 20907–8250
1–800–438–4380
Fax: 301–495–3334
E-mail: adear@alzheimers.org
via Internet: http://www.alzheimers.org/adear

Established by the federal National Institute on Aging, this toll-free line will answer questions about Alzheimer's disease and related disorders, including symptoms and diagnosis, current research findings, and drug testing and clinical trials. An information specialist also can help you locate organizations that provide support and services to Alzheimer's patients and their families, including your nearest Alzheimer's Disease Center (ADC). Twenty-eight ADCs operate in medical institutions across the country, providing information, diagnosis, and medical management at varying costs. ADCs also offer patient and family support groups and opportunities to participate in drug trials and other clinical research projects.

Helpful Publications:
Phone for a complete catalog.

"Age Page: Forgetfulness in Old Age, It's Not What You Think." Order #Z–46. Free fact sheet.

"Alzheimer's Disease Fact Sheet." Order #Z–12. Free fact sheet.

"Home Safety for the Alzheimer's Patient." Order #A–11 (in Spanish, #A–21). 32-page booklet with room-by-room discussion of home safety and behavior management techniques. $2.50.

"Multi-Infarct Dementia Fact Sheet." Order #Z–43. Free fact sheet.

AMC Cancer Information and Counseling Line
American Medical Center (AMC)
1600 Pierce Street
Denver, CO 80214
1–800–525–3777 or 303–233–6501
Fax: 303–233–9562

Sponsored by AMC, a nonprofit cancer research center focusing on prevention and control, this toll-free line offers callers information, advice, literature, and referrals to appropriate local resources.

American Academy of Dermatology
P.O. Box 4014
Schaumburg, IL 60168–4014
847–330–0230

This professional association provides referrals to local dermatologists.

Helpful Publications:
Phone or write for a complete listing or to request single copies of these free pamphlets.
"Hair Loss." Order #PAM21.
"Herpes Zoster (Shingles)." Order #PAM32.
"Mature Skin." Order #PAM28.
"Moles." Order #PAM04.
"Psoriasis." Order #PAM13.
"Urticaria—Hives." Order #PAM22.

American Academy of Family Physicians
8880 Ward Parkway
Kansas City, MO 64114–2797
816–333–9700

This national association of family practitioners requires that members complete a minimum of 150 hours of approved continuing education every three years. Contact for referrals to member physicians in your area.

American Academy of Orthopaedic Surgeons
6300 North River Road
Rosemont, IL 60018–4262
847–823–7186

This professional organization of orthopedists—doctors who specialize in the diagnosis and treatment of injuries or diseases of the musculoskeletal system—will send you information on disorders affecting the bones, joints, ligaments, muscles, and tendons.

Helpful Publications:
Phone for a complete listing. Free public education brochures are available on these topics: "Arthritis," "Common Foot

Problems," "Low Back Pain," "Neck Pain," "Osteoporosis," "Shoulder Pain," "Total Joint Replacement."

American Academy of Physical Medicine and Rehabilitation

1 IBM Plaza, Room 250
Chicago, IL 60611
312–464–9700

Physiatrists (pronounced *fizz-ee-AT-trists*) are physicians who treat patients with physical disabilities and chronic disabling illnesses, including those with arthritis, tendinitis, back pain, spinal cord injuries, brain injuries, stroke, amputations, cancer, and multiple sclerosis. The focus of this medical specialty is on restoring function through various nonsurgical therapies and the use of assistive devices. This national society of physiatrists will answer written requests for information and referrals to local physiatrists.

American Association of Diabetes Educators

444 North Michigan Avenue, Suite 1240
Chicago, IL 60611–3901
312–644–2233
Fax: 312–644–4411

This organization will refer you to local diabetes educators—health professionals who teach people with diabetes how to live healthier, more productive lives.

American Association for Geriatric Psychiatry (AAGP)

7910 Woodmont Avenue, 7th floor
Bethesda, MD 20814–3004
301–654–7850
Fax: 301–654–4137

A professional association of more than 1,400 psychiatrists specializing in the care of older patients, AAGP will provide referrals to geriatric psychiatrists in your area.

American Association of Kidney Patients (AAKP)

100 South Ashley Drive, Suite 280

Tampa, FL 33602
1–800–749-AAKP (1–800–749–2257)

This organization focuses on the needs and concerns of kidney patients and their families, assisting them in locating rehabilitation and other local services, developing local patient and family support groups, conducting educational seminars and conferences, and providing social and educational support through meetings and activities of local chapters. Members receive a newspaper and magazine; brochures on care, treatment, and changing medical technology; discounts on prescription drugs and nutritional supplements; and travel discounts. Annual membership fee: $15.00.

American Board of Medical Specialties
6090-H McDonough Drive
Norcross, GA 30093
1–800–808–2877 or 770–446–5011

Phone for certification information on medical practitioners in twenty-four different categories. You will be asked your zip code and the doctor's name and will be told when the doctor was board-certified and in which specialties.

American Cancer Society (ACS)
1599 Clifton Road NE
Atlanta, GA 30329
1–800-ACS–2345 (1–800–227–2345) or 404–320–3333

This nationwide health organization funds cancer research and helps cancer patients and their families through education, support, and rehabilitation services. Phone the toll-free information line with questions about cancer and to find your nearest ACS office. More than three thousand local offices and 2.5 million volunteers provide cancer education programs; informative booklets, films, and videos; quit-smoking programs; transportation to cancer treatment centers; home care supplies and equipment; home or hospital visits; and support groups.

American Council on Alcoholism (ACA)
2522 St. Paul Street
Baltimore, MD 21218
1–800–527–5344 (helpline) or 410–889–0100
Fax: 410–889–0297

Phone ACA's toll-free helpline for counseling, support, and referrals to professionals, services, and associations working in alcoholism intervention and treatment.

Helpful Publication:
"The Most Frequently Asked Questions about Alcoholism." Free brochure.

American Council of the Blind (ACB)
1155 Fifteenth Street NW, Suite 720
Washington, DC 20005
1–800–424–8666 or 202–467–5081
Fax: 202–467–5085
E-mail: ncrabb@access.degex.net
via Internet: http:\\www.acb.org

A membership organization for people who are blind or visually impaired, ACB operates a toll-free information and referral line on all aspects of blindness. Member benefits include a monthly magazine, available in large print, Braille, audiocassette, and computer disk formats, and group life and health insurance plans. Annual membership fee (member-at-large): $5.00.

American Deafness and Rehabilitation Association
P.O. Box 27
Roland, AR 72135
501–868–8850 (voice/TTY)
Fax: 501–868–8812

This nonprofit association represents professionals who provide services to deaf and hard-of-hearing individuals. Members include rehabilitation personnel, mental health workers, social workers, hearing aid specialists, audiologists, speech therapists, physicians, psychologists, lawyers, and others. Local chapters in fourteen states and the District of Columbia will help you locate service providers in your area.

American Dental Association (ADA)

Council on Access, Prevention and Interprofessional Relations
211 East Chicago Avenue
Chicago, IL 60611
312–440–2860

Contact this division of the American Dental Association for referrals to local dental organizations, which may offer low-cost and/or free services for seniors.

American Diabetes Association (ADA)

1660 Duke Street
Alexandria, VA 22314
1–800-ADA-DISC (1–800–232–3472) or 703–549–1500

A membership organization for diabetics and their families, the American Diabetes Association offers its members information and referrals; insurance counseling; savings on diabetes products; and support through meetings of local chapters. Annual membership fee: $24.00. Phone the 800 number for information on membership, for general information on diabetes risk factors and management, for referral to your local association, or to request a publications catalog.

American Dietetic Association (ADA)

216 West Jackson Boulevard, Suite 800
Chicago, IL 60606–6995
1–800–366–1655 (Nutrition Hotline) or 312–899–0040

The Nutrition Hotline offers recorded messages in English and Spanish on current nutrition issues. Registered dietitians also are available to answer specific questions about diet and nutrition and to provide referrals to dietitians in your area. Be prepared to specify zip code and the type of nutrition counseling needed. Topics of nutrition counseling include allergies, cardiovascular disease, diabetes, digestive disorders, gerontology, high blood pressure, oncology (cancer and chemotherapy), renal (kidneys and dialysis), and weight control.

Helpful Publications:
Phone for a selection of free brochures on a variety of food- and health-related topics.

"Exchange Lists for Meal Planning." Order #0734 (in large print, #0851). 32-page booklet on meal planning for diabetics. $1.50 (in large print, $2.50).

"Staying Healthy: A Guide for Elder Americans." Order #9116. Send a self-addressed stamped envelope for this free pamphlet.

American Foundation for the Blind (AFB)

11 Penn Plaza, Suite 300
New York, NY 10001
1–800-AF-BLIND (1–800–232–5463) or 212–502–7600
TTY: 212–502–7662

Contact AFB for referrals to state or community agencies that specialize in working with people with visual impairments. The organization also will provide lists of sources of devices to help with specific daily living activities and a free packet of basic information and helpful suggestions for visually impaired individuals and family members.

Helpful Publication:
"Aging and Vision: Making the Most of Impaired Vision." Free booklet.

American Foundation for Urologic Disease (AFUD)

300 West Pratt Street, Suite 401
Baltimore, MD 21201–2463
1–800–242–2383 or 410–727–2908

This nonprofit organization supports research and conducts educational programs on urologic disease and disorders, including prostate cancer and other prostate diseases, bladder diseases, incontinence, and sexual dysfunction.

Phone the toll-free line for disease-specific information and publications. Direct written inquiries to the appropriate AFUD council: the Bladder Health Council, the Prostate Health Council, or the Sexual Function Health Council. The foundation also serves as an international clearinghouse for support groups for prostate cancer survivors and their families. Phone the 800 line for referrals to local support groups.

Helpful Publications:
Phone or write for a complete listing or to request copies of these free booklets.
"Answers to Your Questions About Bladder Cancer"
"Answers to Your Questions About Urinary Incontinence (Loss of Bladder Control)"
"Answers to Your Questions About Urinary Tract Infections"
"Enlarged Prostate: BPH and Male Urinary Problems"
"Prostate Disease: Vital Information for Men over 40." Also available in Spanish.

American Geriatrics Society (AGS)
770 Lexington Avenue, Suite 300
New York, NY 10021
212–308–1414
Fax: 212–832–8646
Contact this society of physicians and other professionals involved in the health care of older adults for referrals to licensed geriatricians in your area.

American Health Assistance Foundation
Alzheimer's Family Relief Program
15825 Shady Grove Road, Suite 140
Rockville, MD 20850
1–800–437–AHAF (1–800–437–2423) or 301–948–3244
Fax: 1–800–258–9454
This nationwide program provides direct financial grants of

up to $500 to Alzheimer's disease patients and/or to caregivers who have expenses related to the patient's care and treatment. Applicants may not have assets exceeding $10,000 and must complete a financial statement, with medical and financial needs verified by a physician and social worker or other health professional. The extent of assistance and the number of patients helped depend on the availability of funds, which come from charitable contributions. Phone or write for an application form and further information on eligibility criteria.

Helpful Publications:
The following four booklets are available as a set, for $5.00.
"Alzheimer's Disease: The ABCs of Diagnosis." $2.00.
"Alzheimer's Disease: Legal and Financial Facts You Should Know." $2.00.
"Caring for the Alzheimer's Patient: A Family Guide." $2.00.
"The Hardest Choice: Selecting a Nursing Home for an Alzheimer's Patient." $2.00.

American Hearing Research Foundation
55 East Washington Street, Suite 2022
Chicago, IL 60602
312–726–9670

Contact this nonprofit research foundation for information about hearing disorders and for the addresses of local clinics and specialists providing hearing aid evaluations—impartial evaluations of the hearing improvement an individual can expect from different types of hearing aids.

Helpful Publications:
Phone or write for copies of these free brochures.
"Care of the Ears and Hearing for Health"
"Facts and Fancies About Hearing Aids"
"So You Have Had an Ear Operation . . . What Next?"

American Heart Association (AHA)
7272 Greenville Avenue
Dallas, TX 75231–4596
1–800-AHA-USA1 (1–800–242–8721) or 214–373–6300
Fax: 214–706–1341
via Internet: http://www.amhrt.org

The American Heart Association funds research and sponsors public education programs. Phone the 800 number for information about the prevention and treatment of cardiovascular disease and stroke and to locate your nearest AHA chapter, which will tell you about local health screenings, courses, and special events.

Helpful Publications:
Phone the local chapter or national 800 number to request a complete catalog or copies of these free brochures.

"The American Heart Association Diet: An Eating Plan for Healthy Americans"

"Cholesterol Tracking Record." Wallet-size calendar for recording blood pressure, weight, and serum cholesterol levels.

"Medicine Cabinet Sticker." Lists warning signs of heart attack, emergency action procedures, and emergency phone numbers.

"An Older Person's Guide to Cardiovascular Health and Disease"

"Stroke: A Guide for the Family"

"Walking for a Healthy Heart." Available in a version for people age fifty-five and older.

Stroke Connection
American Heart Association
7272 Greenville Avenue
Dallas, TX 75231–4596
1–800–553–6321

This service of the American Heart Association sponsors a toll-free stroke information and referral line, which offers referrals to local support groups for stroke survivors and their families. The goal of the stroke support groups is to promote independence while reducing some of the losses caused by disability. The Stroke Connection also sponsors a pen pal program, matching stroke survivors and caregivers with others in similar circumstances.

Helpful Publications:
Phone for a complete listing.
"Brain Attack: The Family's Role in Caregiving." 28-page booklet. Free.
"Caring for a Person with Aphasia." 28-page booklet. Free.
"How Stroke Affects Behavior." 38-page booklet. Free.
"The One-Handed Way: Living with the Use of One Hand." 24-page booklet. $2.16.
"What You Should Know About Stroke." 12-page booklet. Free.
Stroke Connection. Bimonthly magazine with news on coping with stroke, health tips, and motivational human interest stories. One-year subscription: $8.00 (free to stroke survivors who are unable to pay fee).
A Stroke of Luck. Informal newsletter for stroke survivors living with aphasia, published three times a year. Subscription free.

American Kidney Fund (AKF)
6110 Executive Boulevard, Suite 1010
Rockville, MD 20852
1–800–638–8299 (helpline) or 301–881–3052
Fax: 301–881–0898
A research, public education, and direct financial aid agency, AKF provides funds to help patients suffering from permanent kidney failure pay for medications, medical supplies, transportation, special diets, and other treatment-related necessities. The agency also awards grants to kidney donors to

help them pay for travel, child care, and other expenses associated with organ donation. Phone the toll-free helpline to speak with a renal social worker or patient service specialist who will provide information on kidney disease and referrals to local support and service resources.

Helpful Publications:
Phone for a complete catalog or to request copies of these free brochures.
"Diabetes and the Kidneys." Order #30 (in large print, #31).
"Diet Guide for the CAPD Patient." Order #40 (in Spanish, #41).
"Diet Guide for the Hemodialysis Patient." Order #42 (in Spanish, #43).
"Facts About Kidney Diseases and Their Treatment." Order #02.
"Facts About Kidney Stones." Order #32.
"High Blood Pressure and Its Effects on the Kidneys." Order #33.
"Kidney Disease: A Guide for Patients and Their Families." Order #03.

American Lung Association
1740 Broadway
New York, NY 10019–4374
1–800-LUNG-USA (1–800–586–4872) or 212–315–8700
Fax: 212–315–8872
Phone the toll-free number to be connected with your local American Lung Association chapter, which will provide information and publications on lung disease prevention, treatment, and therapies, as well as referrals to local quit-smoking programs.

American Mental Health Counselors Association
801 North Fairfax Street, Suite 304
Alexandria, VA 22314
1–800–326–2642 or 703–548–6002

This toll-free line provides referrals to local professional mental health counselors.

American Occupational Therapy Association (AOTA)

4720 Montgomery Lane
P.O. Box 31220
Bethesda, MD 20824–1220
301–652–2682 or 301–652–6611

AOTA is a professional organization for occupational therapists, who help people recovering from illness or injury or coping with aging-related changes to become as independent as possible in home or work environments. Phone for general information and public information brochures on occupational therapy.

American Optometric Association

243 North Lindbergh Boulevard
St. Louis, MO 63141–7881
314–991–4100
Fax: 314–991–4101

This professional organization of doctors of optometry, who diagnose and treat diseases and disorders of the eye, will refer you to your state optometric association, which in turn will help you locate local sources for low-vision services and specialists.

Helpful Publications:
Send a self-addressed stamped business-size envelope with requests for single copies of these free consumer brochures.
"Answers to Your Questions About Bifocals/Trifocals"
"Answers to Your Questions About Cataracts"
"Answers to Your Questions About Dry Eye"
"Answers to Your Questions About Glaucoma"
"Answers to Your Questions About Spots & Floaters"
"Driving Tips for Older Adults"
"Your Vision, the Second 50 Years"

American Osteopathic Association (AOA)
142 East Ontario Street
Chicago, IL 60611
1–800–621–1773 or 312–280–5800
   AOA represents osteopathic physicians (DOs), full-care physicians who emphasize preventive medicine and treatment of the body as an integrated whole. Phone the 800 number for referrals to your state osteopathic association, which will help you locate a DO in your area.

Helpful Publication:
   "What Is a D.O.?" Free brochure.

American Parkinson Disease Association (APDA)
1250 Hylan Boulevard, Suite 4B
Staten Island, NY 10305
1–800–223-APDA (1–800–223–2732) or 718–981–8001
Fax: 718–981–4399
   The largest organization in the world dedicated to Parkinson's disease research, patient advocacy, and public education, APDA manages a nationwide network of information and referral centers, each staffed by a nurse coordinator and supervising physician. Phone the toll-free number for referrals to one of the fifty-one centers, which will answer your questions and provide free literature and referrals to local community and medical resources and support groups.

Helpful Publication:
   "Parkinson's Disease Handbook: A Guide for Patients and Their Families." Free 36-page booklet on symptoms, medications, and other treatments and therapies.

American Physical Therapy Association (APTA)
1111 North Fairfax Street
Alexandria, VA 22314
1–800–999-APTA (1–800–999–2782) or 703–684–2782
Fax: 703–684–7343
Representing licensed physical therapists and physical therapist

assistants, who help people overcome disabilities from chronic disease and injuries, APTA operates a toll-free line for information on physical therapy and the conditions it treats.

Helpful Publications:
Phone for copies of these free 12-page brochures.
"For the Young at Heart: Exercise Tips for Seniors"
"Taking Care of Your Back"
"Taking Care of Your Hand, Wrist, and Elbow"
"Taking Care of Your Knees"
"Taking Care of Your Shoulder"
"Women of All Ages"

American Podiatric Medical Association (APMA)
9312 Old Georgetown Road
Bethesda, MD 20814–1698
1–800-FOOTCARE (1–800–366–8227) or 301–571–9200
Fax: 301–530–2752
    Phone for referrals to APMA state societies, which will provide the names of local podiatrists—doctors who specialize in the diagnosis and treatment of foot injuries and diseases.

Helpful Publications:
Phone to request these free brochures.
"Your Podiatric Physician Talks About Aging"
"Your Podiatric Physician Talks About Foot Health"

American Psychiatric Association
1400 K Street NW
Washington, DC 20005
202–682–6220
    This professional association will put you in touch with your local psychiatric society, for referrals to local psychiatrists, along with information on their educational background, training, and certification.

Helpful Publications:
Order these free brochures by mail.

"Let's Talk Facts About . . ." is a series of brochures on mental illness. Titles include: "Alzheimer's Disease," "Anxiety Disorders," "Choosing a Psychiatrist," "Depression," "Mental Health of the Elderly," "Panic Disorders," "Phobias," "Psychiatric Medications," "Substance Abuse."

American Psychiatric Nurses Association

1200 Nineteenth Street NW, Suite 300
Washington, DC 20036–2401
202–857–1133

Contact this professional association for a list of psychiatric mental health nurses practicing in your area.

Helpful Publication:
"Mental Health Care: A Consumer's Guide." Free brochure.

American Psychological Association (APA)

750 First Street NE
Washington, DC 20002–4242
1–800–374–2721 or 202–336–5500

The world's largest association of psychologists, APA will put you in touch with your local psychological association for referrals to licensed psychologists who work with the elderly.

Helpful Publication:
"Finding Help: How to Choose a Psychologist." Free brochure.

American Society of Hypertension

515 Madison Avenue, Room 1212
New York, NY 10022
212–644–0650
Fax: 212–644–0658

Contact this professional association of physicians and scientists involved in the study, diagnosis, and treatment of hypertension and related cardiovascular diseases for referrals to local hypertension specialists.

American Speech-Language-Hearing Association (ASHA)
10801 Rockville Pike
Rockville, MD 20852–3279
1–800–638–8255 (helpline, voice/TTY) or 301–897–8682 (helpline, voice/TTY, in Maryland, Alaska, and Hawaii)
301–897–5700 (national office, voice/TTY)
Fax: 301–571–0457

The national association for speech-language pathologists and audiologists—professionals who help people with speech, language, and hearing disorders—ASHA operates a helpline to answer questions about communication disorders, rehabilitation, and the fitting, care, and cost of hearing aids. The association also will provide referrals to certified medical specialists in your area.

Helpful Publications:
Phone or write for copies of these free brochures.
"Answers/Questions About Assistive Listening Devices"
"How to Buy a Hearing Aid"

American Tinnitus Association (ATA)
P.O. Box 5
Portland, OR 97207–0005
503–248–9985
Fax: 503–248–0024

This national membership organization supports tinnitus research and will provide referrals to hearing health professionals and local self-help groups. Annual membership fee starts at $25.00. Phone for an information packet.

Helpful Publications:
Phone for a complete catalog; the following brochures are free with membership.
"Coping with the Stress of Tinnitus." $1.00.
"Information About Tinnitus." Available in Spanish. $1.00.

"Noise: Its Effects on Hearing and Tinnitus." $1.00.
"Tinnitus Family Information." $1.00.

Anxiety Disorders Association of America (ADAA)
6000 Executive Boulevard, Suite 513
Rockville, MD 20852
301–231–9350
Fax: 301–231–7392
E-mail: anxdis@aol.com

A nonprofit organization dedicated to promoting the welfare of people with anxiety disorders, ADAA will help you locate appropriate local centers, therapists, and self-help groups. Members receive a quarterly newsletter, discounts on association publications, and statewide listings of professional treatment providers and self-help groups. Annual membership fee: $25.00.

Helpful Publications:
Phone for a complete catalog.
"Anxiety Disorders in the Elderly." Order #P5. $1.00.
"Anxiety Disorders: Helping a Family Member." Order #P6. $1.00.
"Consumers' Guide to Treatment." Order #P1. $1.00.

Arthritis Foundation
1330 West Peachtree Street
Atlanta, GA 30309
1–800–283–7800 (information line)
1–800–933–0032 (member line)
404–872–7100

This national health organization supports arthritis-related research and provides information, support, and referrals. Phone the information line for free booklets on arthritis medications, treatments, and tips for coping with daily activities. Phone the member line to locate your local chapter, which offers numerous volunteer-based services, including self-help classes for individuals with arthritis and their families, exercise classes and videos for people with varying levels of mobility, aquatics exercise programs (many sponsored by local YMCAs and other groups), support groups and clubs, a bimonthly magazine, and lists of local medical specialists and other resources. Annual membership fee: $20.00.

Helpful Publications:
Phone the information line for a complete catalog or copies of these free brochures.
"Arthritis Answers: Basic Information About Arthritis." Order #4001.
"The Family: Making the Difference." Order #9334.
"Managing Your Fatigue." Order #9336.
"Managing Your Health Care." Order #9325.
"Managing Your Pain." Order #9333.

Assistance Dog Institute
P.O. Box 2334
Rohnert Park, CA 94927–2334
1–800–284-DOGS (1–800–284–3647) or 707–585–0300 (voice/TTY)
Fax: 707–585–0445

Assistance dogs include guide dogs for people with visual impairments; hearing dogs, who alert their hearing-impaired owners to sounds; service dogs, who enhance the mobility of people with physical limitations by performing tasks such as pulling wheelchairs and turning on light switches; and social/therapy dogs, who offer unconditional love and acceptance for people who are developmentally disabled or require convalescent care. The Assistance Dog Institute develops improved training for assistance dogs and will help people with special needs find local programs providing dogs.

Association for Macular Diseases
210 East Sixty-fourth Street
New York, NY 10021
212–605–3719

An all-volunteer organization, the Association for Macular Diseases informs, motivates, and offers practical advice and coping strategies to individuals and families trying to adjust to macular disease. The organization publishes a newsletter and medical updates and will provide information and referrals for diagnosis and treatment sources. Annual membership fee: $20.00.

Bassett HealthSource
One Atwell Road
Cooperstown, NY 13326
1–800–298–8900 or 607–547–3900

Operated by Bassett HealthCare, a regional network of health care providers, this toll-free line provides answers to general health questions plus personal advice from registered nurses.

Better Hearing Institute
P.O. Box 1840
Washington, DC 20013
1–800-EAR-WELL (1–800–327–9355) (voice/TTY; Hearing Helpline) or 703–642–0580 (voice/TTY)
Fax: 703–750–9302

Phone this nonprofit educational organization's Hearing Helpline for answers to your questions about hearing loss and help available through medicine, surgery, assistive devices, and other treatment and rehabilitation options. The institute also will provide referrals to local hearing professionals and self-help groups, as well as information about financial assistance for treatment.

Blinded Veterans Association (BVA)
477 H Street NW
Washington, DC 20001–2694
1–800–669–7079 or 202–371–8880

A congressionally chartered veterans service organization, BVA provides a variety of services to blind and legally blind veterans and their families. Volunteers will help veterans access rehabilitation programs and other services available through the Department of Veterans Affairs (VA) and local agencies. The organization also provides information on conditions that cause vision loss, information on benefits and estate planning, personal counseling, assistance in pursuing claims before the VA, and a bimonthly newsletter in large print and on audiocassette. Annual membership fee: $8.00 (service-connected blindness) or $6.00 (associate membership, non-service-connected blindness). All BVA services are provided free of charge; membership is not a prerequisite for service.

Braille Institute
741 North Vermont Avenue
Los Angeles, CA 90029
1–800-BRAILLE (1–800–272–4553) or 213–663–1111

Phone the Braille Institute's toll-free line for information and nationwide referrals for services pertaining to blindness. In southern California the institute offers a range of direct services to individuals who are legally blind or visually impaired, including educational programs that teach the skills needed for independent living, adjustment support and counseling, and access to a library of thousands of popular titles in Braille and on audiocassette and flexible disk.

Cancer Care
1180 Avenue of the Americas
New York, NY 10036
1–800–813-HOPE (1–800–813–4673) (counseling line) or
212–221–3300
Fax: 212–719–0263
E-mail: info@cancercareinc.org.
via Internet: http://cancercareinc.org

Cancer patients and their families may phone the toll-free counseling line to speak with professionally trained social workers and receive emotional support, problem-solving assistance, information, and referrals to local services for additional assistance. Callers have the option of participating in ongoing telephone support groups and educational seminars. On the local level Cancer Care's offices in New York, New Jersey, and Connecticut provide free professional social work counseling and guidance to cancer patients and their families, as well as financial assistance to eligible families.

Cancer Control Society (CCS)

2043 North Berendo Street
Los Angeles, CA 90027
213–663–7801 or 213–663–7805

This nonprofit society's mission is public education in the prevention and control of cancer and other diseases through nutrition, diagnostic tests, and nontoxic alternative therapies. For a requested donation of $10.00, CCS will send an information packet containing a doctor list, patient list, diet sheet, prevention literature, publications list, and more. Referrals and information also may be given by phone.

Cancer Information Service

National Cancer Institute
Building 31, Room 10A24
9000 Rockville Pike
Bethesda, MD 20892
1–800–4-CANCER (1–800–422–6237)
TTY: 1–800–332–8615

Supported by the National Cancer Institute, the federal government's primary agency for cancer research, this toll-free line provides up-to-date information and publications on early detection, risk reduction, treatment options, and clinical trials, plus referrals to cancer-related community services, programs, and treatment facilities. Spanish-speaking operators are available.

Helpful Publications:
"Cancer Tests You Should Know About: A Guide for People 65 and Over." Free 14-page booklet, including checklist of periodic cancer tests.
"What You Need to Know About Cancer." Free

32-page booklet on cancer detection, causes, prevention, and treatment.

PDQ (Physician's Data Query)
PDQ is a computer database developed by the National Cancer Institute, containing the latest information on state-of-the-art treatments and drugs for all forms of cancer, health problems caused by cancer and its treatments, clinical trials, and listings of cancer specialists and organizations with cancer care programs. Information specialists at the Cancer Information Service have access to some PDQ information, including clinical trial listings and descriptions of treatments and anticancer drugs. They also will explain ways you can access additional PDQ data. Access is available through some hospitals, university libraries, and large public libraries; via fax machine through CancerFax (301–402–5874); and via Internet and other electronic information services through CancerNet. For a contents list of CancerNet IDs, send an E-mail message to: cancernet@icicb.nci.nih.gov. Enter the word HELP in the body of the mail message (or SPANISH for information in Spanish).

Cochlear Implant Club International (CICI)
P.O. Box 464
Buffalo, NY 14223–0464
716–838–4662 (voice/TTY)
Local chapters of this nonprofit organization for cochlear implant users and their families provide fellowship, moral support for those considering or approaching surgery, practical suggestions for wearing and maintaining processors, and friendly assistance to implantees' family members. Organization members receive a newsletter with human interest stories, user tips, and news on research and developments. Contact for referrals to your local chapter and for information on cochlear implants.

Compeer

Monroe Square, Suite B–1
259 Monroe Avenue
Rochester, NY 14607
1–800–836–0475 or 716–546–8280

Through 115 programs in thirty-three states, Compeer matches trained volunteers in friendship relationships with people of all ages who are receiving mental health treatment. The volunteers help reduce loneliness and isolation and form a link to the community. Clients must be referred by mental health professionals. Phone the 800 number for information on a nearby program.

Consumer Health Information Research Institute Hotline (CHIRI)

300 Pink Hill Road
Independence, MO 64057
816–228–4595

This patient and family advisory group is set up to help consumers avoid physical and financial harm from health quackery. Phone to check out alternative or complementary health therapies.

Coronary Club

Cleveland Clinic Foundation
9500 Euclid Avenue
Cleveland, OH 44195
1–800–478–4255 or 216–444–3690

People who have or are at risk for heart disease may join this nonprofit membership organization to receive benefits that include a one-year subscription to a monthly newsletter by Cleveland Clinic cardiac specialists and discounts on products such as exercise equipment, cookbooks, and videos. Annual membership fee: $29.00.

Corporate Angel Network (CAN)

Westchester County Airport
Building One

White Plains, NY 10604
914–328–1313
Fax: 1–800–328–4226

CAN arranges free air transportation for cancer patients to and from recognized cancer treatment centers, using available seats on corporate aircraft flying on business trips. Financial need is not a requirement, but there are a few restrictions; for example, patients must be able to walk unassisted and must not require special services or life-support systems. Requests are taken only within three weeks of a definite appointment or discharge date.

Council of Citizens with Low Vision International (CCLVI)

c/o American Council of the Blind
1155 Fifteenth Street NW
Washington, DC 20005
1–800–733–2258

Outreach programs sponsored by this international network of individuals with low vision include a toll-free information and referral line, activities and support groups at local chapters throughout the United States and Canada, and a quarterly newsletter in large print and on audiocassette. Annual membership fee: $10.00.

Deafness Research Foundation

15 West Thirty-ninth Street
New York, NY 10018–3806
212–768–1181 (voice/TTY)
Fax: 212–768–1782

This voluntary organization funds research into treatments of deafness and other ear disorders and will provide information on hearing disorders plus referrals to local physicians.

Delta Society

289 Perimeter Road East
Renton, WA 98055–1329
206–226–7357
TTY: 1–800–809–2714

Fax: 206–235–1076

E-mail: deltasociety@cis.compuserve.com

Delta links people with disabilities to resources for obtaining a service dog. The 800 line also provides immediate information and assistance to people with service dogs who are denied access to housing or public places.

Department of Veterans Affairs (VA)

Blind Rehabilitation Service (117B)
810 Vermont Avenue NW
Washington, DC 20420
202–273–8483

Veterans and their families may contact this VA office for information about the VIST (Visual Impairment Services Team) program and other benefits available to legally blind veterans. VIST is a community-based service that provides diagnosis, treatment, and referrals to rehabilitation centers for comprehensive training in adjustment to sight loss.

DEPRESSION Awareness, Recognition, Treatment (D/ART)

National Institute of Mental Health
5600 Fishers Lane, Room 10–85
Rockville, MD 20857
1–800–421–4211 or 301–443–4140

Phone this professional and public education program for information and free publications on symptoms, diagnosis, and treatment of depression.

Helpful Publications:
Phone or write for copies of these free brochures.

"A Consumer's Guide to Services." Order #ADM 92–0214.

"Helpful Facts About Depression." Order #ADM 89–1536.

"If You're Over 65 and Feeling Depressed . . . Treatment Brings New Hope." Order #ADM 90–1653.

Descriptive Video Service
WGBH Educational Foundation
125 Western Avenue
Boston, MA 02134
1–800–333–1203
E-mail: dus@wgbh.org
via Internet: http://www.boston.com/wgbh/dvs

This national nonprofit organization provides narrated descriptions of a program's or movie's key visual elements during pauses in the soundtrack, making television and home video accessible to blind and visually impaired people. Contact for a free program guide and a catalog of home video titles, available in large print and braille.

Disabled American Veterans
P.O. Box 14301
Cincinnati, OH 45250
606–441–7300

For veterans who suffered some degree of disability while serving in times of war or armed conflict, this privately funded membership organization offers personal counseling on VA compensation and other benefits, assistance in assembling evidence and presenting claims, transportation to VA medical facilities, disaster relief in times of natural disaster, and special programs addressing problems associated with aging. Lifetime membership fee: age 41–60, $125.00; age 61–70, $100.00; age 71 and over, $75.00 (payable in installments).

EAR Foundation
1817 Patterson Street
Nashville, TN 37203
1–800–545–HEAR (1–800–545–4327) (voice/TTY)
Fax: 615–329–7935

This not-for-profit organization is committed to public awareness, education, and support for hearing- and balance-impaired people. The foundation's Meniere's Network is a national network of support groups allowing Meniere's patients to share their experiences and coping strategies.

Electronic Industries Foundation
Assistive Devices Division (ADD)
2500 Wilson Boulevard
Arlington, VA 22201–3834
703–907–7600
ADD is a network of private companies that produce electronic products and services to assist individuals who have physical, mental, or sensory limitations. Contact for information on ADD manufacturers and the types of products and services available.

Helpful Publication:
Send a self-addressed stamped envelope to: Electronic Industries Foundation, 919 Eighteenth Street NW, Suite 900, Washington, DC 20006.
"Extend Their Reach: Electronic Devices Can Mean a World of Difference to Those with Special Needs." Free 28-page booklet on electronic devices for people with disabilities, with resource list of manufacturers.

Foundation of Dentistry for the Handicapped
1800 Glenarm Place, Suite 500
Denver, CO 80202
303–298–9650
Fax: 303–298–9649
More than five thousand dentists and dental laboratories in thirteen states volunteer through this program to provide free dental care and dental appliances to elderly and disabled people who cannot afford needed treatment. The program currently serves Alaska, California, Colorado, Illinois, Indiana, Louisiana, Michigan, Mississippi, New Jersey, Ohio (Cincinnati only), Oregon, Rhode Island, and Wyoming. Contact for information on eligibility and for referrals to participating dentists.

Foundation for Glaucoma Research
490 Post Street, Suite 830
San Francisco, CA 94102
1–800–826–6693 or 415–986–3162
Fax: 415–986–3763

226

This nonprofit foundation supports and conducts research and operates a national telephone-based peer support network for glaucoma patients and their families. Phone the toll-free number for information on diagnosis, treatment, research, and support services.

Helpful Publications:
Gleams. Quarterly newsletter on glaucoma-related topics. Subscription free.
"Understanding and Living with Glaucoma." Free 36-page booklet.

Friend's Health Connection
P.O. Box 114
New Brunswick, NJ 08903
1–800–48FRIEND (1–800–483–7436) or 908–418–1811
via Internet: http://www.48friend.com
People of all ages with any chronic illness, disorder, or handicap are connected with others, to find emotional support through communicating via letters, phone, tapes, and E-mail. Members are matched according to health problem, symptoms, interests, hobbies, lifestyle, and other personal characteristics. One-time fee: $10.00.

Guide Dog Foundation for the Blind
371 East Jericho Turnpike
Smithtown, NY 11787–2976
1–800–548–4337 or 516–265–2121
Fax: 516–361–5192
The Guide Dog Foundation breeds and trains Labradors and Golden Retrievers to become companions, friends, and "eyes" for people who are either totally blind or have serious visual limitations. Applicants must be in good physical and mental health and able to provide adequate housing and care for the dog. Medical and ophthalmologic reports and personal and agency references are required with the application. Student and dog train together in a twenty-five-day residential program. There is no cost to the applicant. Phone or write for a packet of

information, including an application and an audiotape about the program.

Guide Dogs of America
13445 Glenoaks Boulevard
Sylmar, CA 91342
1–800–459–4843 or 818–362–5834
Fax: 818–362–6870

Guide Dogs of America breeds and trains Labrador Retrievers, Golden Retrievers, and German Shepherds and matches them with blind or visually impaired partners. Students and guide dogs train together for twenty-eight days at the organization's California facility. Applicants must submit physician reports. There is no charge to the recipient for the dog, residential training, special equipment, or follow-up.

Guide Dogs for the Blind
P.O. Box 151200
San Rafael, CA 94915–1200
415–499–4000
Fax: 415–499–4035

This nonprofit charitable organization breeds and trains German Shepherds, Labradors, and Golden Retrievers to become guide dogs for legally blind people who are able to travel independently and are suited to working with and caring for a dog. Applicants must provide medical and personal references. The guide dog, transportation, room and board for a twenty-eight-day student-dog training program, and a $200 annual veterinary stipend are provided free of charge to applicants accepted into the program. Contact for an application and for information, which is available in print and on audiocassette.

Hearing Aid Helpline
International Hearing Society
20361 Middlebelt Road
Livonia, MI 48152
1–800–521–5247

Operated by the professional organization that represents hearing aid specialists, this toll-free helpline answers questions about hearing loss and hearing aids and provides referrals to local certified hearing aid specialists.

Helpful Publication:
"The World of Sound: Facts About Hearing and Hearing Aids." Free brochure.

Hear Now
9745 East Hampden Avenue, Suite 300
Denver, CO 80231–4923
1–800–648-HEAR (1–800–648–4327) (voice/TTY) or
303–695–7797 (voice/TTY)
Fax: 303–695–7789

Hear Now makes hearing aids and cochlear implants accessible to deaf and hard-of-hearing people with limited financial resources. The organization provides the devices and arranges for associated hearing health care professionals to fit them free of charge. Applicants must have a documented hearing loss. Financial need is determined according to level of family income, excessive medical expenses, and the cost of the needed hearing technology. Phone the toll-free number for information about additional requirements and to request an application for assistance.

Helen Keller National Center for Deaf-Blind Youths and Adults
111 Middle Neck Road
Sands Point, NY 11050
516–944–8900
TTY: 516–944–8637

Serving individuals who are deaf-blind or at risk for developing both vision and hearing impairments, this federally funded center provides diagnostic evaluation, short-term rehabilitation and personal adjustment training, and job preparation and placement. Services are offered through the New York headquarters, ten regional offices, and forty affiliates. The South Central office, in Dallas (214–490–9677), has an Older Adults Program that provides educational courses, information, and referrals for deaf-blind older adults and their caregivers. Phone the national headquarters for information on local offices and programs.

IBM Independence Series Information Center
11400 Burret Road
Austin, TX 78758
1–800-IBM–4832 (1–800–426–4832)
TTY: 1–800–426–4833

This service provides information on computer products designed to help people with disabilities, including visual and hearing impairments, achieve greater independence.

International Association of Cancer Victors and Friends (IACVF)
7740 West Manchester Avenue, Suite 203
Playa Del Rey, CA 90293
310–822–5032

Supporting nontoxic, holistic cancer therapies, IACVF provides referral lists of patients who have successfully controlled their disease through such therapies, clinics and doctors offering holistic treatment, and member chapters offering information and support throughout the United States, Canada, and Australia.

International Foundation for Functional Gastrointestinal Disorders
P.O. Box 17864
Milwaukee, WI 53217
414–964–1799
Fax: 414–964–7176
E-mail: iffgd@execpc.com
via Internet: www.execpc.com\iffgd

This nonprofit education and research foundation offers support and information to individuals and families affected by functional gastrointestinal disorders, including irritable bowel syndrome and bowel incontinence. Members receive a quarterly newsletter, fact sheets, and support via telephone or E-mail. Annual membership fee: $20.00.

Helpful Publications:
The following fact sheets are free to members; nonmembers send $1.00 and a self-addressed stamped envelope with each request.

"IBS Brochure." Order #101. Describes causes, management, and treatment of irritable bowel syndrome.

"Living with and Managing Fecal Incontinence." Order #104.

"Regaining Control." Order #103. Discusses treatments for managing bowel incontinence.

Lifesaver Charities
P.O. Box 2533
Garden Grove, CA 92640
714–530–7100
Fax: 714–530–0830
Lifesaver Tags are small, tear-resistant, washable tags that can be filled out with information on an individual's identity, allergies, medications, doctor, and emergency contacts, and either sewn into clothing or laced into shoes. Send $1.00 and a self-addressed stamped envelope for ten tags.

Lighthouse National Center for Vision and Aging (NCVA)
111 East Fifty-ninth Street, 11th floor
New York, NY 10022
1–800–334–5497 (voice/TTY) or 212–821–9200 (voice) or 212–821–9713 (TTY)
Fax: 212–821–9707
E-mail: scohen@lighthouse.org
Phone NCVA's toll-free number to learn about age-related eye disorders and to locate local low-vision clinics, training for independent living, adaptive products, and self-help groups for older people with visual impairments. The Lighthouse provides direct services to visually impaired individuals in the New York City area. Also see listing under "Specialty Catalogs."

Helpful Publications:

Phone for a complete catalog; send orders to: Publications Department, The Lighthouse, 36–20 Northern Boulevard, Long Island City, NY 11101.

"Cataract Information." Order #P420. Free brochure.

"Factsheet on Glaucoma." Order #P440. Free flyer.

"Sound and Sight: Your Second Fifty Years." Order #P166. Practical guidebook on coping with dual sensory loss. $5.00.

"Whatever Works." Order #P840. Practical solutions to help people with impaired vision cope with everyday tasks. $5.00.

Lions Clubs International

300 Twenty-second Street
Oak Brook, IL 60521–8842
630–571–5466

Contact for the address of your state Lions Club office, which will provide applications for financial assistance for eye care to needy individuals who are visually impaired. The assistance comes from local Lions Clubs; since their funding varies, applying is no guarantee of acceptance.

Lung Line Information Service

National Jewish Center for Immunology and Respiratory Medicine
1400 Jackson Street
Denver, CO 80206-2762
1–800–222-LUNG (1–800–222–5864) or 303–355–5864

Phone this automated information line to listen to recorded messages about asthma, emphysema, allergies, respiratory infections, tuberculosis, and other lung diseases. You also can speak with a registered nurse, who will answer your questions about respiratory diseases and immunology or will refer you to another source that can. Lung Line operators provide limited referrals to respiratory physicians nationwide.

Macular Degeneration International
2968 West Ina Road, Number 106
Tucson, AZ 85741
602–797–2525

This nonprofit organization sponsors educational and support programs for individuals with early-onset or late-onset (age-related) macular degeneration. Members receive a resource manual and periodic updated inserts; a listing of services, programs, and consumer products catalogs; an introductory audiotape; and a biannual newsletter. Annual membership fee: $25.00.

Medic Alert U.S.
2323 Colorado Avenue
Turlock, CA 95382
1–800–344–3226 or 209–668–3333
Fax: 209–669–2495

Medic Alert members receive a distinctive necklace or bracelet and wallet card detailing special medical conditions and the member's ID number. If the wearer becomes incapacitated and requires emergency medical assistance, emergency personnel can contact Medic Alert's twenty-four-hour response center for instant access to medical records. Once contacted, Medic Alert notifies the patient's physician and family. There is a $35.00 enrollment charge and $15.00 annual fee; membership is available free to indigent people with special medical conditions.

Mended Hearts
7272 Greenville Avenue
Dallas, TX 75231–4596
214–706–1442

This support organization for heart disease patients and their families functions through 250 chapters throughout the United States. Members visit patients and families in hospitals and offer support through monthly chapter meetings. Contact for the location of your nearest chapter.

Helpful Publication:
    Heartbeat. Quarterly newsletter on issues of interest to heart patients. One-year subscription: $10.00.

Merrill Lynch Deaf/Hard-of-Hearing Investor Services
P.O. Box 9010
Princeton, NJ 08543–9010
1–800–765–8331 (TTY, customer service—complaints, concerns, suggestions)
1–800–333–4825 (TTY, Deaf/Hard-of-Hearing Bulletin Board — 24-hour information on products and services)
1–800–765–4833 (TTY) or 1–800–765–4464 (voice amplification, referrals to local financial consultants; free financial brochures and captioned videotapes)
609–282–1212, ext. 3121 (voice, general information)
    Merrill Lynch is the only full-service financial service firm with a program for the deaf and hard-of-hearing community. All financial consultants are trained in the use of TRS (Telecommunications Relay Service). Deaf financial consultants are available, and representatives on TTY lines will answer inquiries relating to account updates, mortgages, and refinancing. A number of captioned videotapes are available free of charge on retirement planning, estate planning, and other topics.

National Alliance for the Mentally Ill (NAMI)
200 North Glebe Road, Suite 1015
Arlington, VA 22203–3754
1–800–950-NAMI (1–800–950–6264) or 703–524–7600
Fax: 703–524–9094
    A membership organization for individuals diagnosed with mental illness, as well as their family and friends, NAMI supports research, advocates improved services, and sponsors a nationwide network of support groups. Membership fees vary and may be set according to ability to pay. Phone the toll-free number with your questions about mental illness and for referrals to local NAMI chapters, support groups, and services.

National Arthritis and Musculoskeletal and Skin Diseases Information Clearinghouse
National Institutes of Health
1 AMS Circle
Bethesda, MD 20892–3675
301–495–4484

This resource center of the National Institutes of Health provides information about federal research and scientific advances related to arthritis, osteoporosis, and other bone diseases; autoimmune diseases; skin diseases; musculoskeletal diseases; connective tissue diseases; and muscle diseases.

Helpful Publications:
Phone for a complete listing or to order these free information packets, which contain reprinted materials from various sources.
"Arthritis." Order #AR–27.
"Back Pain." Order #AR–78.
"Bursitis/Tendinitis." Order #AR–166.
"Gout." Order #AR–99.
"Hair Loss in Women." Order #AR–157.
"Hip Replacement." Order #AR–149.
"Osteoarthritis." Order #AR–73.

National Asian Pacific Center on Aging (NAPCA)
Melbourne Tower
1511 Third Avenue, Suite 914
Seattle, WA 98101
206–624–1221

For older people who speak an Asian language, this nonprofit agency maintains a library of brochures and articles on topics such as cancer and other diseases, health tips, and nutrition. Tell the operator the topic and language you are interested in, and you will receive free copies of relevant publications.

National Association for Continence (NAFC)
P.O. Box 8310
Spartanburg, SC 29305–8310
1–800-BLADDER (1–800–252–3337) or 864–579–7900
Fax: 864–579–7902

People with incontinence and their families may join NAFC to receive by mail a list of local health professionals who specialize in diagnosis and treatment, a directory of incontinence organizations and product dealers, personal answers to questions about bladder control problems, and a subscription to the organization's quarterly newsletter. Annual fee: $15.00 (people who cannot afford the fee receive a complimentary newsletter subscription).

Helpful Publications:
Phone for a complete catalog and ordering information.

"Aging and Incontinence." Order #4. Fact sheet. $1.50.

"Bladder Retraining." 6-week program for men and women. $3.00.

"Loss of Bladder Control: Your Guide to Treatment Options." Order #1. Fact sheet. $1.50.

"Pelvic Muscle Exercises for Men and Women." Order #3. Fact sheet. $1.50.

National Association of the Deaf (NAD)
814 Thayer Avenue
Silver Spring, MD 20910
301–587–1788
TTY: 301–587–1789
Fax: 301–587–1791

This consumer organization advocates better services for deaf and hard-of-hearing people. Members receive a list of information on NAD's programs, services, and activities, plus a newsletter and other publications. Annual membership fee (age sixty and older): $15.00. Phone for information and referrals to your state NAD affiliate and other resources.

Captioned Films / Videos
National Association of the Deaf (NAD)
1447 East Main Street
Spartanburg, SC 29307
1-800-237-6213
TTY: 1-800-237-6819
Fax: 1-800-538-5636

Phone this federally funded service of NAD for a free catalog of more than four thousand open-captioned films and videos. Most are educational films for young people, but the catalog includes about seven hundred general interest videos for all ages. Films and videos may be borrowed free of charge by people with hearing impairments.

National Association of Hospital Hospitality Houses
3111 West Jackson Street
Muncie, IN 47304
1-800-542-9730 or 765-288-3226
Fax: 317-287-0321

If your loved one requires medical treatment at a distant hospital, this association's toll-free line will give you information on hospital hospitality houses—programs providing safe, comfortable lodging and other supportive services for family members. Lodging may be available free or for a small charge.

National Association for Visually Handicapped (NAVH)
22 West Twenty-first Street
New York, NY 10010
212-889-3141
Fax: 212-727-2931

or

National Association for Visually Handicapped (NAVH)
3201 Balboa Street
San Francisco, CA 94121
415-221-3201
Fax: 415-221-8754

A national voluntary organization, NAVH serves partially seeing Americans. Phone for referrals to national and state resources, including low-vision clinics and talking book libraries. Members receive a discount catalog on visual aids, newsletters and medical updates, discounts on other NAVH publications, and use of a 5,200-volume large-print lending library. In the New York and San Francisco areas members may attend free seminars and receive free consultations by phone or in person. Annual membership fee: $40.00.

Helpful Publications:
Phone for a complete catalog; prices below are for non-members.

"Aging and Sensory Loss: A Tragedy or a Pain in the Neck?" Discusses eyesight and hearing loss in advanced age. $2.25.

"Cataracts." $2.25.

"Diabetic Retinopathy." $2.00.

"Diseases of the Macula." $2.00.

"Glaucoma: The Sneak Thief of Sight." $2.25.

"A Patient's Guide to Visual Aids and Illumination." Discusses devices that make reading easier for the partially seeing. 75¢

National Clearinghouse for Alcohol and Drug Information (NCADI)

P.O. Box 2345
Rockville, MD 20847–2345
1–800–729–6686 (English and Spanish) or 301–468–2600
TTY: 1–800–487–4889
Fax: 301–468–6433

Contact this national clearinghouse for information and publications on an array of topics related to alcohol, tobacco, and other drugs.

Helpful Publications:
"ATOD Resource Guide: Older Americans." Order #MS443. Free 20-page booklet with guidelines and resources to help prevent alcohol and prescription drug abuse among older adults.

"If Someone Close Has a Problem with Alcohol or Other Drugs." Order #PH317 (on audiocassette, order #AV222). Free 8-page booklet.

"Using Your Medicines Wisely: A Guide for the Elderly." Order #PHD500. Free 26-page booklet.

National Coalition for Cancer Survivorship (NCCS)
1010 Wayne Avenue, Suite 505
Silver Spring, MD 20910–9796
301–650–8868
Fax: 301–565–9670

A membership organization for people who have been diagnosed with cancer and for their loved ones, NCCS aims to inform, serve, and advocate on behalf of cancer survivors, to help them live the best quality of life possible following their diagnosis. Member benefits include a resource network linking cancer survivors to community support services, regional meetings for cancer survivors, personal responses to inquiries, and a quarterly newsletter on cancer survivorship issues. Annual membership fee: $35.00 (those unable to pay may join for any amount they can afford).

Helpful Publication:
"Teamwork: The Cancer Patient's Guide to Talking with Your Doctor." Free brochure.

National Council on Patient Information and Education
666 Eleventh Street NW, Suite 810
Washington, DC 20001–4542
202–347–6711
Fax: 202–638–0773

Concerned with improving communication between health care professionals and patients about prescription medicines, this coalition of health professional organizations has a variety of free brochures plus a wallet card providing a personal record of allergies, blood type, and emergency numbers.

Helpful Publications:
Phone or write for a complete listing or to request these free publications.

"A Consumer's Guide to Prescription Medicine Use."

"'Get the Answers' Wallet Card." Available in English and Spanish.

"Medicine: Before You Take It, Talk About It." Information designed for older consumers.

National Diabetes Information Clearinghouse (FDIC)
One Information Way
Bethesda, MD 20892–3560
301–654–3327
Fax: 301–907–8906

A service of the National Institute of Diabetes and Digestive and Kidney Diseases, one of the National Institutes of Health, this clearinghouse responds to written and phone inquiries about diabetes and provides referrals to diabetes organizations, including support groups.

Helpful Publications:
Phone for a complete catalog of free publications.

"Insulin-Dependent Diabetes." Order DM–51. 36-page booklet on diagnosis, treatment, and complications.

"Noninsulin-Dependent Diabetes." Order #DM–81. 35-page booklet on diabetes management, glucose monitoring, and complications.

Information packets, including fact sheets and article reprints, are available on:

"Alcohol and Diabetes." Order #DM–158.

"Diabetes and Hypertension." Order #DM–142.

"Health Insurance and Diabetes." Order #DM–144.

"Travel and Diabetes." Order #DM–149.

National Digestive Diseases Information Clearinghouse (NDDIC)
Two Information Way
Bethesda, MD 20892–3570

301–654–3810

Fax: 301–907–8906

This service of the National Institute of Diabetes and Digestive and Kidney Diseases responds to written and phone inquiries about the prevention and management of digestive diseases and provides referrals to digestive disease organizations, including support groups.

Helpful Publications:
Phone for a complete catalog of free publications.

"Age Page: Constipation." Order #DD–36. Fact sheet on causes, treatments, and the role of diet.

"Age Page: Digestive Do's and Don'ts." Order #DD–08. Fact sheet on causes and treatments of common digestive disorders.

Information packets, including fact sheets and article reprints, are available on:

"Abdominal Pain." Order #DD–151.

"Digestive Diseases: General Information." Order #DD–123.

"Liver Diseases: General Information." Order #DD–127.

National Empowerment Center (NEC)
20 Ballard Road
Lawrence, MA 01843–1018
1–800-POWER–2-U (1–800–769–3728)
TTY: 1–800–889–7693
Fax: 508–681–6426
E-mail: empower@world.std.com

NEC maintains a national directory of peer support groups, drop-in centers, and statewide organizations for people with mental disabilities.

National Eye Care Project (NECP)
P.O. Box 429098
San Francisco, CA 94142–9098
1–800–222-EYES (1–800–222–3937)

Free medical eye care is available to older adults who do not have or cannot afford a personal eye physician. U.S. citizens or legal residents age sixty-five or older are eligible to participate in the program if they do not have access to an ophthalmologist they have seen in the past and are not enrolled in a prepaid health care plan or eligible for treatment at a government care facility. Participants are matched to a volunteer NECP ophthalmologist in their area, who will provide a medical eye exam and treatment for any condition or disease diagnosed. Some services, such as hospital treatment, prescriptions, and eyeglasses, are not included. Phone the toll-free number to determine eligibility and receive free information about eye diseases commonly affecting people over age sixty-five.

National Eye Institute (NEI)
Information Office
Building 31, Room 6A32
31 Center Drive MSC 2510
Bethesda, MD 20892–2510
301–496–5248
A component of the federal National Institutes of Health, NEI supports and conducts research into disorders and diseases of the visual system. Contact for information about research into specific eye diseases, a list of free brochures on eye disorders, and referrals to other eye health-related organizations.

National Federation of the Blind (NFB)
1800 Johnson Street
Baltimore, MD 21230–4998
410–659–9314
Fax: 410–685–5653
The nation's largest organization of blind people, NFB has more than seven hundred local chapters in large cities throughout the United States. Members help newly blinded individuals adjust, learn how to continue most former activities, and remain in their own homes. The federation also provides information about eye diseases and causes of blindness, laws and regulations concerning the blind, and services available through government and private agencies in each state. The

Materials Center offers more than eight hundred publications in print and Braille and on audiocassette covering all aspects and issues of blindness, including about one hundred publications available at no cost. Also see listing under "Specialty Catalogs."

Helpful Publications:
Phone for a catalog of free publications in print and Braille and on audiocassette, computer disk, and talking book disk.

"Blindness and Disorders of the Eye."

Braille Monitor. Monthly magazine available in print and Braille and on audiocassette, with news and issues of special significance to the blind and people losing their sight.

"Comments on Clothing."

If Blindness Comes. Available in large print and on audiocassette, book includes extensive information about blindness, services, programs, and resources.

Kernel Books. Free volumes of inspirational true-life stories told by blind people; issued once or twice a year. Current titles include: *What Color Is the Sun, The Freedom Bell, As the Twig Is Bent, Making Hay,* and *The Journey.* Available in large print and Braille and on audiocassette.

Newsline. Daily digital talking newspaper reproduces the texts of *USA Today,* the *Chicago Tribune,* and the *New York Times.* The spoken text may be accessed by touch-tone phone. Service currently is available only in the District of Columbia, Maryland, and Louisiana, but will be expanding across the country as funding becomes available.

Diabetics Division of the National Federation of the Blind
1800 Johnson Street, Suite 300
Baltimore, MD 21230–4998
410–659–9314

This support and information network serves blind and sighted diabetics and their families. Volunteers in local chapters provide free counseling and information on local resources, aids, and appliances.

Helpful Publications:
Phone for a complete listing of free publications.

"Diabetic Food Exchange List." Available in Braille and on audiocassette.

Voice of the Diabetic. Quarterly magazine for blind diabetics, with tips on diet, diabetes control, self-reliance, and independence. Available in print and on audiocassette.

National Foundation for Depressive Illness
P.O. Box 2257
New York, NY 10116-2257
1–800–248–4344
Fax: 212–268–4434

Phone this toll-free line to hear a recorded message on recognizing the symptoms of depressive and manic-depressive illness. You can write the organization to request a packet of further information, which includes article reprints; a referral list of physicians, treatment centers, and support groups in any area you specify; and a bibliography of suggested readings. Enclose a self-addressed stamped ($1.01 postage) business-size envelope. The foundation requests at least a $5.00 donation but will send its packet at no cost to those who cannot afford the fee.

National Fraternal Society of the Deaf
1300 West Northwest Highway
Mount Prospect, IL 60056
847–392–9282 (voice)
TTY: 847–392–1409
Fax: 847–392–9298

This fraternal society sells low-cost life insurance for people who are deaf or hearing-impaired and their hearing relatives. More than eighty local lodges nationwide also sponsor community projects, including donations of clothing, food items, and assistive devices to low-income people with hearing impairments.

National Health Information Center (NHIC)
P.O. Box 1133
Washington, DC 20013–1133
1–800–336–4797 or 301–565–4167
Fax: 301–984–4256
E-mail: nhicinfo@health.org
via Internet: http://nhic-nt.health.org

A service of the U.S. Department of Health and Human Services, NHIC links consumers who have health and medical questions with the organizations best able to respond. An information specialist will search the center's database of government and private health-related organizations and give you names, addresses, phone numbers, and brief descriptions of appropriate groups. The service is useful and the information specialists helpful, but be prepared to wait on hold for several minutes.

Helpful Publications:
"Dietary Guidelines for Americans." Order #40003 (in Spanish, #40002). $1.00.

"Healthfinders: Long-Term Care." Order #A0028. $1.00.

"Healthfinders: 1995 Federal Health Information Centers and Toll-free Numbers for Health Information." Order #A0001. $1.00.

National Heart, Lung and Blood Institute (NHLBI)
P.O. Box 30105
Bethesda, MD 20824–0105
1–800–575-WELL (1–800–575–9355 [information line]) or
301–251–1222
Fax: 301–251–1223

This branch of the federal National Institutes of Health focuses on improving public health through education on cardiovascular disease risk reduction. Phone the information line for recorded messages in English and Spanish about how to prevent and treat high blood pressure and high blood cholesterol.

Helpful Publications:
Phone for a complete catalog of free publications.

"Age Page: Stroke Prevention and Treatment." Order #55–487. 2-page fact sheet.

"Check Your Smoking IQ: An Important Quiz for Older Smokers." Order #91–3031. 2-page quiz sheet.

"Facts About Blood Cholesterol." Order #94–2696. 28-page booklet.

"Facts About How to Prevent High Blood Pressure." Order #94–3281. 20-page booklet.

"High Blood Pressure & What You Can Do About It." Order #55–22A. 31-page booklet.

"Stay Young at Heart Recipe Cards." Order #55–648. 4-page booklet.

National Hypertension Association (NHA)
324 East Thirtieth Street
New York, NY 10016
1–800–575-WELL (1–800–575–9355 [information line])
or 212–889–3557
Fax: 212–447–7032

This nonprofit organization devoted to hypertension research, education, and detection cosponsors a toll-free information line with the National Heart, Lung and Blood Institute (see above) and offers additional information through its national headquarters.

Helpful Publications:
"Hypertension and You: What You Need to Know." Free brochure.

"Your Blood Cholesterol Level: What It Means for Your Heart." Free brochure.

National Information Center on Deafness (NICD)
Gallaudet University
800 Florida Avenue NE
Washington, DC 20002–3695
202–651–5051
TTY: 202–651–5052
Fax: 202–651–5054

A centralized source of accurate, up-to-date information, NICD answers questions and provides publications on a wide array of topics related to deafness and hearing loss. The staff also will refer callers to medical experts and local programs and services. NICD is a service of Gallaudet University, the country's only liberal arts university for deaf students.

Helpful Publications:
Phone for a free catalog and ordering information.

"Aging and Hearing Loss: Some Commonly Asked Questions." Order #506. 8-page booklet. $1.50.

"Communication Tips for Adults with Hearing Loss." Order #392. 8-page booklet. $1.50.

"Hearing Aids and Other Assistive Devices: Where to Get Assistance." Order #538. Resource list of agencies and organizations offering financial assistance. $1.00.

"Managing Hearing Loss in Later Life." Order #398. 6-page fact sheet. $1.50.

"Residential Facilities for Deaf Adults." Order #423. $2.00.

National Information Center on Hearing Loss
Swarthmore Medical Center
300 South Chester Road
Swarthmore, PA 19081
1–800–622-EARS (1–800–622–3277)

Contact this group for information and publications on hearing loss, treatments, and hearing aids. The organization also will send listings of local ear, nose, and throat doctors, audiologists, and hearing instrument specialists, and will provide referrals to support groups for people with hearing impairments.

National Institute on Aging (NIA)
31 Center Drive
Building 31, #5C27
Bethesda, MD 20892–2292
301–496–1752

A division of the National Institutes of Health, NIA supports and conducts research into the diseases and other special problems and needs of the aged, with an emphasis on strategies to maintain health and independence in later years. Specialists will answer your health-related questions by phone.

Helpful Publications:
For a complete catalog or to order copies of these free fact sheets write: NIA Information Center, P.O. Box 8057, Gaithersburg, MD 20898–8057, or phone 1–800–222–2225; TTY: 1–800–222–4225.

"Age Pages" are quick, practical fact sheets on a variety of health-related topics. Titles include: "Arthritis Advice," "Cancer Facts for People over 50," "Constipation," "Dealing with Diabetes," "Finding Good Medical Care for Older Americans," "Food Facts for Older People," "A Good Night's Sleep," "Medicines: Use Them Wisely," "Osteoporosis: The Bone Thinner," "Sexuality in Later Life."

National Institute on Deafness and Other Communication Disorders Information Clearinghouse (NIDCD)
One Communication Avenue
Bethesda, MD 20892–3456
1–800–241–1044 or 301–496–7243
TTY: 1–800–241–1055
Fax: 301–402–0018

One of the institutes of the National Institutes of Health, NIDCD supports and conducts research into disorders of hearing, speech, balance, smell, and taste. Contact the clearinghouse for information and publications related to these areas.

Helpful Publications:
Phone for a complete catalog of free publications.

"Age Page: Hearing and Older People." Order #DC–24 (in Spanish, #DC–24S).

"Because You Asked About Smell and Taste Disorders." Order #DC–69.

"Facts About Telecommunications Relay Services." Order #DC–12.

"Hearing and Hearing Loss Information Packet." Order #DC–103.

"Update on Dizziness." Order #DC–04.

National Institute of Mental Health (NIMH)

Information Resources and Inquiries Branch
Parklawn Building, Room 7-99
5600 Fishers Lane
Rockville, MD 20857
1–800–64PANIC (1–800–647–2642) or 301–443–4513
TTY: 301–443–8431
Fax: 301–443–5158
E-mail: nimhpubs@nih.gov

This government agency, a component of the National Institutes of Health, supports research on mental illness and mental health. Phone for information and publications on symptoms and treatments of anxiety and panic disorders, paranoia, Alzheimer's disease, depression, manic-depressive illness, and other mental health topics.

Helpful Publications:
Phone for a complete catalog.

"Alzheimer's Disease." Order #NIH95–3676. 40 pages.

"Anxiety Disorders." Order #NIH94–3879 (in Spanish, #SP95–3879). 24 pages.

"A Consumer's Guide to Mental Health Services." Order #NIH94–3585 (in Spanish, #SP90–0214). 21 pages.

"Useful Information on Sleep Disorders." Order #ADM87–1541. 36 pages.

National Institute of Neurological Disorders and Stroke (NINDS)
P.O. Box 5801
Bethesda, MD 20824
301–496–5751

A division of the federal National Institutes of Health, NINDS supports research on brain and nervous system disorders. Contact for free information, fact sheets, and research reports on chronic pain, dizziness, epilepsy, Parkinson's disease, shingles, stroke, and other disorders.

National Kidney Foundation (NKF)
30 East Thirty-third Street
New York, NY 10016
1–800–622–9010 or 212–889–2210

The major voluntary health agency concerned with kidney and urinary tract diseases, the National Kidney Foundation sponsors research and offers support and educational services to patients and their families. Local affiliates provide screening and early detection programs, transportation to and from dialysis centers, and direct financial assistance to low-income patients. Most also help organize patient and family support groups. Contact the national office for information about kidney and urinary tract diseases and to locate your nearest NKF affiliate.

Helpful Publications:
Phone for a complete catalog of free brochures.
"High Blood Pressure and Your Kidneys." Order #02–04 (in Spanish, #02–41). 8 pages.
"What Everyone Should Know About Kidneys and Kidney Disease." Order #01–01 (in Spanish, #01–02). 16 pages.
"Your Kidneys: Master Chemists of the Body." Order #01–03. 12 pages.

National Kidney and Urologic Diseases Information Clearinghouse (NKUDIC)
Three Information Way
Bethesda, MD 20892–3580

301–654–4415
Fax: 301–907–8906

Direct your written or phone inquiries about kidney and urologic diseases to this service of the National Institute of Diabetes and Digestive and Kidney Diseases, one of the National Institutes of Health. The clearinghouse also will provide referrals to kidney and urologic associations, including support groups.

Helpful Publications:
Phone for a complete catalog of free publications. Information packets, including fact sheets and article reprints, are available on:

"Kidney Disease and Hypertension." Order #KU–71.
"Prostatitis." Order #KU–52.
"Urinary Incontinence." Order #KU–55.
"Urinary Tract Infections in Women." Order #KU–66.

National Mental Health Association (NMHA)

1021 Prince Street
Alexandria, VA 22314–2971
1–800–969-NMHA (1–800–969–6642) or 703–684–7722
Fax: 703–684–5968

NMHA acts as a clearinghouse for information related to mental health, referring callers with questions to the agencies and organizations best suited to provide answers. Phone the twenty-four-hour toll-free information line for referrals to local and national mental health organizations and mental health providers or to request a catalog of free brochures, available on more than two hundred mental health topics.

National Mental Health Consumers' Self-Help Clearinghouse

1211 Chestnut Street, Suite 1000
Philadelphia, PA 19107
1–800–553–4-KEY (1–800–553–4539) or 215–751–1810
TTY: 215–751–9655
Fax: 215–636–6310
E-mail: thekey@delphi.com

Operated by the Mental Health Association of Southeastern Pennsylvania, this national clearinghouse provides information and technical assistance to mental health consumers seeking to launch self-help groups, plus referrals to existing self-help groups and to local mental health associations.

Helpful Publication:
    "The Elderly and Mental Health." $2.00

National Osteoporosis Foundation (NOF)
1150 Seventeenth Street NW, Suite 500
Washington, DC 20036–4603
1–800–223–9994 or 202–223–2226
Fax: 202–223–2237

Members of this organization receive an Osteoporosis Prevention Kit plus the free quarterly newsletter the *Osteoporosis Report.*

Helpful Publications:
Phone or write for these free publications.
    "Risk Factor Card"
    "Stand UP to Osteoporosis"

National Parkinson Foundation
1501 Northwest Ninth Avenue
Bob Hope Road
Miami, FL 33136–1494
1–800–327–4545 (out of state) or 1–800–433–7022 (in Florida) or 305–547–6666
Fax: 305–548–4403
E-mail: mailbox@npf.med.miami.edu
via Internet: http://www.parkinson.org

Thirty-one national Parkinson Foundation Centers of Excellence conduct research and provide treatment, therapy, rehabilitation, and educational services to Parkinson's disease patients and their families. A network of support groups and other outreach activities brings information and services to patients and families throughout the country. Phone to locate local services and support groups and to request free educational materials on Parkinson-related topics.

National Rehabilitation Information Center (NARIC)
8455 Colesville Road, Suite 935
Silver Spring, MD 20910–3319
1–800–346–2742 or 301–588–9284 (voice/TTY)
Fax: 301–587–1967

An information specialist at this library and information center will provide referrals to local resources; for example, a list of rehabilitation facilities or independent living centers in your area. NARIC also will search its bibliographic database of more than forty-three thousand pamphlets, fact sheets, and other documents published by a variety of organizations on topics including physical and psychiatric disabilities, independent living, medical rehabilitation, and assistive technology. The search can be tailored to your interests, with a descriptive listing provided of all relevant documents. Cost is $10.00 for the first one hundred citations. Lists are available in large print or Braille and on audiocassette or PC-compatible disk. NARIC also is able to conduct searches of the ABLEDATA database (see above).

Helpful Publications:
Free consumer resource guides are available on these topics: "Head Injury," "Home Modification," "Spinal Cord Injury," "Stroke."

National Stroke Association (NSA)
96 Inverness Drive East, Suite I
Englewood, CO 80112–5112
1–800-STROKES (1–800–787–6537) or 303–649–9299
TTY: 303–649–0122
Fax: 303–649–1328
via Internet: http://www.stroke.org

NSA's goal is to reduce the incidence and severity of stroke through prevention, medical treatment, rehabilitation, family support, and research. Phone for information and referrals to medical professionals, rehabilitation facilities, and support groups for survivors and caregivers. NSA members receive an informative quarterly newsletter, discounts on other publications, a guide to products and services for stroke survivors, and a free personalized stroke risk assessment and prevention plan. Annual membership fee: $20.00.

Helpful Publications:
Phone for a complete catalog.

"Adaptive Resources: A Guide to Products and Services." Order #BB3. Annual 48-page listing of adaptive resource products and manufacturers. 50¢.

"The Brain at Risk: Understanding and Preventing Stroke." Order #BC6. 27-page booklet. 50¢.

"Home Exercises for Stroke Survivors." Order #BB2. 28-page illustrated booklet. 50¢.

"Living at Home After a Stroke." Order #BB1. 24-page guide for survivors and caregivers. 50¢.

"Stroke Treatment & Recovery." Order #BA5. 16-page booklet. 50¢.

National Women's Health Network
514 Tenth Street NW, Suite 400
Washington, DC 20004
202–347–1140

This advocacy organization operates a clearinghouse of women's health information, which members can write or phone with questions about their health care. Members also receive a bimonthly newsletter on developments in women's health. Annual membership fee: $25.00.

New Eyes for the Needy
549 Millburn Avenue
P.O. Box 332
Short Hills, NJ 07078–0332
201–376–4903
Fax: 201–376–3807

This volunteer charitable organization gives indigent people vouchers for free prescription eyeglasses, which are dispensed by practitioners in their local areas. Applications for assistance must be made through a social service department, and the recipient must have a prescription from a recent eye exam.

Paralyzed Veterans of America (PVA)

801 Eighteenth Street NW
Washington, DC 20006
1–800–424–8200 (member information)
202-USA–1300 (202–872–1300)
TTY: 1–800–795–4327
Fax: 202–785–4452

Veterans with paralysis caused by spinal cord injury or disease have an advocate in this nonprofit organization. PVA provides free assistance and representation to veterans with a spinal cord dysfunction who are seeking health care and other benefits. The organization also assists veterans and their families with tasks essential to daily living, such as finding attendant care and housing. PVA's Architecture and Barrier Free Design Program will send you a packet of information on locating accessible housing or adapting the home for people with disabilities. Other member benefits include social and recreational activities at forty local chapters throughout the United States. Membership is free for the first year; fees for subsequent years vary among chapters.

Helpful Publications:
Phone for a complete catalog of free publications.
"An Introduction to Spinal Cord Injury: Understanding the Changes"
"General Housing Package." Collection of articles on kitchen and bathroom design and adapting the home for wheelchair users.
"Making Your Home Accessible: Assessing Your Needs for Home Modifications"

Parkinson's Disease Foundation (PDF)

Columbia-Presbyterian Medical Center
650 West 168th Street

New York, NY 10032
1–800–457–6676 or 212–923–4700

This corporation conducts and funds research into the causes and treatment of Parkinson's disease and related disorders, including Alzheimer's disease and Lou Gehrig's disease (amyotrophic lateral sclerosis). Contact for information on home care and physical therapy and for referrals to local support groups and physicians experienced in the treatment of Parkinson's disease.

Helpful Publications:

"Exercises for the Parkinson Patient with Hints for Daily Living." Free brochure.

"The Parkinson Patient at Home." Free brochure.

Parkinson's Disease Foundation Newsletter. Free newsletter for patients and family.

Prevent Blindness America
500 East Remington Road
Schaumberg, IL 60173–5611
1–800–331–2020
Fax: 847–843–8458
via Internet: www.prevent-blindness.org

Contact this national volunteer eye health and safety organization for information and publications on vision, eye health, and eye safety. Affiliate offices in more than forty states sponsor support groups for individuals coping with age-related eye diseases. Most provide free adult vision screening at senior centers, community health centers, and similar sites.

Helpful Publications:
Limit is three free single copies; some publications are available in large print.

"A Checklist for Your Eye Doctor Appointment." Order #AB15.

"Family Home Eye Test." Order #AB45.

"LifeSight: Growing Older with Good Vision." Order #AB55.

"Signs of Possible Eye Trouble in Adults." #AB65.

PRIDE Foundation

391 Long Hill Road
P.O. Box 1293
Groton, CT 06340–1293
860–445–1448 or 860–445–7320

This nonprofit agency provides custom-designed clothing patterns and modifies off-the-rack clothing for the comfort and ease of wheelchair users and others with physical disabilities.

R. A. Bloch Cancer Foundation

4410 Main Street
Kansas City, MO 64111
816–932–8453 (Cancer Hot Line)
Fax: 816–931–7486

Newly diagnosed cancer patients may phone the Cancer Hot Line to talk with individuals who have had cancer, who will offer emotional support and encouragement, information, and advice. On the local level the R. A. Bloch Cancer Support Center provides a range of free support programs for Kansas City–area cancer patients and their families.

Seeing Eye

P.O. Box 375
Morristown, NJ 07963–0375
201–539–4425
Fax: 201–539–0922

Seeing Eye, the world's oldest guide dog school, trains dogs as companions and guides. Blind and visually impaired individuals who are in good physical condition may apply for a dog. If accepted, the student trains with the dog for twenty to twenty-seven days at the school. Students are asked to pay $150.00 to cover a small portion of the costs of the dog, equipment, training, room and board, and round-trip transportation; no one is denied service for lack of funds.

Self Help for Hard of Hearing People (SHHH)

7910 Woodmont Avenue, Suite 1200
Bethesda, MD 20814

301–657–2248
TTY: 301–657–2249
Fax: 301–913–9413

The largest consumer membership organization for individuals who do not hear well, SHHH has a nationwide support network of 260 groups and chapters whose members meet to learn about hearing loss and coping strategies. The national office will respond to inquiries about hearing loss and give referrals to local health professionals and other resources. Member benefits include a hearing health care plan with discounts on hearing care services, hearing aids, and other products and services; a bimonthly newsletter; and discounts on other SHHH publications. Annual membership fee: $25.00.

Helpful Publications:
Phone for a complete catalog; prices below are for non-members.
"A Consumer's Guide for Purchasing a Hearing Aid." $1.65.
"It's Our Hearing Loss: What Families Need to Know and Do." $1.75.
"Older Adults with Hearing Loss." $3.75.
"Persuading Your Spouse/Relative/Friend to Acknowledge Hearing Loss and Seek Help." $1.95.

Simon Foundation for Continence
P.O. Box 815
Wilmette, IL 60091
1–800–23-SIMON (1–800–237–4666) or 847–864–3913
Fax: 847–864–9758

This not-for-profit educational organization is dedicated to helping people find cures and management techniques for incontinence. Members receive a quarterly newsletter and other publications. Annual membership fee: $15.00.

Helpful Publications:
Phone for a complete catalog; send a self-addressed

stamped business-size envelope and $1.00 for each of these article reprints.

"Advanced Age Is Not a Cause for Incontinence." Order #1.

"Are You Ready to Talk to Your Doctor About Incontinence?" Order #7.

"Finding an Incontinence Product to Suit Your Needs." Order #2.

Skin Cancer Foundation

245 Fifth Avenue, Suite 1403
New York, NY 10016
212–725–5176
Fax: 212–725–5751

Concerned solely with skin cancer, this nonprofit foundation supports research and conducts public and medical educational programs. Patients and their families may join the Inner Circle, a membership program, to gain access to a hotline that answers specific questions about skin cancer. Members receive a quarterly newsletter about sun protection and skin health plus periodic reports on research developments in diagnosis, treatment, and prevention. Annual membership fee starts at $100.00.

Helpful Publications:
Send a self-addressed stamped envelope for each copy of these free brochures.

"The ABCDs of Moles & Melanomas." Order #BR–4. 6-page brochure with photographs.

"Simple Steps to Sun Safety." Order #BR–14. 6-page brochure.

"Skin Cancer: If You Can Spot It, You Can Stop It." Order #BR–13. 8-page brochure with body map for recording self-exams.

Stroke Clubs International (SCI)

805 Twelfth Street
Galveston, TX 77550
409–762–1022

More than nine hundred independently run Stroke Clubs serve stroke victims and their families through counseling, education, and mutual support. Contact the main office for referrals to the Stroke Club nearest your area.

Telecommunications for the Deaf (TDI)
8719 Colesville Road, Suite 300
Silver Spring, MD 20910–3919
301–589–3786
TTY: 301–589–3006
Fax: 301–589–3797
A nonprofit organization dedicated to improving technology and accessibility for all who rely on visual telecommunications, TDI publishes the *National Directory of TTY Numbers,* with business, organization, and residential TTY numbers and addresses, plus fax numbers, E-mail addresses, relay service numbers, and information about the Internet. Residential listings cost $15.00 per year; the directory costs $20.00, plus $4.00 shipping and handling.

Tele-Consumer Hotline
901 Fifteenth Street NW, Suite 230
Washington, DC 20005
1–800–332–1124 (voice/TTY) or 202–347–7208
(voice/TTY)
Fax: 202–408–1134
Phone this hotline for information about different types of telephone services available to assist people who are deaf, hard of hearing, or have a disability that interferes with use of telephone equipment. Operators also will provide referrals to relay services.

United Ostomy Association (UOA)
36 Executive Park, Suite 120
Irving, CA 92614
714–660–8624
An association of ostomy groups throughout the United States and Canada, UOA gives advice and information to

ostomates and their families. Local ostomy chapters provide person-to-person help for new ostomates through volunteer visitors. Most groups meet monthly for educational programs, mutual aid, and moral support.

United Way of America

701 North Fairfax Street
Alexandria, VA 22314–2045
703–836–7100

Your local United Way organization may operate or support an information and referral service that can help you locate community resources providing medical and mental health services, rehabilitation, alcohol and drug abuse treatment, and services for individuals with disabilities. Look in your phone directory or contact the national office for the location of your local United Way.

Vision Foundation

818 Mount Auburn Street
Watertown, MA 02172
617–926–4232

An information and support network, Vision Foundation sponsors mutual aid groups and telephone support programs for older people who are coping with sight loss or progressive eye disease. The organization offers referrals to local vision resources plus a newsletter and literature in large print and on audiocassette. Annual membership fee: $30.00 (for individuals on fixed incomes, $15.00).

Wander Watch Alert 24

P.O. Box 35287
Sarasota, FL 34242–5287
1–800–881–8502 or 941–349–6583

To help safeguard people with Alzheimer's disease, brain injury, or other impairments, this system uses an ankle band containing a microtransmitter that sends a silent coded radio signal to the caregiver's home receiver, allowing the caregiver to calculate the distance the wearer is from the receiver and sounding an alarm when the wearer travels beyond a selected range. The waterproof, four-ounce anklet is worn continuously; a tamper alarm sounds if it is forcibly removed. The complete system costs about $750.00. Phone the 800 number for the name of a local authorized dealer, or look in your phone directory under "Security Control" or "Burglar Alarms."

REGIONAL

Organizations on this list provide services in limited geographic areas. You may be able to find groups offering similar services in your relative's community.

AgeWell Resource Center
Westgate Mall
2341-M Schoenersville Road
Bethlehem, PA 18107
610–954–3999
Fax: 610–954–3525

Free and low-cost programs for older adults in the Lehigh Valley area of Pennsylvania include health screenings, flu immunizations, individual counseling by health professionals, support groups for individuals with various health problems, and a quarterly newsletter of health-related information.

Associated Services for the Blind
919 Walnut Street
Philadelphia, PA 19107
215–627–0600
Fax: 215–922–0692
E-mail: asbinfo@libertynet.org
via Internet: http://www.libertynet.org/~asbinfo

For blind and visually impaired people in the Delaware Valley, Associated Services for the Blind offers free information, support, and educational courses in computer skills, English as a second language, accessing telephone services, and other subjects. Through the Radio Information Center, which reaches

Pennsylvania, New Jersey, and Delaware, listeners may hear readings of major daily and neighborhood newspapers and popular magazines. Also see "New Vision Store" listing under "Specialty Catalogs."

Boston Center for Independent Living (BCIL)

95 Berkeley Street, Suite 206
Boston, MA 02116
617–338–6665
TTY: 617–338–6662
Fax: 617–338–6661

Most of BCIL's services are provided in eastern Massachusetts, with the focus on enabling people of all ages who have disabilities to live independently in the community. The organization also answers questions related to health care, housing, skills building, and other issues of independence for the disabled.

Brookdale Center on Aging

425 East Twenty-fifth Street
New York, NY 10010–2590
212–481–7670

Brookdale Center, a university-based gerontology center, runs a number of programs in the New York metropolitan area providing social activities for people suffering from Alzheimer's disease. Phone for contact names and locations.

Chemocare

231 North Avenue West
Westfield, NJ 07090–1428
1–800–55-CHEMO (1–800–552–4366) (out of state) or
908–233–1103 (in New Jersey)
TTY: 908–233–7510
Fax: 908–233–0228

This New-Jersey based program matches patients who are undergoing treatment for cancer with trained volunteers who have survived a similar experience and resumed their normal lives. More than three hundred volunteers offer emotional support and encouragement to patients and families through personal visits and by phone.

Consumer Health
5720 Flatiron Parkway
Boulder, CO 80301-2834
1–800-DOCTORS (1–800–362–8677) or 847–433–6847

Phone this hospital-supported computer database service for free assistance in locating a doctor or dentist suited to your relative's needs. Counselors will ask questions to help guide your search, then provide a variety of information about recommended professionals, including educational background and training, certification, procedures performed in the office, specialties, hospital affiliations, fees and payment methods, treatment style, and philosophy of practice. The service is currently available in fifteen cities.

Family Caregiver Alliance Association (FCA)
425 Bush Street, Suite 500
San Francisco, CA 94108
415–434–3388
E-mail: info@caregiver.org
via Internet: http://www.caregiver.org

This nonprofit organization assists families of adults who have Alzheimer's disease, head injury, stroke, Parkinson's disease, brain tumor, or another chronic or progressive brain disorder. Services cover the six-county San Francisco Bay area and include educational programs, care planning, legal consultations, individual and group counseling, and limited financial assistance for respite care. FCA also is the lead agency for California's Caregiver Resource Center network, a statewide system of centers offering a broad range of free and low-cost services to caregivers of adults with brain disorders. Contact for the location of Caregiver Resource Centers throughout the state.

Other Helpful Free or Low-Cost Publications

Accent on Living is a quarterly magazine for people with disabilities, featuring health care news, product reports, travel and vacation guides, self-improvement tips, and human interest stories. One-year subscription: $12.00. Contact: Accent on Living, P.O. Box 700, Bloomington, IL 61702 (1–800–787–8444).

The American Association of Retired Persons (AARP) offers many comprehensive, free publications on health-related topics. For a free catalog or to request the following titles, contact: AARP Fulfillment, 601 E Street NW, Washington, DC 20049 (1–800–424–3410).

"Coping and Caring: Living with Alzheimer's Disease." Order #D12441.
"Facts About Hearing Loss." Order #D14869.
"Facts About Vision Loss." Order #D14870.
"Pep Up Your Life: A Fitness Book for Seniors." Order #D549.

Caring for the Caregiver: A Guide to Living with Alzheimer's Disease. Free 171-page guidebook covers many issues involved in caring for an Alzheimer's patient at home. Contact: Parke-Davis, Warner-Lambert Company, 201 Tabor Road, Morris Plains, NJ 07950 (1–800–223–0432).

"Center Watch" is a World Wide Web page that lists current clinical trials by region and disorder. Patients may sign up for confidential notification of specific clinical trials. This page can be reached at http://www.w2.centerwatch.com on the Internet.

For a catalog of free and low-cost health- and consumer-related government publications, write: Consumer Information Center–6A, P.O. Box 100, Pueblo, CO 81002. There is a $1.00 service charge per total order for free booklets from the following list:

"Choosing Medical Treatments." Order #537C. Free 5-page booklet on alternative therapies.

"Hocus-Pocus as Applied to Arthritis." Order #540C. Free 7-page booklet on fraudulent "cures."

"Pocket Guide to Federal Help for Individuals with Disabilities." Order #117C. 34-page booklet on federal programs for rehabilitation, employment, housing, and more. $1.50.

"Thrifty Meals for Two." Order #120C. 69-page booklet with menus and recipes for the older couple on a limited budget. $2.50.

"Unproven Medical Treatments Lure Elderly." Order #546C. Free 6-page booklet on medical frauds.

"Eating Well to Stay Well." Order #4181. Free 48-page booklet with diet and lifestyle suggestions to help seniors sustain health. Contact: National Council on the Aging, Information Office, 409 Third Street SW, Suite 200, Washington, DC 20024 (202–479–6653).

The Food and Nutrition Information Center offers free "Nutri-Topics"—source lists of recommended articles, books, brochures, and pamphlets, with ordering information—on these topics: "Nutrition and Cancer," "Nutrition and Cardiovascular Disease," "Nutrition and the Elderly," "Weight Control and Obesity." Contact: Food and Nutrition Information Center, U.S. Department of Agriculture, National Agricultural Library Building, Room 304, Beltsville, MD 20705–2351 (301–504–5719).

Send 75¢ in postage stamps for each of the following booklets to: Heart Disease Research Foundation, 50 Court Street, Brooklyn, NY 11201 (718–649–6210).

"How Personality Factors and Exercise Relate to Cardio-Vascular Diseases"

"The Prevention of Cardio-Vascular Diseases"

"13 Triggering Factors Preceding Myocardial Infarctions (Heart Attack) and Stroke"

"How to Select the Right Doctor." Free 15-page brochure. Write: Georgetown Medical Directory, 2233 Wisconsin Avenue NW, Suite 333, Washington, DC 20007.

"How to Talk to an Older Person Who Has a Problem with Alcohol or

Medications." Free 12-page booklet on signs of misuse and abuse and how to help. Contact: Hazelden Information Center, P.O. Box 11, Center City, MN 55012–0011 (1–800–436–2273).

"Incontinence: Everything You Wanted to Know but Were Afraid to Ask." Free brochure. Contact: Alliance for Aging Research, 2021 K Street NW, Suite 305, Washington, DC 20006 (202–293–2856).

The National Association for Human Development offers three booklets on graduated levels of exercise instruction, at $3.00 each. For ordering information phone 202–328–2191.
      "Basic Exercises for People over 60" (Series I)
      "Moderate Exercises for People over 60"(Series II)
      "Exercise-Activity for People over 60" (Series III)

To order the following low-cost booklets, contact: National Consumers League, 1701 K Street NW, Suite 1200, Washington, DC 20006 (202–835–3323).
      "Food & Drug Interactions." Also available in Spanish. $1.00.
      "Questions to Ask: Taking Charge of Your Health." $1.00.
      "When Medicines Don't Mix: Preventing Drug Interactions." Also available in Spanish. $1.00.

"The Nursing Home, Alzheimer's, and You." Free brochure. Send self-addressed stamped envelope to: American Association of Homes and Services for the Aging, 901 E Street NW, Suite 500, Washington, DC 20004–2011.

Nutrition Action Healthletter is published ten times a year by Center for Science in the Public Interest, a nonprofit public interest membership organization. The magazine covers nutrition research findings, deceptive food advertising and labels, unhealthy ingredients, and healthy diet tips. One-year subscription, which includes a free copy of the booklet "Eating Smart Shopping Guide": $10.00. Contact: Center for Science in the Public Interest, 1875 Connecticut Avenue NW, Suite 300, Washington, DC 20009–5728 (202–332–9110).

The Parkinson's Disease Web Page offers on-line information on

Parkinson's disease. This page can be reached on the Internet at: http://neuro-chief-e.mgh.harvard.edu/parkinsonweb/Main/PDmain.htm/

Technical File is the only technical magazine specifically directed at blind individuals. Published quarterly in Braille and on audiocassette and floppy disk, it contains articles on electronics and sensory aids assembly for blind professionals and hobbyists. For subscription information contact: Smith-Kettlewell Eye Research Institute, Rehabilitation Engineering Research Center, 2232 Webster Street, San Francisco, CA 94115 (415–561–1619).

"10 Simple Ways to Improve Your Memory." Free brochure. Contact: Memory Assessment Clinics, 8311 Wisconsin Avenue, Bethesda, MD 20814–3126 (301–657–0030).

The U.S. Public Health Service offers a number of informative free booklets on health care topics. For a free catalog or to request copies of the following guides, contact: Agency for Health Care Policy and Research, Publications Clearinghouse, P.O. Box 8547, Silver Spring, MD 20907 (1–800–358–9295).

> "Depression Is a Treatable Illness: Patient Guide." Order #93–0553 (in Spanish, #93–0554).
> "Preventing Pressure Ulcers: Patient Guide." Order #92–0048 (in Spanish, #93–0014).
> "Recovering After a Stroke: Patient and Family Guide." Order #95–0664 (in Spanish, #95–0665).
> "Treating Pressure Ulcers: Consumer Guide." Order #95–0654 (in Spanish, #95–0655).
> "Treating Your Enlarged Prostate: Patient Guide." Order #94–0584 (in Spanish, #94–0585).

"What You Need to Know About . . ." is a series of free 10-page booklets on these topics: "Breast Cancer," "Heart Attacks," "Strokes." Contact: America's Pharmaceutical Research Companies, 1100 Fifteenth Street NW, Washington, DC 20005 (1–800–862–4110). Information is also available on the Internet at www.phrma.org

Worst Pills Best Pills is a monthly newsletter on prescription and nonprescription drugs, including usefulness, possible adverse side effects, which drugs should not be taken together, and which should not be taken at all. One-year subscription: $12.00. Contact: Public Citizen Health Research Group, 1600 Twentieth Street NW, Washington, DC 20009–1001 (202–588–1000).

Publications for the Visually Impaired

The following organizations publish and/or distribute reading materials in formats accessible to people who are blind or visually impaired or have a physical disability that prevents the easy use of printed matter. Many donate their materials free of charge; proof of disability usually is required for free service.

American Bible Society
1865 Broadway
New York, NY 10023
212–408–1200
Donates free Bibles in large print, Braille, or recorded form.

American Printing House for the Blind
1839 Frankfort Avenue
P.O. Box 6085
Louisville, KY 40206–0085
1–800–223–1839 or 502–895–2405
Fax: 502–899–2274
Free weekly editions of *Newsweek* magazine, with full content of articles, on audiocassette. Also phone for a free catalog of books in large print and Braille and on audiocassette and computer disk.

Aurora Ministries, Bible Alliance
P.O. Box 621
Bradenton, FL 34206
941–748–3031
Fax: 941–748–2625
Donates free Bibles on audiocassette, available in forty different languages.

Blindskills
P.O. Box 5181
Salem, OR 97304–0181
1–800–860–4224 or 503–581–4224
Fax: 503–581–0178
Publishes *Dialogue,* quarterly magazine on adjustment techniques, mobility, independence, health, recreation, products, and services to enhance quality of life. Available in large print and Braille and on audiocassette.

Choice Magazine Listening
85 Channel Drive
Port Washington, NY 11050
516–883–8280
Produces free bimonthly audio anthologies of articles, short stories, and poetry, playable on the National Library Service cassette player (see below).

Christian Record Services
P.O. Box 6097
Lincoln, NE 68506–0097
402–488–0981
TTY: 402–488–1902
Fax: 402–488–7582
Publishes Bible study guides and inspirational magazines, booklets, and journals in large print and Braille and on flexible disk.

Christian Services for the Blind
P.O. Box 26
1124 Fair Oaks Avenue
South Pasadena, CA 91031–0026
818–799–3935
Fax: 818-403-9460
Offers four different Christian magazines on audiocassette, playable on the National Library Service cassette player (see page 272), plus a lending library of several hundred Christian books on audiocassette and in Braille.

Horizons for the Blind
16A Meadowdale Shopping Center
Carpentersville, IL 60110
847–836–1400 (voice/TTY)
Fax: 847–836–1443
Instruction books and booklets on crafts, gardening, food preparation, and household appliance operation, available in large print and Braille and on audiocassette.

In Touch Networks
Jewish Guild for the Blind
15 West Sixty-fifth Street
New York, NY 10023
1–800–456–3166 or 212–769–6270
"America's Newsstand of the Air" broadcasts readings of news articles from newspapers and magazines twenty-four hours a day. In the tristate area of New York, New Jersey, and Connecticut, listeners pick up the closed-circuit signal on special pretuned receivers, available from In Touch for $88.00. Beyond a fifty-five-mile radius from the transmission site in New York City, listeners hear the broadcast via satellite through FM cable-radio, often accessible through the television set for subscribers to a cable package that includes audio. Program schedules are available in large print and Braille and on audiocassette.

Jewish Braille Institute of America
100 East Thirtieth Street
New York, NY 10016
212–889–2525
Fax: 212–689–3692
Publications on Judaism, in large print and Braille and on audio-cassette.

Johanna Bureau for the Blind and Physically Handi-capped
8 South Michigan Avenue, Suite 300
Chicago, IL 60603–3305
312–332–6076

Fax: 312–332–0780
Library of titles, mostly textbooks, in Braille, which may be purchased at a cost of 15¢ per Braille page. Will also transcribe new materials, at 15¢ per Braille page.

John Milton Society for the Blind
475 Riverside Drive, Room 455
New York, NY 10115
212–870–3336
Free Bible study materials, worship services, and quarterly digest of inspirational articles, in large print and Braille and on audiocassette, playable on the National Library Service tape player (see below).

Lutheran Braille Workers
P.O. Box 5000
Yucaipa, CA 92399
909–795–8977
Fax: 909–795–8970
Free Bibles and other Christian books in large print and Braille, available in forty different languages.

National Braille Association
3 Townline Circle
Rochester, NY 14623–2513
716–427–8260
Fax: 716–427–0263
About 2,000 general interest, music, and textbook titles in Braille may be purchased at a cost of 15¢ per Braille page and $1.00 binding per volume. Catalog is available in print and on audiocassette.

National Library Service for the Blind and Physically Handicapped
Library of Congress
1291 Taylor Street NW
Washington, DC 20542
1–800–424–8567 or 202–707–5100

Fax: 202–707–0712
Federally funded library program distributes Braille and recorded reading materials to a network of regional and local libraries, which have access to the entire collection and circulate materials free of charge to eligible borrowers. Also available are music materials and free subscriptions to more than seventy magazines on audio disk or in Braille. Special playback equipment is loaned free to readers. Ask your local public librarian about applying for service.

New York Times Mail Subscriptions
P.O. Box 9564
Uniondale, NY 11555-9564
1–800–631–2580
Publishes *New York Times Large Type Weekly*, a weekly newspaper including *New York Times* news articles, editorials, book and film reviews, columns, and crossword puzzle. One-year subscription: $58.00.

Reader's Digest Fund for the Blind
Large-Type Publications
P.O. Box 241
Mount Morris, IL 61054–9982
1–800–877–5293
Publishes monthly *Reader's Digest* magazine in Braille and on audiocassette (free of charge) and in large print (one-year subscription: $11.95). Also available are *Reader's Digest Condensed Books: Large Type Reader,* with selections from Reader's Digest Condensed Books and other Reader's Digest publications. Published every two to three months; five-volume subscription: $9.89.

Readings for the Blind
29451 Greenfield Road, Suite 216
Southfield, MI 48076–2294
810–557–7776
Customized service provides tape recordings of otherwise inaccessible print material.

Thorndike Press/G. K. Hall
200 Old Tappan Road
Old Tappan, NJ 07675–7095
1–800–223–2336
Phone for a free sales catalog of large-print books, including current and classic fiction and nonfiction.

Vision World Wide
5707 Brockton Drive, Suite 302
Indianapolis, IN 46220–5481
1–800–431–1739 or 317–254–1332
Fax: 317–251–6588
Publishes *Vision Enhancement,* a quarterly magazine with news on medical and psychological issues, assistive devices and technology, news briefs of happenings around the world, motivational stories, and resource guides. Available in large print and on audiocassette and computer disk. One-year subscription: $20.00.

World at Large
P.O. Box 190330
Brooklyn, NY 11219
718–972–4000
Publishes *World at Large* magazine, a biweekly newsmagazine in large print, with current articles from *Time, U.S. News & World Report,* and the *Monitor.* One-year subscription: $39.00.

Xavier Society for the Blind
154 East Twenty-third Street
New York, NY 10010
1–800–637–9193 or 212–473–7800
Fax: 212–473–7801
Free religious and inspirational materials, including *Catholic Review,* a bimonthly selection of articles from Catholic periodicals, available in large print and Braille and on audiocassette.

Lending Libraries

Lending libraries generally require applicants to submit written verification of their disability by an authority such as a doctor, ophthalmologist, registered nurse, or staff at a hospital or social agency.

Books Aloud

P.O. Box 5731
San Jose, CA 95150–5731
408–277–4878 or 408–277–4839
Fax: 408–277–4818
Collection: 5,000-plus general interest titles on audiocassette
Distribution: Automatic monthly circulating library; client specifies the number of books and categories desired; specific titles can be reserved
Loan period: 30 days
Cost: $25.00 donation requested from new clients
Catalog: Large print and audiocassette

JGB Cassette Library

Jewish Guild for the Blind
15 West Sixty-fifth Street
New York, NY 10023
1–800–284–4422 or 212–769–6200
Fax: 212–769–6266
Collection: About 1,500 titles on audiocassette, including contemporary and classic fiction, nonfiction, mysteries, biographies, humor, poetry, science fiction, romance, and more
Distribution: Client orders by title from catalog; may also request librarian to select from selected categories
Loan period: 30 days
Cost: $25.00 per year; free to clients who meet Medicaid eligility requirements.
Catalog: Large print
Other services: Free monthly mailings of compilations of cover stories from *Time* and *People* magazines on audiocassette

Kings Tape Library for the Blind
202 West Grangeville Boulevard
Hanford, CA 93230–2951
209–582–4843
Collection: Several hundred fiction and general interest nonfiction titles on audiocassette and voice-indexed (playable on four-track tape player)
Distribution: Client sends list of requested titles from catalog; books are sent one at a time
Loan period: 4 weeks
Cost: Free
Catalog: Large print and audiocassette

Martha Arney Library for the Blind
3911 Hayes Street NE
Minneapolis, MN 55421
612–788–0508
Collection: More than 1,000 nondenominational Christian and general interest books on audiocassette
Distribution: Client selects titles from reading list; books are sent one at a time
Loan period: 4 weeks
Cost: Free
Catalog: Print and audiocassette

Recording for the Blind & Dyslexic
20 Roszel Road
Princeton, NJ 08540
1–800–221–4792 or 609–452–0606
Fax: 609–987–8116
Collection: 80,000 textbooks and other educational books in most subject areas, including fiction, drama, and poetry in many languages, on computer disk and audiocassette (playable on four-track tape player)
Distribution: Client borrows selected audiocassette titles from catalog; books on computer disk may be purchased at varying prices
Loan period: Up to one year
Cost: $50.00 one-time registration fee

Catalog: Annual print catalog (three-book set), $49.95; quarterly supplement on audiocassette, $16.00 per year
Other services: Some books not in catalog may be recorded on request; four-track tape players available for purchase

Taped Ministries NW
122 SW 150th Street
Burien, WA 98166–1956
206–243–7377

Collection: Several hundred Christian books, devotionals, and magazines on audiocassette
Distribution: Client selects titles from list; two to four books are sent at a time
Loan period: Up to eight weeks
Cost: Free
Catalog: Large print

Volunteers of Vacaville
P.O. Box 670
Vacaville, CA 95696–0670
707–448–6841, ext. 2044

Collection: More than 2,500 mystery, science fiction, western, and best-seller titles on audiocassette
Distribution: Client specifies categories; four recently recorded titles in selected category sent each month
Loan period: 60 days
Cost: $20.00 per year
Catalog: Print, audiocassette
Other services: Book club titles may be purchased for 50¢ per cassette; members may send up to three personal books to be recorded each month (completed cassettes may be borrowed for 120 days or purchased at 50¢ per cassette). Braille-writers serviced and repaired.

Specialty Catalogs

The following organizations and retailers offer free print catalogs of products for people who are visually impaired, hearing impaired, or physically challenged and for older people with special needs. Some companies also offer their catalogs in large print or on audiocassette.

Ann Morris Enterprises
890 Fams Court
East Meadow, NY 11554–5101
1–800–454–3175 or 516–292–9232
Fax: 516–292–2522
Products for people with vision loss, including housewares, kitchen items, pet supplies, collectibles, medical supplies, writing supplies, computer accessories, talking items

Can-Do Products
Independent Living Aids
27 East Mall
Plainview, NY 11803
1–800–537–2118
Fax: 516–752–3135
Products for people who are blind or visually impaired, including talking items, lighting accessories, kitchen aids, household items, games, writing supplies, health care items, vision and hearing assistive devices

Carolyn's Products for Enhanced Living
P.O. Box 14577
Bradenton, FL 34280–4577
1–800–648–2266
Fax: 941–739–5503
Low-vision products, including talking items, magnifiers, lamps, computer accessories, household and personal products, health care items, games

Crestwood Company
6625 North Sidney Place
Milwaukee, WI 53209–3259
414–352–5678
Fax: 414–352–5679

Communication aids, including handheld talking devices, voice amplifiers, eating and drinking aids

Dr. Leonard's HealthCare Catalog
42 Mayfield Avenue
P.O. Box 7821
Edison, NJ 08818–7821
1–800–785–0880
Assistive devices for the elderly or disabled, health and beauty items

Duraline Medical Products
324 Werner Street
P.O. Box 67
Leipsic, OH 45856–1039
1–800–654–3376 or 419–943–2044
Fax: 419–943–3637
Incontinence products

Enrichments Product Catalog
P.O. Box 5050
Bolingbrook, IL 60440–5050
1–800–323–5547
Assistive devices for daily living activities, including kitchen tools, exercise products, mobility assists, wheelchair accessories, health care and incontinence products, bathroom and grooming aids, dressing aids, easy-change clothing

HDIS
1215 Dielman Industrial Court
St. Louis, MO 63132
1–800–538–1036
Incontinence products

Healthy Living
6836 Engle Road
P.O. Box 94512
Cleveland, OH 44101–4512

1–800–800–0100
Incontinence products

Hear-More
P.O. Box 3413
Farmingdale, NY 11735
1–800–881–4327 (voice/TTY) or 516–752–0738
(voice/TTY)
Fax: 516–752–0689
Amplifiers, alerting systems, closed-caption decoders, communication and computer devices, speech enhancers, and other products for the deaf and hearing impaired

Hear You Are
125 Main Street
Route 46
Netcong, NJ 07857
1–800–278–EARS (1–800–278–3277) or 201–347–7662
(voice/TTY)
Fax: 201–691–0611
Assistive listening devices

Lighthouse Low Vision Products
36–20 Northern Boulevard
Long Island City, NY 11101
1–800–829–0500
Low vision products, including talking and easy-read items, writing supplies, small appliances and tools, household items, games, personal grooming aids, mobility assists, health care products

LS&S Group
P.O. Box 673
Northbrook, IL 60065
1–800–468–4789 or 847–498–9777
TTY: 1–800–317–8533
Fax: 847–498–1482
Products for visually and hearing-impaired people, including CCTV and computer adaptive devices, talking items, tape

recorders/players, magnifiers and lighting, mobility aids, health care products, household items, TTYs, signalers, closed-caption decoders

Lucent Technologies Accessible Communications Products Center
1224 Fernridge Parkway
Creve Coeur, MO 63141
1–800–233–1222
Equipment to enhance telephone communications, including amplifiers, auxiliary ringers, TTYs

Maxi Aids & Appliances for Independent Living
42 Executive Boulevard
P.O. Box 3209
Farmingdale, NY 11735
1–800–522–6294 or 516–752–0521
Fax: 516–752–0689
Wide variety of aids and appliances, including high-tech products, for people who are visually impaired, blind, hearing impaired, or have other special needs

National Federation of the Blind
1800 Johnson Street
Baltimore, MD 21230–4998
410–659–9314
Fax: 410–685–5653
Assistive devices and equipment for people with limited eyesight, including writing materials, "talking" items, kitchen items, games

New Vision Store
Associated Services for the Blind
919 Walnut Street, 1st floor
Philadelphia, PA 19107
215–629–2990
Devices to assist blind or visually impaired people with daily living activities, including talking items, magnifiers, canes, cassette recorders, writing supplies

Science Products
P.O. Box 888
Southeastern, PA 19399
1–800–888–7400 or 610–296–2111
Low-vision aids, including magnifiers, eyewear, telescopes and monoculars, lighting, self-care products, convenience items

Sears Home HealthCare Catalog
20 Presidential Drive
Roselle, IL 60172
1–800–948–8800
Personal care items, assistive devices, exercise equipment, medical goods, postmastectomy clothing, diabetic and skin care products, incontinence products, mobility assists, games

TFI Engineering
529 Main Street
Boston, MA 02129
617–242–7007
Fax: 617–242–2007
Talking items, medical devices, tape recorders/players, health care products, computers

Toll-Free Health Helplines

Phone these toll-free helplines for a variety of services—usually provided free of charge—related to specific chronic conditions, illnesses, or special needs.

Alcohol Abuse Hotline　　　　　　800–252–6465
[24-hour information, referrals to treatment resources]

Alcohol and Drug Helpline　　　　800–821–4357
[24-hour information, referrals to treatment centers]

Alcohol Rehabilitation for the Elderly　800–354–7089
[information, limited counseling, referrals to local medical resources and support groups, publications]

**American Academy of Allergy
and Immunology**   800–822–2762
[referrals to doctors, publications]

**American Association of Oral and Maxillofacial
Surgeons**   800–467–5268
[publications on mouth- or jaw-related surgery]

American Brain Tumor Association   800–886–2282
[referrals to doctors and support groups, publications]

**American Institute for Cancer Research
Nutrition Hotline**   800–843–8114
[information on nutrition related to cancer prevention and
therapy, referrals to organizations and support groups, pub-
lications]

**American Leprosy Missions
(Hansen's disease)**   800–543–3131
[information, publications]

American Liver Foundation   800–223–0179
[information, referrals to doctors, publications]

American Lupus Society   800–331–1802
[information packet]

American Paralysis Association   800–225–0292
[information, referrals, publications]

**American Society for Dermatologic
Surgery**   800–441–2737
[information, referrals to doctors, publications]

American Trauma Society   800–556–7890
[referrals to support groups, publications]

Amyotrophic Lateral Sclerosis Association
(Lou Gehrig's Disease)   800–782–4747
[information; referrals to doctors, home care agencies, support groups; publications]

Asthma and Allergy Foundation
of America   800–727–8462
[information, referrals to other hotlines, publications]

Asthma Information Line   800–822–2762
[referrals to doctors, publications]

Brain Injury Association   800–444–6443
[information]

Crohn's and Colitis Foundation
of America   800–932–2423
[information, referrals to doctors and support groups, publications]

Epilepsy Foundation of America   800–332–1000
[counseling, referrals, mail-order discount pharmacy, publications, newsletter]

Grief Recovery Helpline   800–445–4808
[counseling, referrals, support, publications]

Hansen's Disease Center   800–642–2477
[referrals to doctors, clinics, treatment centers; publications]

Histiocytosis Association   800–548–2758
[publications, newsletter]

Huntington's Disease Society
of America   800–345–4372
[information, support, referrals]

Impotence World Association   800–669–1603
[information packet, referrals]

Leukemia Society of America   800–955–4572
[referrals to local chapters, publications, newsletter]

Life Extension Foundation   800–327–6110
[information, publications, mail-order health products]

Lupus Foundation of America   800–558–0121
[information packet, referrals to local chapters]

Meat and Poultry Hotline   800–535–4555
[information on safe handling of meat and poultry, publications]

**Medical Rehabilitation
Education Foundation**   800–438–7342
[information, publications]

Meniere's Network   800–545–4327
[information, publications]

Myasthenia Gravis Foundation   800–541–5454
[information, limited referrals, support, publications]

National AIDS Clearinghouse   800–458–5231
(TTY: 800–243–7012)
[information on clinical trials and funding sources, referrals, publications; sponsored by Centers for Disease Control]

National AIDS Hotline   800–342–2437
(TTY: 800–243–7889)
[counseling; referrals to legal, financial, medical resources, support groups; publications; sponsored by Centers for Disease Control]

**National Alliance of Breast Cancer
Organizations**   800–719–9154
[information packet, publications]

National Aphasia Association   800–922–4622
[information, support, publications]

**National Clearinghouse for Alcohol
and Drug Information**   800–729–6686
      (TTY: 800–487–4889)
[limited counseling, referrals, publications, newsletter]

National Council on Alcoholism and Drug Dependence
      800–622–2255
[referrals to local treatment programs, publications]

**National Drug Information Treatment
and Referral Hotline**   800–662–4357
      (TTY: 800–228–0427)
*[24-hour referrals; sponsored by Center for Substance Abuse
Treatment]*

National Headache Foundation   800–843–2256
[referrals to doctors, publications, newsletter]

National Indian AIDS Hotline   800–283–2437
*[counseling; referrals to doctors, clinics, support groups;
newsletter; available to everyone]*

**National Information Center for Orphan Drugs
and Rare Diseases**   800–300–7469
[referrals to drug companies]

National Lymphedema Network   800–541–3259
*[information; counseling; referrals to health care profession-
als, treatment centers, exercise programs, support groups;
support; publications; newsletter]*

National Multiple Sclerosis Society   800–344–4867
*[information; counseling; referrals to doctors, clinics, local
chapters; publications]*

**National Organization for Rare
Disorders**   800–999–6673
[information on financial assistance program, publications]

286

National Psoriasis Foundation   800–723–9166
[counseling; referrals to doctors, clinics, support groups; publications]

National Resource Center for the Prevention of Alcohol, Tobacco, Other Drug Abuse, and Mental Illness in Women   800–354–8824
[information packet]

National Spinal Cord Injury Association   800–962–9629
[limited counseling; referrals to doctors, living centers, support groups, financial assistance; publications]

National Spinal Cord Injury Association Hotline   800–526–3456
[counseling; referrals to rehabilitation programs, clinics, equipment centers, support groups; publications]

Office of Minority Health Resource Center   800–444–6472
[information, referrals to organizations and funding sources, publications]

Oley Foundation
(long-term specialized nutritional therapy)   800–776–6539
[publications, newsletter]

Phoenix Society National Organization for Burn Survivors   800–888–2876
[support; counseling; referrals to medical and legal assistance resources, support groups; publications; newsletter]

Polycystic Kidney Foundation   800–753–2873
[information kit]

Seafood Hotline   800–332–4010
[recorded information on safe food handling, referrals to related hotlines, publications]

Sjogren's Syndrome Association   800–475–6473
[information, referrals to physicians and support groups, publications]

Spondylitis Association of America   800–777–8189
[information, publications]

Thyroid Foundation of America   800–832–8321
[limited counseling, referrals to doctors and clinics, publications]

Tourette Syndrome Association   800–237–0717
[information, referrals to doctors]

**Transplant Recipients International
Organization**   800–874–6386
[newsletter]

United Scleroderma Foundation   800–722–4673
[information, limited counseling, referrals to doctors and support groups, publications]

Vestibular Disorders Association   800–837–8428
[information]

**Y-Me National Breast Cancer
Organization**   800–221–2141
[information, counseling, referrals to doctors and clinics, support for patients and partners, publications]

Chapter Six

Enriching
the Later Years

After my mother passed away, Blanche, one of her dear friends, began calling me two or three times a day, just to talk . . . and talk. Obviously she was lonely. She lived alone in an apartment building and didn't really have any family left. I called the senior citizen coordinator at the senior center, and this lovely woman got her involved in some wonderful activities. They have bridge, they have bingo, they have swimming at the Y. She even takes a class in line dancing! Recently she went to an intergenerational senior prom at the high school. The kids at the high school—the juniors and seniors—host it. The boys dance with the women, and the girls dance with the older men who come. The coordinator gets somebody to drive her to some of the activities and I've taken her to others. Oh, she loves it!

Active and Involved

Maintaining a positive outlook on life is important at any age, but it can be particularly challenging in later years. Many of your relative's close friends may have moved away or died. Diminished capacities may have forced the gradual letting go of activities that once filled the day and gave a sense of satisfaction and accomplishment. It's easy to slip into boredom, self-absorption, or depression as links to the outside world come undone. With some effort and ingenuity, however, you can help your loved one forge new ties and maintain an active, positive spirit.

Here are some tips to get you started, followed by a look at a few activities that may be especially appealing and rewarding to healthy, independent adults:

- Draw your parent into a discussion of the things he or she enjoyed doing when you were growing up. Reading, gardening, playing a musical instrument, painting, craft work, carpentry, dancing, traveling—what pleasurable activities has your parent given up in recent years, and why? Together you should be able to come up with ways for your loved one to resume former interests, perhaps on a revised or limited scale. Checklist #18 may serve as a conversation starter and activity planner.

- Watch for ways to turn a talent or an interest into a new and rewarding pastime. If your father enjoys storytelling, a handsome journal, writing supplies, and some encouragement could get him started recording boyhood memories or family history. If your mother is always snapping pictures of the grandchildren, you might suggest organizing photo albums or entering favorite shots in a local photography contest or county fair. A good cook might find an attractive, enduring way to record treasured family recipes.

- Help your parent set up a convenient workplace for crafts and hobbies. Make sure lighting is adequate for safety and all necessary supplies are on hand.

- Look for ways to share your relative's handiwork—as gifts for family or friends, sale items in yard or church sales, or through local fairs, festivals, or consignment shops.

- Thoroughly explore the social and recreational programs available in your parent's community. Local services might include those discussed in Chapter 2, such as friendly visitors, senior companions, adult day care, transportation to shopping centers and other community sites, senior centers, and so on. Community organizations may sponsor day trips, exercise classes, intergenerational programs, and other get-togethers. Besides offering an enjoyable way to pass the time, these programs can foster new friendships, increased independence, and a sense of belonging.

- If your loved one is confined to home or bed, fight boredom by encouraging visitors. Friends may come to chat; family members, perhaps a grandchild, might arrange a daily session of card playing or reading aloud. Music, radio, television, videotapes, a bedside telephone, and books or other reading materials can help fill the day and raise spirits. If your loved one has a visual or physical impairment that makes reading difficult, see the listings in Chapter 5 under "Publications for the Visually Impaired" and "Lending Libraries."

Enrichment Through Education

Has your parent ever expressed regrets about missing out on a complete education? Does she or he have an abiding interest in astronomy, military history, literature, or some other subject? More than a million people age sixty-five and older are enrolled in some form of higher education, proving that the capacity to learn continues through life.

Perhaps it is time to encourage your loved one to finally earn that advanced degree or take noncredit courses at a nearby educational institution. Nearly all colleges and universities offer continuing education courses. These not only stimulate the mind but can broaden social contacts and give a terrific sense of accomplishment. A nearby museum, library, YMCA, or religious or civic group may sponsor short-term educational programs. For older people who would rather learn at their own pace, in their own comfortable armchair, correspondence courses offer a fine alternative to institutional learning. Also check your parent's local newspaper and the bulletin boards at the local library and senior center for news of lectures and discussion series.

Enrichment Through Employment

For the older person who has always worked, retirement may be a welcome relief . . . or a big bore. If your relative seems bored, restless, listless, or irritable since retiring and has no plans, hobbies, or interests to fill those suddenly empty days, part-time work may offer several advantages. Work gets your parent out of the house, restores a sense of purpose and usefulness, and provides money to supplement income. With about 12 percent of all Americans over age sixty-five living below or near the poverty level, many older people simply have to work. For others, extra income can mean money for vacations and other otherwise unaffordable luxuries. A word of caution: Social Security and some pension benefits are reduced after a certain earnings ceiling is passed. Your parent should check with the Social Security Administration, a financial adviser, and/or former employers about current earnings limits.

The Directory of Resources includes several organizations providing employment training and work experience projects for seniors. Local businesses also may offer part-time, seasonal, or consulting work or flexible options such as job sharing for older workers.

Enrichment Through Volunteerism

Millions of older people volunteer their time, talents, and energies in a wide variety of community service projects. Older volunteers deliver meals to the homebound; restock library shelves; run thrift shops and fund-raisers; provide career, financial, or tax counseling; tutor young students; and serve as special friends to children with disabilities. The range of activities is as broad as the diversity of volunteers' interests and skills. It is not unusual for an older person to both receive and give volunteer aid. A homebound senior may benefit from home-delivered meals and volunteer chore services and at the same time make daily telephone reassurance calls to latchkey children or donate homemade craft items to programs for the needy.

Volunteerism fosters community involvement, friendships, and a sense of purpose. For the individual on the receiving end of charitable services, it offers an opportunity to reduce feelings of dependence by giving something back. Volunteering can allow your aging relative to make productive use of a lifetime store of skills and experience, in a flexible

To Drive or Not to Drive?

One of the most deeply felt impairments of aging may be the loss of driving skills. For many people in rural and some suburban areas, driving is a lifeline, and losing the car can mean the abrupt end of activities essential to body and spirit.

Caregivers may dread the day when a parent will have to stop driving and at the same time worry about the possibility of auto accidents. Warning signs of a major accident in the making include:

- One or more fender benders—minor accidents in parking lots, at stop signs, etc.
- One or more traffic citations for minor violations
- Difficulty interpreting traffic signs
- Difficulty spotting road obstructions, pedestrians, and other vehicles
- Drifting into other traffic lanes
- Abruptly stopping without cause
- Poor judgment in traffic situations, such as failure to yield right of way or misjudging merges into oncoming traffic

If you have concerns about your relative's driving, you might suggest enrolling in a safety course for older drivers. These classroom courses teach older people how to adjust their driving habits to compensate for diminishing physical or perceptual skills. Home study materials also are available for self-assessment of abilities and improvement of skills outside the classroom. See the Directory of Resources for organizations to contact for local information.

When it is obvious that confused behavior or a physical disability makes continued driving dangerous but you are unable to convince your aging relative to give up the keys, try enlisting the help of a trusted family friend, doctor, or clergy. The doctor, for example, might calmly and clearly explain the medical reasons why your relative should no longer drive. In extreme cases caregivers have resorted to extreme measures—talking to a local sheriff or police officer about lifting the license, "losing" the keys, or disabling the vehicle. Obviously, these are options to consider only when all else fails and your loved one is endangering self and others.

If it seems likely that your parent will have to give up driving, begin to look into transportation alternatives early. This difficult topic will be easier to broach if you have a list of suggested alternatives. These might include public transportation, community transportation services for seniors, and commitments from family members, friends, and neighbors to provide a lift to the grocery store, appointments, and recreational activities.

schedule that calls for as much or as little commitment as energy and inclinations allow.

To find out about volunteer opportunities in your relative's area, check the local newspaper or contact the Area Agency on Aging (see Appendix B). Also see the national and regional volunteer programs listed in the Directory of Resources.

✔ *CHECKLIST #18: BOREDOM BEATERS*

If chronic illness or disability has narrowed your relative's world, here is a list of pastimes that may help. First review the list with your loved one, checking off activities he or she once enjoyed or might like to try now. Then go back over the items checked and, if physical limitations make an activity seem difficult or impossible, consider whether some adaptations or special equipment could put it back within reach. For example, your parent might try container gardening if a whole outdoor plot is no longer practical. The ability to read or perform craft work could be restored with large-print or recorded books or specially designed craft instructions and supplies. The former traveler who is no longer comfortable going it alone might take pleasure in exploring as part of a tour group or on a cruise. Also review the Directory of Resources in Chapter 5, which includes organizations providing aids and devices to help individuals with visual, hearing, and other physical impairments continue to enjoy hobbies and other recreational activities.

ACTIVITY	POSSIBLE MODIFICATIONS/ADAPTATIONS
Reading	
Listening to music	
Playing a musical instrument	
Gardening	
Woodwork/carpentry	
Painting	

ACTIVITY	POSSIBLE MODIFICATIONS/ADAPTATIONS
Photography	
Sewing	
Knitting/crocheting	
Other crafts or hobbies	
Cooking/baking	
Card games	
Board games	
Puzzles	
Writing—correspondence	
Writing—journal, stories, poetry	
TV viewing	
Moviegoing	
Theatergoing	
Dining out	
Shopping	
Walking/nature walks	
Dancing	
Swimming	

ACTIVITY	POSSIBLE MODIFICATIONS/ADAPTATIONS
Golf	
Racquet sports	
Other sports	
Camping out	
Visiting friends and family	
Traveling/sightseeing	
Volunteer work	
Schoolwork/educational activities	
Office work	

Directory of Resources

The following groups sponsor community volunteer and employment projects and educational, social, and recreational programs. Also see Chapter 2 for organizations that provide information and services related to programs such as friendly visitors, senior companions, senior centers, transportation services, and adult day care. Chapter 5 lists groups providing information, advice, and products to help people with physical limitations pursue recreational activities.

NATIONAL

Organizations on this list offer their services nationwide or over a significant area of the country.

AAA Foundation for Traffic Safety
1440 New York Avenue NW, Suite 201
Washington, DC 20005
202–638–5944

Many AAA offices offer Mature Operator Programs—classroom courses for individuals age fifty-five and older to enhance driving knowledge and skills. Contact your local AAA office for information.

Helpful Publications:
Order these booklets from your local AAA office or by writing the address above.

"Concerned About an Older Driver? A Guide for Families and Friends." 18-page booklet gives facts about driving and tips for helping an older person drive safely. $5.00.

"Drivers 55 Plus: Test Your Own Performance." 16-page handbook for self-evaluating skills. $2.00.

American Association of Retired Persons (AARP)
601 E Street NW
Washington, DC 20049
1–800–424–3410 or 202–434–2300
TTY: 202–434–6561

Members of this organization for people age fifty and older may use their talents to serve their communities in a variety of volunteer programs. AARP's Volunteer Talent Bank matches registrants with local volunteer positions in their area of interest. Regional offices also conduct employment programs, including job search workshops and work experience projects for low-income seniors. Annual membership fee: $8.00.

55 Alive/Mature Driving
American Association of Retired Persons (AARP)
601 E Street NW
Washington, DC 20049
1–800–424–3410 or 202–434–2300
TTY: 202–434–6561

A driver refresher course for people over age fifty,

this AARP community outreach program covers normal age-related physical changes, rules of the road, and safety precautions.

Helpful Publication:
For a copy of this free booklet write AARP Fulfillment at the address above.

"Older Driver Skill Assessment and Resource Guide." Order #D14957. Questions and self-tests for assessing driving skills.

Catholic Charities USA

1731 King Street, Suite 200
Alexandria, VA 22314
703–549–1390

Social and recreational programs at Catholic Charities senior centers are offered free to all older adults, regardless of religious affiliation, through 1,200 independent agencies nationwide. Local agencies also will refer you to area senior programs and social organizations for seniors. To locate a nearby agency, look in your phone directory under "Catholic Charities" or "Catholic Social Services," or phone the main office.

Catholic Golden Age

430 Penn Avenue
Scranton, PA 18503
1–800–836–5699 or 717–342–3294
Fax: 717–963–0149

Catholics age fifty and older who join CGA may participate in meetings, outings, educational programs, religious observations, and community projects at about two hundred local chapters nationwide. Membership also includes financial benefits such as discounts on products and services. Annual membership fee: $8.00.

Centers for Disease Control and Prevention (CDC)

U.S. Department of Health and Human Services
Atlanta, GA 30333
404–332–4559

298

Phone this federal center's twenty-four-hour hotline for information for international travelers. Information available by recorded message or fax includes vaccine recommendations, disease information by world region, and food and water precautions.

Center for the Study of Aging
706 Madison Avenue
Albany, NY 12208
518–465–6927
Fax: 518–462–1339

Dedicated to improving older adults' quality of life, consultants from this national nonprofit foundation help develop health, wellness, and physical activity programs at senior centers, adult day care centers, and other sites. Contact to locate quality programs in your area.

Eldercare Locator
1–800–677–1116

For referrals to community resources offering seniors recreational and social activities, phone this nationwide directory assistance service, sponsored by the National Association of Area Agencies on Aging. You'll need to give the operator your relative's county and city name or zip code.

Elderhostel
75 Federal Street
Boston, MA 02110–1941
617–426–8056

Healthy, adventurous individuals age fifty-five and older participating in Elderhostel's educational programs take week-long noncredit courses and live on campus at colleges, universities, conference centers, environmental study centers, and other educational institutions throughout the United States and abroad. Elderhostel will match participants who have physical disabilities with institutions that are able to accommodate them. The typical charge for a five-night U.S. program is $320.00. Also available are Elderhostel Service Programs, which offer older adults the opportunity to learn "on the job" as they volunteer in public service programs ranging from compiling data on whales and dolphins in Texas to teaching English to schoolchildren in Jamaica.

Family Friends
NCOA Intergenerational Programs
National Council on the Aging
409 Third Street SW, Suite 200
Washington, DC 20024
202–479–6675

This national volunteer program brings individuals age fifty-five and older into the homes of children who are medically fragile or in need of special services. Phone for information on local volunteer opportunities.

Generations United
c/o Child Welfare League of America
440 First Street NW, Suite 310
Washington, DC 20001–2085
202–638–2952
Fax: 202–638–4004

A national coalition of more than 130 organizations, Generations United promotes programs that bring together old and young. These include volunteer opportunities in which older people work with children, for example, by serving as tutors or mentors in schools or youth groups, by providing telephone reassurance to latchkey children, or by working side by side in community service projects. Contact the national office for information on programs in your parent's area.

Gray Panthers
2025 Pennsylvania Avenue NW, Suite 821
Washington, DC 20006
202–466–3132
Fax: 202–466–3133

A national intergenerational organization of activists working for social change in issues such as health care, jobs, and the environment, Gray Panthers offers its members a newspaper and periodic updates plus the opportunity to work on area issues through fifty-five local chapters nationwide. Annual membership fee: $20.00.

International Senior Citizens Association
255 South Hill Street, Suite 409
Los Angeles, CA 90012
213–625–5008
Fax: 213–625–7115

Affiliated with the United Nations, this worldwide organization of seniors and seniors groups promotes closer bonds and better understanding among older people throughout the world. Members receive a quarterly newsletter, the opportunity to participate in social and cultural programs at local chapters, and group travel programs. Annual membership fee: $10.00.

National Asian Pacific Center on Aging
Melbourne Tower
1511 Third Avenue, Suite 914
Seattle, WA 98101
206–624–1221

Serving Asian and Pacific Islander seniors age fifty-five and older, this nonprofit agency runs employment programs in the Pacific Northwest, California, the Chicago-Great Lakes area, the District of Columbia–Virginia area, Boston, Philadelphia, and New York. Some programs are federally funded and open only to low-income workers.

National Association for Hispanic Elderly
(Asociacion Nacional Pro Personas Mayores)
3325 Wilshire Boulevard, Suite 800
Los Angeles, CA 90010
213–487–1922
Fax: 213–385–3014

Through fourteen regional offices, this private nonprofit corporation brings information and services to older people of Hispanic origin. Project Ayuda provides part-time jobs for low-income seniors in ten states and the District of Columbia with the goal of helping these workers develop jobs skills and find permanent employment. The Senior Environmental Employment program places older workers in technical and nontechnical jobs with the Environmental Protection Agency. Phone for referrals to your regional office and for information on model projects in local communities throughout the country.

National Caucus and Center on Black Aged (NCBA)

1424 K Street NW, Suite 500
Washington, DC 20005
202–637–8400
Fax: 202–347–0895

A nonprofit interracial membership organization with offices in ten states and the District of Columbia, NCBA sponsors employment and training programs that place low-income workers age fifty-five and older in a variety of jobs, ranging from nurse's aide, electrician, carpenter, and receptionist to housing management and assignments with the Environmental Protection Agency.

National Senior Service Corps (NSSC)

1201 New York Avenue NW
Washington, DC 20525
1–800–424–8867 or 202–606–5000

Senior Corps is a network of federally supported programs that help people age fifty-five and older find volunteer service opportunities in their communities. Foster Grandparents offer support to children with special physical and emotional needs. Senior Companions provide assistance and friendship to help elderly homebound individuals live independently. The Retired and Senior Volunteer Program (RSVP) involves seniors in projects that match their personal interests and make use of their skills and life experience. RSVP volunteers perform a wide variety of services, from leading local museum tours to planting community gardens to tutoring at-risk youth. Phone for a list of nearby programs and the phone number of your local project coordinator.

National University Continuing Education Program
Peterson's Publishing Group
202 Carnegie Center
P.O. Box 2123
Princeton, NJ 08543–2123
1–800–338–3282 or 609–243–0111, ext. 225
Fax: 609–452–0966
via Internet: http://www.petersons.com

For the older adult with reasonably strong reading and writing skills who would like an opportunity to expand personal knowledge, Peterson's publishes the *Independent Study Catalog,* with detailed information on more than 10,000 home study courses offered by 100 educational institutions. Cost: $16.95 plus $4.75 shipping and handling.

Presbyterian Church USA
100 Witherspoon Street
Louisville, KY 40202–1396
502–569–5000

Healthy, active older adults with the Presbyterian Older Adult Ministry Network offer volunteer services and spiritual support to elderly people who need help living independently. Phone for information on local volunteer programs and for the name and phone number of the local Older Adult Ministry resource person.

Senior Community Service Employment Program (SCSEP)
U.S. Department of Labor
Employment and Training Administration
Office of Special Targeted Programs
200 Constitution Avenue NW, Room N4641
Washington, DC 20210
202–219–5904
TTY: 1–800–326–2577

Low-income adults age fifty-five and older may find part-time employment through this federally funded program. Enrollees usually are placed in community service jobs, where they receive on-the-job training, personal and employment counseling, and assistance in finding permanent employment in the private sector. In local areas the program is sponsored by various project grantees, including the American Association of Retired Persons, National Asian Pacific Center on Aging, National Association for Hispanic Elderly, and National Caucus and Center on Black Aged (see above). Contact SCSEP for program information and to locate your area's sponsor.

REGIONAL

Organizations on this list provide services in limited geographic areas. You may be able to find groups offering similar services in your relative's community.

Aging in America
1500 Pelham Parkway South
Bronx, NY 10461
718–824–4004

At seven senior centers in the Bronx, Aging in America provides a wide variety of recreational programs and social opportunities, including classes and discussion groups, dancing and aerobics, arts and crafts, and games. Activities are free or available for a small fee. The agency also offers employment and volunteer opportunities for seniors.

Elder Craftsmen
921 Madison Avenue
New York, NY 10021
212–861–5260

Members age fifty-five and older are trained to make craft items such as baby quilts, toys, and clothing, which are donated to needy individuals and families in New York City. Crafters work in senior centers or independently at home. Experienced older crafters may be paid for the items they make. Elder Craftsmen also will provide a mailing list of retail shops around the country that take items on consignment from local older crafters.

Jewish Association for Services for the Aged (JASA)
40 West Sixty-eighth Street
New York, NY 10023
212–724–3200

For New York City adults age fifty-five and older of all faiths, JASA offers a variety of social activities, including trips, classes, breakfast and luncheon clubs, and cultural and educational programs. Staff members speak English, Spanish, and Yiddish.

SageNet (Senior Action in a Gay Environment)
305 Seventh Avenue
New York, NY 10001
212–741–2247
Fax: 212–366–1947
E-mail: sageny@aol.com

This network of twelve independent affiliate groups provides social and support programs and direct services to older gay men and lesbians. Social programs at the pioneer organization in New York City include workshops, excursions and trips, luncheons and supper clubs, friendly home visits, a senior center, and a pen pal network. Other SageNet groups operate in cities in Arizona, Connecticut, Florida, Massachusetts, Minnesota, Nebraska, New York, Vermont, Wisconsin, and Ontario, Canada. Contact the New York City office for information about the Sage network and to locate your nearest office.

United Senior Action
1211 South Hiatt Street
Indianapolis, IN 46221
317–634–0872
Fax: 317–687–3661

Members of this statewide organization advocating on behalf of older Hoosiers can participate in efforts to influence public policy through phone and letter campaigns, meetings and presentations, and legislative lobbying.

Chapter Seven

Facing
Final Days

The hospice were very caring people, very supportive. They would speak with my husband maybe twenty, twenty-five minutes. They took his temperature, pulse—just the very fundamental care—then they would report his physical condition to the doctor. It was more an emotional and mental lift than physical for him and also for me. He had worries and things on his mind. I was able to tell them little things that I wouldn't have said to anyone. They were like a personal friend. We had the same woman nearly every time. We became very comfortable with her. The last time she came she told me that he was failing and that I should call my children, if they lived out of town, to have them come to see him. After he died, she came over to see me, which was lovely, just wanted to see how I was doing. I have nothing but praise for the hospice. I couldn't have gotten through it without them. I think they made me stronger.

Breaking the Silence

Talking about death is painful. Most of us stop cold at the prospect of bringing up such a topic. But if you are caring for someone who has a terminal illness, it's a topic that already is very much on your loved one's mind. Most likely, when you are able to face up to your own fears, pain, and embarrassment and signal your willingness to listen, you will find that your relative or friend is eager to discuss a weighty list of concerns. Even if an older person is healthy and active, planning for the inevitable still can give comfort. It's natural for the elderly to fear being overwhelmed by disability and losing control of their destiny. You can ease that fear by taking steps to ensure that your loved one's final days will be spent in dignity, with personal concerns heard and final wishes observed.

Advance Directives

The best way to make sure that an aging relative's or friend's final wishes are followed is to encourage your loved one to both express preferences verbally and put them in writing. Chapter 4 covers the essential legal tools every person should prepare for financial decision making. Another important document, the advance directive, deals with decisions related to medical care. By stating in advance preferences about medical treatments, the advance directive allows individuals to control their own health care even if they become too ill to speak for themselves.

There are two legally recognized types of advance directive: the living will and the durable power of attorney for health care.

A living will is a statement of an individual's preferences about medical care in the event of terminal illness. It specifically states how far physicians should go in providing life-sustaining care for a patient who is dying. The document may rule out or permit measures such as surgery, resuscitation, feeding tubes, and other treatment options as well as specifying measures for relief of pain. In most cases the intent of the living will is to make known that the patient who is terminally ill and has no hope of cure does not want life prolonged by artificial or "heroic" measures. Such a document gives the incapacitated person a continued voice in health care choices and makes it easier for the family to make difficult decisions on their relative's behalf.

A durable power of attorney for health care, also called a health care power of attorney or health care proxy, designates another person—usually a family member—to act as an incapacitated patient's representative, or proxy, in granting or refusing consent for health care procedures. This document may very specifically detail the kinds of treatments and procedures the health care proxy has the authority to approve or refuse, or it may be

308

general, giving the proxy full discretion. The health care power of attorney is more comprehensive than the living will, since it applies to all health care decisions, not just life-prolonging treatments. The document can allow the health care proxy to place the patient in a nursing home, for example, or to insist upon specific medically feasible treatments, in keeping with the patient's stated wishes. The health care power of attorney takes effect not only in cases of terminal illness but also when a nonterminal condition such as Alzheimer's disease or severe stroke prevents the patient from making informed choices regarding her or his own care.

The durable power of attorney for health care is legally recognized in all states. Forty-seven states and the District of Columbia have living will statutes, with provisions that vary from state to state. For example, some statutes broaden the living will's effectiveness by permitting the document to designate a health care proxy. In some states it is wise to prepare both forms of advance directive. Before making that decision, your parent should become familiar with applicable state laws, requirement, and limitations. An elder law attorney can provide that information, as can a few of the organizations listed in the Directory of Resources.

Technically, your parent does not need an attorney's services to prepare an advance directive. Some experts do advise seeking legal assistance in appointing a health care proxy or in cases of particularly complicated illness or where family members are likely to bitterly dispute health care decisions. State-specific forms for living wills and health care powers of attorney may be obtained from an attorney or from several sources listed in the Directory of Resources. Forms also may be available from the Area Agency on Aging (see Appendix B), state attorney general's office, and some doctors' offices and retirement and nursing homes. Health care providers funded by Medicare or Medicaid are required to give all patients written information on state laws regarding advance directives.

In preparing an advance directive, it is important to be as detailed as possible about the types of treatment preferred or rejected. Frequently used terms such as "heroic measures" and "extraordinary care" may be too vague to provide guidance in specific health care situations. State requirements regarding witnessing and filing advance directives vary, but in most cases the document must be signed, dated, and witnessed by two people who are not related to the signer and are not potential heirs. Your parent should give copies of advance directives to personal physicians, family members, and the health care proxy. An additional copy should be kept in an easily located spot and a small card kept in the purse or wallet, stating where advance directives are located and who, if anyone, is the designated health care proxy. Advance directives can be revoked or amended at any time, in accordance with state law. Changes should be noted in writing, dated, and signed.

Hospice Care

Not too many years ago, most people died at home, cared for by their families. Along came advances in medical technology, which sometimes delayed death while leaving patients with a very poor quality of life. Gravely ill people often spent their final days in a hospital, hooked up to machines and cut off from family, friends, and the comfort of familiar surroundings. Today, in response to that trend, about two thousand organizations in the United States provide a relatively new kind of compassionate care, called hospice care, for dying people and their families.

Hospice is a comprehensive array of medical and social services designed to help terminally ill patients and their loved ones cope with the physical, emotional, psychological, and spiritual distress of life-threatening illness. Services are performed by a team of medical professionals and volunteers, which may include a physician, registered nurse, licensed practical nurse, home health aides, therapists, social workers, counselors, homemakers, and clergy. Hospice programs may be based in hospitals, home health care agencies, nursing homes, or independent agencies; there also are a number of all-volunteer organizations. Services usually are provided in the patient's home, with the family network—including relatives, life partners, and close friends—considered an integral part of the care team. The hospice physicians, nurses, and other staff and volunteers direct, coordinate, and assist with care, but family members generally handle routine daily care tasks. With help and training by hospice workers, family members administer medications, bathe and feed the patient, and attend to other personal needs. Final decisions over care remain with the patient and family.

The majority of hospice patients are in the final stages of cancer, but hospice also serves people with heart, respiratory, or neurological disorders; AIDS; and other terminal conditions. In most cases patients have an illness that is no longer responding to aggressive, cure-oriented treatments, and they have been diagnosed as having six months or less to live. The emphasis of hospice is on care rather than cure. The program does not seek to prolong life or to hasten death but rather to help patients live out the end of their lives in a loving environment, alert, pain-free, and in comfort and dignity.

Individual hospice programs vary, but the range of services includes:

- Physician and nursing care
- Medical supplies and appliances
- Symptom relief and management, including drugs for pain relief, administered so that the patient remains as comfortable and alert as possible
- Physical, occupational, and speech therapy
- Emotional support, including spiritual counseling as desired
- Trained volunteers to assist with errands and provide support, companionship, and respite
- Continuous care during short-term periods of crisis
- Twenty-four-hour on-call availability
- Short-term inpatient care when necessary
- Counseling and bereavement services, including continuing support for the family after the patient's death

Hospice programs usually do not include surgery, routine intravenous therapy, blood transfusions, or respirator use, except when such procedures might relieve pain and make the patient more comfortable.

In-home hospice is nearly always less costly than conventional hospital care. Most nonprofit hospices offer their services to all patients, regardless of ability to pay. Other programs, particularly those that are part of large organizations such as hospitals or nursing homes, may require insurance, Medicare, or private payment. Medicare covers hospice care provided by a Medicare-approved hospice program, if the patient is eligible for Medicare Part A and has been certified as terminally ill, with a life expectancy of six months or less. The patient must sign a statement choosing hospice care instead of standard Medicare benefits for treatment of the terminal illness. Hospice care also is covered by most private health insurance policies and, in many cases, by Medicaid.

For further details on Medicare hospice benefits and on Medicare-certified hospice programs serving your area, contact the Medicare Hotline, Social Security Administration (see Directory of Resources), or state health department. Several organizations providing information about hospice and referrals to local hospice programs are listed in the Directory of Resources. You also might look in your phone directory under "Hospice," or ask your parent's doctor, a local hospital, or the local social services department for referrals. Checklist #19 includes questions to ask when selecting a hospice program.

Funeral Planning

A funeral is the third most expensive purchase, after a home and car, that most people ever make. Yet decisions about the funeral usually are made hastily, in a time of emotional turmoil. If your loved one has not expressed preferences in advance, you may end up agonizing over the arrangements, quarreling with siblings, and spending thousands more than necessary for a funeral unlike anything your parent would have wanted.

It is possible to avoid needless extravagance and still ensure a dignified funeral service. The key is facing up to this admittedly unpleasant topic while your aging relative or friend is living and you are able to make informed and clear-headed choices. You might take advantage of a discussion about updating the will or preparing an advance directive to ask if your parent has preferences about funeral arrangements. Basic questions to address include:

- Should there be burial or cremation?
- Are there preferences regarding cemetery and funeral home?
- Has a cemetery plot been purchased?
- Should there be a funeral service? A memorial service?
- Are there any special wishes regarding how the funeral and burial or cremation should be conducted?

It also will be helpful for your parent to make a record of the information needed to prepare an accurate obituary. Some people choose to write their own obituary and/or a eulogy to be read at the funeral or memorial service.

While preplanning the funeral is wise, prepaying may not be the best choice. Buyers of prepaid funeral contracts have lost some or all of their money when their plans changed, they moved to another state, or the company selling the contract went out of business. A better alternative might be to set up a small joint savings account containing funds to pay for the funeral, with the principal caregiver as cosigner. Funeral benefits also may be available through an existing life insurance policy, pension plan, or union or fraternal society.

Whether you are making advance plans or planning a funeral on short notice, the Better Business Bureau recommends taking these precautions:

- Phone or visit a number of funeral homes and ask for an itemized list of services and costs.

- Don't be afraid to ask questions at the funeral home. You have the right to know what you are paying for.

- Consider bringing along a friend to the funeral home who is not as emotionally involved with the death and can help you make clear decisions.

- Ask to be shown the full variety of caskets available, all of which may not be on display.

- Be aware that, except in certain specified cases, embalming is not required by law and the funeral home is required to obtain permission before proceeding. In some instances embalming may be an unnecessary expense, such as when the body is to be cremated or buried within twenty-four hours.

 ## CHECKLIST #19: SELECTING A HOSPICE PROGRAM

Use this checklist to evaluate hospice services and compare the programs offered by different hospice organizations:

❏ *What area does the hospice serve?*
Many programs accept only patients from within a specific geographic area.

❏ *Does the hospice specialize in dealing with certain types of illness?*
Some hospices, for example, provide care only for people with AIDS.

❑ *Will the hospice develop a professional plan of care?*
This evaluation should be performed by an experienced registered nurse or social worker, in the home, in conjunction with consultations with the family doctor and/or other involved health professionals. You and your relative are entitled to a written copy of the care plan, which should spell out the hospice's duties and work schedule.

❑ *Who will be on the hospice care team?*
Ask if your relative will see one person consistently or many different care providers. Also find out if your relative's personal physician will remain involved in care, and if not, who will provide medical direction and how often your relative will see a hospice doctor.

❑ *What are the qualifications of the staff and volunteers?*
You'll want to know what training the nurses have in treating dying patients, how often a nurse will visit the home, and if a nurse is on call twenty-four hours a day. Also ask if social workers, clergy, and volunteers have any special training in working with the dying.

❑ *What are the responsibilities of the family caregiver?*
Ask what duties you (or another primary caregiver) will be expected to perform and what resources are available to assist and relieve you.

❑ *Does the hospice provide bereavement counseling and support for the family?*
Support for the family should include continued contact and comfort after the death. Many hospices sponsor caregiver support groups; some provide volunteers to stay with the patient so the caregiver can attend meetings.

❑ *What happens if there is an emergency in the middle of the night?*
You will want to know if after-hours calls are answered by a hospice staff member or an answering service, and how quickly help is available.

❑ *Is the hospice Medicare-certified?*
Medicare covers only care provided by an approved hospice program. Find out what out-of-pocket expenses Medicare patients are expected to pay.

314

❏ *What are the fees and how are they applied—per day, per visit, or at some other rate?*
If your relative has private insurance, ask whether the hospice will accept whatever the insurance company pays as payment in full. If your relative has no insurance coverage, there may be a payment plan or a sliding-scale fee based on ability to pay. The hospice should be able to provide a written statement outlining services, fees, and payment procedures.

❏ *Will the hospice handle the billing with Medicare or private insurance carriers?*
If not, find out if someone from the hospice can help you with insurance forms and other financial questions and problems.

❏ *Does the hospice meet state licensing requirements?*
Your state department of health will provide information on applicable regulations. Also ask if the program has any kind of outside review or accreditation, and confirm the information with the organizations named.

❏ *Will the hospice provide references from professionals such as hospital staff or a social worker with a community agency?*
Talk to these people about their experiences with the hospice's services. Also check with the local Better Business Bureau for the hospice's complaint record.

Directory of Resources

Several of the following organizations offer support and services, including hospice referrals, to people with terminal illnesses, their family members, and the bereaved. Others provide information and publications related to advance directives. Also see the Directory of Resources in Chapter 4 for resources providing referrals to attorneys and legal aid services for help in preparing these forms.

NATIONAL

Organizations on this list offer their services nationwide or over a significant area of the country.

American Association of Retired Persons (AARP)
Widowed Persons Service
601 E Street NW
Washington, DC 20049
1–800–424–3410 or 202–434–2300
TTY: 202–434–6561

Volunteers with this AARP community outreach program work with religious, social service, and mental health agencies to provide educational, support, and referral services to the newly widowed.

Helpful Publications:
Order these free brochures and booklets by writing AARP Fulfillment at the address above.

"Final Details: A Guide for Survivors When Death Comes." Order #D14168.

"On Being Alone: Guide for Widowed Persons." Order #D150.

"Prepaying Your Funeral: Some Questions to Ask." Order #D13188.

"Who Decides If You Can't: Planning Family Medical Decisionmaking." Order #D15294.

Choice in Dying
200 Varick Street
New York, NY 10014
1–800–989-WILL (1–800–989–9455) or 212–366–5540
Fax: 212–366–5337

A leading advocate for the right of individuals to make their own decisions about medical care at the end of life, Choice in Dying pioneered the living will and has distributed ten million copies of these documents over the past twenty-five years. The organization offers advance directives tailored to the laws of each state. You also may call the toll-free number with questions about advance directives, their applicability under various circumstances, and how to ensure that a loved one's wishes are honored by the health care system. Members receive notification of any changes in the laws that affect their advance directives, amended forms when necessary, a quarterly newsletter, and publication discounts. Annual membership fee: $25.00.

Helpful Publications:

"Dying at Home." Order #QA300. 19-page booklet on medical, legal, and psychological concerns. $5.00

"Medical Treatments & Your Living Will." Order #QA400 (in Spanish, #SP400). 9-page booklet on benefits and burdens of various types of life support.

"State-Specific Advance Directive Packet, with Instruction Booklet." Order #AD100. Specify state. $3.50.

"You and Your Choices: Advance Directives." Order #QA100 (in Spanish, #SP100). 10-page booklet on importance and purpose of advance directives. $3.50.

Council of Better Business Bureaus (CBBB)

4200 Wilson Boulevard
Arlington, VA 22003
703–276–0100
Fax: 703–525–8277

Ask the CBBB for the location of your local Better Business Bureau, and contact that office to ask about the complaint records of hospice programs and funeral homes.

Foundation for Hospice and Homecare

513 C Street NE
Washington, DC 20002–5809
202–547–6586
Fax: 202–546–8968

This national organization has an array of programs to serve the dying, disabled, and disadvantaged. Its National Certification Program sets standards for and accredits home care aides. Contact for referrals to local home health care agencies providing hospice care.

Helpful Publication:

Send a self-addressed stamped envelope, with 64¢ postage, for this free brochure.

"All About Hospice Care: A Consumer's Guide."

Hospice Association of America (HAA)
228 Seventh Street SE
Washington, DC 20003
202–546–4759
Fax: 202–547–9559
Contact this national organization representing hospices and other caregivers of terminally ill patients and their families for information on selecting and financing hospice care and to locate local hospice services.

Helpful Publication:
Send a self-addressed stamped envelope, with 52¢ postage, for this free brochure.
"Hospice: A Consumer's Guide"

HospiceLink
Hospice Education Institute
190 Westbrook Road
Essex, CT 06426–1511
1–800–331–1620
Phone HospiceLink for information about the principles and practices of hospice care and for support, sympathy, and referrals to local hospice care programs.

Joint Commission on Accreditation of Health Care Organizations
One Renaissance Boulevard
Oakbrook Terrace, IL 60181
630–916–5800
The Joint Commission evaluates and accredits U.S. health care organizations, including hospice programs that have voluntarily agreed to meet certain performance standards and undergo periodic surveys. Phone the number above for information on a hospice's current accreditation status. To register a complaint about an accredited hospice, phone 630–916–5642.

Medicare Hotline
1–800–638–6833
TTY: 1–800–820–1202
    Phone this federally operated hotline for referrals to Medicare-certified hospice programs and information on Medicare hospice benefits.

National Association for Home Care (NAHC)
228 Seventh Avenue SE
Washington, DC 20003
202–547–7424
Fax: 202–547–3540
E-mail: celiap@nahc.org
    Contact the national office of this trade organization representing home care agencies, home care aide organizations, and hospices for the location of your state office, which will give you referrals to local hospice programs.

National Hospice Organization
1901 North Moore Street, Suite 901
Washington, DC 22209
1–800–658–8898 (Hospice Helpline) or 703–243–5900
Fax: 703–525–5762
    Phone the Hospice Helpline for referrals to hospice programs in your area and for information on hospice insurance benefits.

Helpful Publications:
Phone for a complete catalog; to fax publication orders, phone 1–800–499–6464; brochures cost 79¢ each plus 7 percent shipping and handling.
    "About Grief." Order #710038 (in Spanish, #710046).
    "About Hospice." Order #710053 (in Spanish, #710061).
    "About Hospice Under Medicare." Order #710079 (in Spanish, #710087).

"Advance Medical Directives." Order #710012 (in Spanish, #710020).

National Institute for Jewish Hospice (NIJH)
8723 Alden Drive, Suite 652
Los Angeles, CA 90048
1–800–446–4448 or 310–467–7423
Fax: 619–322–3817
    NIJH's twenty-four-hour toll-free line offers counseling to the Jewish terminally ill and their families and will provide referrals to hospices, hospitals, health professionals, and clergy.

Helpful Publications:
California residents add sales tax.
    "Caring for Jewish Terminally Ill." $3.00.
    "For Families of the Jewish Terminally Ill." $3.00.
    "The Jewish Orphaned Adult." $3.00.
    "The NIJH Jewish Living Will." Free handbook with living will and advance medical directive forms.
    "Realities of the Dying." $3.00.

Social Security Administration
1–800–772–1213
TTY: 1–800–325–0778
Phone for information and publications related to Medicare hospice benefits.

THEOS (They Help Each Other Spiritually)
322 Boulevard of the Allies, Suite 105
Pittsburgh, PA 15222
412–471–7779
Fax: 412–471–7782
    This national network of about seventy-five local chapters helps widowed individuals of all ages and their families to rebuild their lives through mutual self-help.

Visiting Nurse Associations of America
3801 East Florida Avenue, Suite 900
Denver, CO 80210
1–800–426–2547 or 1–888–866–8773

Phone the toll-free number to locate your nearest Visiting Nurse Association, which will manage and coordinate the details of in-home hospice care.

Other Helpful Free or Low-Cost Publications

Order the following booklets by contacting: American Bar Association Commission on Legal Problems of the Elderly, 740 Fifteenth Street NW, 8th floor, Washington, DC 20005 (202–662–8690).

"Health Care Powers of Attorney: An Introduction and Sample Form." $1.75.

"Health and Financial Decisions: Legal Tools for Preserving Personal Autonomy." Free brochure on powers of attorney, trusts, advance directives, and other planning tools.

Order the following pamphlets by contacting: Catholic Health Association of the United States, 4455 Woodson Road, St. Louis, MO 63134–3797 (314–427–2500).

"Advice on Advance Directives: Helping You Prepare for Your Healthcare." Order #100 (in Spanish, #101). 25¢.

"Durable Power of Attorney for Healthcare." Order #230 (in Spanish, #231). 25¢.

"A Consumer Guide to Hospice Care." 32-page booklet discusses hospice services and organizations, costs and standards; includes consumer checklist. $4.00. Contact: National Consumers League, 1701 K Street NW, Suite 1200, Washington, DC 20006 (202–835–3323).

"Funerals: A Consumer Guide." Order #367C. 4-page brochure on laws regarding funeral costs and services. 50¢. Write: Consumer Information Center–6A, P.O. Box 100, Pueblo, CO 81002.

The Hospice Foundation Educational Series includes these free booklets: "The Basics of Hospice," "Coping with Fears Related to Terminal Illness," "How to Select a Hospice." Contact: Hospice Foundation of America, 777 Seventeenth Street, Suite 401, Miami, FL 33139 (1–800–854–3402 or 305–538–9272).

"Medicare Hospice Benefits." Order #591B. Free booklet. Write: Consumer Information Center, Department 33, Pueblo, CO 81009.

"Planning a Funeral." Free brochure. Contact: Funeral Service Consumer Assistance Program, National Foundation of Funeral Service, 2250 East Devon Avenue–250, Des Plaines, IL 60018 (1–800–662–7666 or 847–827–6337).

"Planning for Incapacity: A Self-Help Guide." 40-page booklet includes living will and durable power of attorney for health care forms. Specify state. $5.00. Write: Legal Counsel for the Elderly, P.O. Box 96474, Washington, DC 20090–6474.

Chapter Eight

Care for the Caregiver

My mother had had surgery, so she came and stayed with me. I was working so I had to have somebody come in and be with her during the day, because she couldn't really function on her own. That lasted for about three weeks. It was hard on the family having a sick person in the house. I made arrangements for her to go home and I talked to my brother. Then we talked to my other brother, who wasn't working, and asked him to come up and stay with my mother. So that's what happened. My one brother lived with Mother during the week, and my other brothers rotated coming on the weekend. I was there as often as I could be, after work and every weekend. I stayed with her when one person left until the other got there. It was stressful but we managed. We were all right there to support one another.

Caregiver "Maintenance"

You, the caregiver, are remarkably important. Another adult's well-being depends on you. If you become so involved with that person's needs that you neglect your own, however, you may not last through the months or years of hard work and responsibility that lie ahead. It's like maintaining a vehicle: Put off the tune-ups or drive those extra miles without fueling up, and someday, when you step on the gas, the power won't be there. Taking good care of yourself is really just routine "life maintenance." It's not selfish or inessential. On the contrary, it's one of your most important obligations as a caregiver.

Like all aspects of caregiving, caring for yourself takes some advance planning. You'll need to set up a system for sharing responsibilities, organize your day to make the most of free time, and learn some coping strategies to get over the rough spots. Following are guidelines for setting up a network of family, friends, and outside resources to help meet your loved one's needs. Also included are fill-in forms to give you a picture of where your days go and enable you to manage your time more efficiently.

The Support Network

Your relative probably has an informal support network already in place. Your job is to identify and organize all those people who might lend a hand. Family usually is the logical place to start. Even if you are your relative's primary caregiver, all family members share the responsibility for care.

A family conference can provide a good opportunity for brainstorming about options and dividing up chores. Sit down with your older relative first, if possible, to make a list of supports needed. Again, don't forget your own needs. If you are a full-time caregiver, the support network should include visitors who will stay with your parent from time to time to give you a chance to run errands, enjoy friends or hobbies, or simply spend some time alone.

Once you've identified care-receiver and caregiver needs, ask your parent and siblings to meet for a discussion about sharing responsibilities. Each person might agree to take on a specific care area—providing transportation, handling finances, researching housing options, etc. Even young children, especially those who live nearby or in the same house as an aging relative, can make a contribution, perhaps by sharing snacktimes, reading aloud from letters or the newspaper, or helping with house or yard chores. Your siblings who live at a distance also can make a commitment, for example, to write or phone on a regular basis, to get their children to write, and/or to help financially as needed. Take notes during your family conference and send all family members a copy. You may want to plan regular follow-up meetings to review and revise your family care plan.

Don't be surprised if your family planning sessions are awkward. Unresolved childhood conflicts often resurface at such get-togethers, especially when open communication among family members isn't the general rule. You may find yourself spending more time arguing about ancient history than resolving current difficulties. Try to focus on positive actions and problem solving and to express your needs honestly and without reproach. Make sure that everyone gets an equal chance to be heard and that no one—including yourself!—is pressured to take on any caregiving role unwillingly. Chances are good that the time spent working together will lead to improved communication and closeness, benefiting not only your parent but the rest of the family, too.

There's also a good chance that, even with full family cooperation, extra help will be required to meet all your relative's physical, emotional, and social needs. More than likely, your parent has longtime friends, neighbors, and social contacts from a church, synagogue, or other community group who would be willing to lend a hand. Don't forget the extended family. Aunts, uncles, cousins, nieces, and nephews might be willing to help if asked. You also may have friends who've said, "Anytime I can help . . ." Well, the time is now! Make a list of all those people who are providing or might provide support, noting addresses and phone numbers. Contact each name on the list, either to confirm and show your appreciation for their services or to express your concerns about your parent and give them a chance to help. Don't be shy about initiating these contacts. Often friends and neighbors will be glad to assist but have hesitated to offer, perhaps because they were unaware of needs, uncertain what they could do, or afraid of interfering. You may want to ask these contacts if they have a particular service in mind or run through the list of your relative's needs. Even a small commitment, such as spending a couple of hours each week visiting with your parent or giving a ride to and from the doctor's office, can relieve you of one more responsibility and enhance your parent's quality of life. Be sure to ask your relative's friends if they can think of anyone else you might call and to leave your phone number with each member of this informal support team.

Community resources are the third and final link in your caregiver support chain. Chapter 2 includes descriptions of commonly available community services and tips for locating them in the local community.

Respite care, which gives caregivers a break by providing a few hours of companionship for the care-receiver, may be available through adult day care centers, a home health care agency, a hospice, a local government or community program, or informally through your network of family and friends. Some hospitals, nursing homes, and assisted living facilities offer residential respite care, allowing caregivers to take an extended break or vacation. The Area Agency on Aging (see Appendix B), department of social services or public health, or a local religious organization or senior center should be able to help you locate respite care resources. See Chapter 2 for tips on locating and evaluating adult day care services.

Mutual support groups can serve as an excellent source of information, support, and comfort for both care-receivers and caregivers. National associations for people with specific illnesses or medical conditions—Alzheimer's disease, cancer, stroke, etc.—often sponsor local support groups for family members. In many communities there are support groups set up specifically for adult children caring for aging parents. Through sharing common experiences, caregivers often are able to overcome feelings of loneliness and isolation, learn coping strategies and more efficient ways to handle care, find out about good community resources and professional services, and gain strength in an atmosphere of mutual acceptance and encouragement. Support groups may meet once a week or once a month; they may be small or large, formal or spontaneous. It might take a lot of work and schedule juggling for you to find the time to attend meetings, but for many caregivers the emotional benefits are well worth the effort. To locate a support group in your area, contact the local chapter of a national organization dealing with your relative's specific health problem (see Chapter 5, Directory of Resources), the Area Agency on Aging (see Appendix B), the department of health or social services, a local hospital, a national or regional self-help clearinghouse (see Appendix E), or one of the organizations listed in this chapter's Directory of Resources.

Following are some additional tips that may help you seek and accept help with caregiving responsibilities and remain mindful of your own essential needs.

- Your physical health is a key concern. If caregiving disrupts your night's sleep, try to work in daytime naps or break periods. You might ask a sibling or friend to take over for a night or for a couple of hours in the afternoon. Regular moderate exercise will help you sleep better as well as relieving frustrations and strengthening you for physical tasks. Also do your best to eat a well-balanced diet. Remind yourself that your body needs the proper fuel to keep up with your demanding routine.

- Emotional well-being is closely linked with physical health. Caregivers often experience conflicting and confusing emotions—anger, guilt, resentment, impatience, sadness, love, dislike. Rather than wasting time punishing yourself for negative feelings, accept them as normal, spontaneous responses to your situation. It may help to talk over your feelings with a spouse, sibling, close friend, or professional counselor.

- When stresses accumulate, try to find some time alone to unwind. A walk outdoors, reading a good book, listening to music, or taking a quiet drive may help you to relax. Some caregivers find release in meditation, relaxation techniques, or prayer.

- Keep up with your friendships, outside interests, and hobbies. These not only give pleasure but also provide a healthy perspective on your situation, reminding you that you are more than "just" a caregiver.

- Don't feel guilty about needing help with or a break from caregiving. Few people can carry the entire load on their own. Consider that your parent too may benefit from an occasional break. A substitute caregiver may bring a fresh and more enthusiastic approach than you are able to maintain and may be better at performing specific tasks such as handling finances or offering relaxed companionship.

- Arrange your day to take full advantage of all outside assistance. The Weekly Planner forms at the end of this chapter can help you organize your days, set priorities, and find more time for yourself.

- Encourage your loved one to be as independent as possible. While it may seem quicker and easier to dress or feed your relative than to stand by while she or he struggles, in the long run doing too much for the care-receiver only lowers that person's self-esteem and adds to your burdens. Allow your parent to independently perform as many daily living activities as possible, even if things don't get done as quickly or competently as you might prefer.

- Keep your expectations realistic. You cannot restore health, spare your loved one every pain, or solve every problem. Neither can you perform all tasks perfectly. Set your sights instead on making your parent more comfortable, improving the quality of life, and remaining a sympathetic ally in good times and bad.

Long-Distance Caregiving

Which is more difficult—caring for an aging relative who lives nearby or being involved in the care of a loved one from a distance? Each situation has its challenges. While the on-site caregiver may face near-constant physical stresses, the long-distance caregiver often suffers from the added guilt and frustration of being unable to help with day-to-day problems. The following tips may help you cope with the difficult task of caregiving from afar:

- Before visiting your relative, set up appointments with local agencies and service providers. For names and phone numbers, use the Eldercare Locator (1–800–677–1116), local branches of national organizations dealing with eldercare issues (see resource directories in the appropriate chapters), and a copy of your parent's local phone directory. If possible, arrange for any needed services to start when you arrive, so that you can help evaluate them and make any necessary changes.

- During your visit be observant about health and safety issues. Is your parent eating well? Is the house reasonably clean and in good repair? Do friends stop by and phone? If what you see raises concerns, address them respectfully but frankly. Ask your loved one how he or she is managing and what supports might solve current or potential problems. Ask to meet the important people in your relative's life — friends, neighbors, doctors, clergy, and so on. If you are uncertain how your parent is coping in your absence, these people may offer insight. They also may be willing to help out in providing caregiving support. Be sure to leave your phone number with each of these contacts, and ask them to call you if problems arise.

- Consider hiring a private geriatric care manager to do the things you would do for your loved one if you lived closer. Chapter 1 includes a discussion of geriatric care management and guidelines for finding and selecting a GCM.

- Set up a regular schedule for phoning your relative, and ask other family members to do their part in phoning, writing, and visiting.

- Take care of yourself. Recognize that being a long-distance caregiver is stressful. You have a right to be proud of the support arrangements you are able to put in place from afar.

- Look for the positive aspects of your caregiving relationship. Focus on what you are doing for your parent, not on what you cannot do. Amid all the stresses of caregiving, stop from time to time and pat yourself on the back. Your hard work is enriching the final years of someone you love.

Using Your "Weekly Planner"

Caregivers tend to be very generous with their time, taking on so many obligations that they end up drained and exhausted. When you find that happening to you—or, ideally, *before* it happens—some sensible planning can help to wrestle your schedule back under control. Time management in itself takes some time. In the long run, though, it can save you hours and effort, conserving your energy for priority tasks and ensuring that enough time remains for yourself and your family.

Begin by using the charts that follow to record what you do every hour of every day for one week (you'll just use the "Activity" columns for now). Before filling in the forms, you may want to make some extra copies for future use. Remember to tuck your daily log in your pocket or purse whenever you leave the house so that you can jot down time spent on outside activities.

At the end of the week go back over your daily logs and note whom each of your activities benefited. Which were caregiving tasks performed for your relative or older friend? Which chores did you perform for your spouse or children? Your employer? Which activities involved attending to your own personal needs or spending enjoyable time with family, friends, or on your own?

Now fill in the last two columns. Which of your daily activities could you delegate to someone else, and to whom? There will be some chores only you are able to perform and some you will feel that you must do personally or that you enjoy doing. But it's likely that each day includes tasks that someone else could take over, whether that someone is a sibling, family friend, another member of your parent's informal support team, or a volunteer or paid worker from a community program or private agency. Also look for activities that might be performed more simply or efficiently or dropped altogether. Rather than baking for a school fund-raiser, you might pick up inexpensive cupcakes at the supermarket. A quick phone call could substitute for a letter or invitation, catalog shopping for a trip to the mall. Would anyone care if the lawn was mowed or the house cleaned a little less frequently? Can you talk your way out of a volunteer job that you were talked into and don't really enjoy? Substitute activities you do enjoy for some of the tasks you trim from your schedule. Also look for short blocks of time that can be used to advantage. You might stretch out your morning shower into a relaxing soak in the tub, or plan to walk in a nearby park while waiting for your parent at the doctor or your child at an after-school activity.

Once you have reviewed your first week's schedule, you are ready to begin planning a more sensible, less draining second week. This time you'll fill in your Weekly Planner *before* the week begins. Make a list of your top priorities for the week; these should always include time for yourself and time with your own family and friends. Then schedule time for the responsibilities that remain on your list after you've delegated some chores and eliminated or consolidated others. Keep in mind your goal of maintaining a healthy balance between personal and caregiving activities.

Organizing your time will get easier each week, and it will help you feel competent and in control. Keep your planning flexible. Don't expect to accomplish everything on schedule, and be prepared to adjust your day to accommodate changes in plans. If you find yourself carrying over some activities from week to week unaccomplished, consider whether they might be delegated, performed some alternate way, or put aside until a future date. And, by all means, when others ask or expect you to take on an added duty, pull out your schedule and use it to show them—and yourself—whether their request is reasonable or out of the question.

Weekly Planner

Week's Schedule (Week of _____ to _____)

This week's priorities:

_____

_____

_____

_____

_____

MONDAY

	Activity	Performed for whom?	Could it be delegated? To whom?	Could it be or done more efficently? How?
6:00 a.m.				
7:00 a.m.				
8:00 a.m.				
9:00 a.m.				
10:00 a.m.				
11:00 a.m.				
12:00 p.m.				
1:00 p.m.				
2:00 p.m.				
3:00 p.m.				
4:00 p.m.				
5:00 p.m.				
6:00 p.m.				
7:00 p.m.				
8:00 p.m.				
9:00 p.m.				
10:00 p.m.				
11:00 p.m.				
12:00-6:00 a.m.				

TUESDAY

	Activity	Performed for whom?	Could it be delegated? To whom?	Could it be or done more efficently? How?
6:00 a.m.				
7:00 a.m.				
8:00 a.m.				
9:00 a.m.				
10:00 a.m.				
11:00 a.m.				
12:00 p.m.				
1:00 p.m.				
2:00 p.m.				
3:00 p.m.				
4:00 p.m.				
5:00 p.m.				
6:00 p.m.				
7:00 p.m.				
8:00 p.m.				
9:00 p.m.				
10:00 p.m.				
11:00 p.m.				
12:00-6:00 a.m.				

WEDNESDAY

	Activity	Performed for whom?	Could it be delegated? To whom?	Could it be or done more efficently? How?
6:00 a.m.				
7:00 a.m.				
8:00 a.m.				
9:00 a.m.				
10:00 a.m.				
11:00 a.m.				
12:00 p.m.				
1:00 p.m.				
2:00 p.m.				
3:00 p.m.				
4:00 p.m.				
5:00 p.m.				
6:00 p.m.				
7:00 p.m.				
8:00 p.m.				
9:00 p.m.				
10:00 p.m.				
11:00 p.m.				
12:00-6:00 a.m.				

THURSDAY

	Activity	Performed for whom?	Could it be delegated? To whom?	Could it be or done more efficently? How?
6:00 a.m.				
7:00 a.m.				
8:00 a.m.				
9:00 a.m.				
10:00 a.m.				
11:00 a.m.				
12:00 p.m.				
1:00 p.m.				
2:00 p.m.				
3:00 p.m.				
4:00 p.m.				
5:00 p.m.				
6:00 p.m.				
7:00 p.m.				
8:00 p.m.				
9:00 p.m.				
10:00 p.m.				
11:00 p.m.				
12:00-6:00 a.m.				

FRIDAY

	Activity	Performed for whom?	Could it be delegated? To whom?	Could it be or done more efficently? How?
6:00 a.m.				
7:00 a.m.				
8:00 a.m.				
9:00 a.m.				
10:00 a.m.				
11:00 a.m.				
12:00 p.m.				
1:00 p.m.				
2:00 p.m.				
3:00 p.m.				
4:00 p.m.				
5:00 p.m.				
6:00 p.m.				
7:00 p.m.				
8:00 p.m.				
9:00 p.m.				
10:00 p.m.				
11:00 p.m.				
12:00-6:00 a.m.				

SATURDAY

	Activity	Performed for whom?	Could it be delegated? To whom?	Could it be or done more efficently? How?
6:00 a.m.				
7:00 a.m.				
8:00 a.m.				
9:00 a.m.				
10:00 a.m.				
11:00 a.m.				
12:00 p.m.				
1:00 p.m.				
2:00 p.m.				
3:00 p.m.				
4:00 p.m.				
5:00 p.m.				
6:00 p.m.				
7:00 p.m.				
8:00 p.m.				
9:00 p.m.				
10:00 p.m.				
11:00 p.m.				
12:00-6:00 a.m.				

SUNDAY

	Activity	Performed for whom?	Could it be delegated? To whom?	Could it be or done more efficently? How?
6:00 a.m.				
7:00 a.m.				
8:00 a.m.				
9:00 a.m.				
10:00 a.m.				
11:00 a.m.				
12:00 p.m.				
1:00 p.m.				
2:00 p.m.				
3:00 p.m.				
4:00 p.m.				
5:00 p.m.				
6:00 p.m.				
7:00 p.m.				
8:00 p.m.				
9:00 p.m.				
10:00 p.m.				
11:00 p.m.				
12:00-6:00 a.m.				

Directory of Resources

The following organizations can help you locate respite care, a support group, and other resources for caregivers. When looking for respite care, you also might try a local hospice program. See the Directory of Resources in Chapter 7 for groups providing hospice referrals. For additional referrals to caregiver support groups, contact a national or regional self-help clearinghouse (see Appendix E) or an organization serving individuals and families coping with specific illnesses or disabilities (see the Directory of Resources in Chapter 5).

NATIONAL

Organizations on this list provide their services nationwide or over a significant area of the country.

Alzheimer's Association
919 North Michigan Avenue, Suite 1000
Chicago, IL 61611–1676
1–800–272–3900
TTY: 312–335–8882
Fax: 312–335–1110
Your local chapter of this national voluntary organization will help you locate respite care and other community resources for Alzheimer's patients and put you in touch with a local family support group.

Helpful Publications:
"Caregiver Stress: Signs to Watch For, Steps to Take." Order #PR 200Z. Free brochure.
"Especially for the Alzheimer Caregiver." Order #ED 221Z. Free brochure.
"Respite Care: How to Find What's Right for You." Order #PF 112Z. 18-page booklet. $1.75.

Children of Aging Parents (CAPS)
Woodbourne Office Campus, Suite 302-A
1609 Woodbourne Road

Levittown, PA 19057–1511
1–800–227–7294 or 215–945–6900
Fax: 215–945–8720

A nonprofit organization of caregivers, CAPS will refer you to a local caregiver support group or, if no group exists in your area, provide a starter pack for organizing one. The organization publishes a bimonthly newsletter, fact sheets, state-by-state resource lists, and other materials for caregivers; members receive a 15 percent discount on publications. Annual membership fee: $20.00.

Helpful Publications:
Prices quoted are for nonmembers.

"Companies and Catalogs Offering Special Products for the Elderly and Disabled." $3.00.

"List of Resources." Guide includes statewide listings of support groups and geriatric care managers, plus information for long-distance caregivers. Specify state. $4.00.

Eldercare America
1141 Loxford Terrace
Silver Spring, MD 20901
301–593–1621

This coalition of organizations, professionals, and concerned individuals advocates improved services for family members who are caring for older relatives. Eldercare America conducts local workshops on family caregiving and will provide speakers or instructors for support group meetings or conferences. Annual membership fee: $35.00.

Eldercare Locator
1–800–677–1116

To locate respite care, adult day care, and other community resources designed to give caregivers a break, phone this nationwide directory assistance service, operated by the National Association of Area Agencies on Aging. You'll need to give the operator your relative's county and city name or zip code.

340

Family Service America (FSA)
11700 West Lake Park Drive
Milwaukee, WI 53224–3099
1–800–221–2681 or 414–359–1040
Fax: 414–359–1074

Family Service America is an international nonprofit association made up of community-based counseling and support organizations dedicated to strengthening family life. Member agencies offer a variety of eldercare programs, caregiver support groups, and counseling to help families cope with the challenges of eldercare. Phone the 800 number for referrals to local FSA agencies and programs.

Friends' Health Connection
P.O. Box 114
New Brunswick, NJ 08903
1–800–48FRIEND (1–800–483–7436) or 908–418–1811
via Internet: http://www.48friend.com

This service will connect you in a supportive relationship with another person caring for a loved one with a chronic illness. Members are matched according to their lifestyles, interests, occupations, and other personal characteristics, to communicate via letters, phone, tapes, and E-mail. One-time fee: $10.00.

National Adult Day Services Association
National Council on the Aging (NCOA)
409 Third Street SW, Suite 200
Washington, DC 20024
202–479–6682

Contact this branch of NCOA, an association of organizations and individuals that work with or on behalf of older adults, for referrals to adult day care centers in your community.

National Family Caregivers Association (NFCA)
9621 East Bexhill Drive
Kensington, MD 20895–3014
1–800–896–3650 or 301–942–6430
Fax: 301–942–2302

A nonprofit membership organization committed to improving family caregiver quality of life, NFCA offers members a twenty-four-hour toll-free helpline, a database network to link caregivers, a resource guide, and an informative newsletter. Annual membership fee: $15.00.

National Senior Service Corps (NSSC)
1201 New York Avenue NW
Washington, DC 20525
1–800–424–8867
Volunteers with the Service Corps' Senior Companion Program provide respite care to relieve live-in caregivers for short periods of time. Phone the toll-free number to locate your local program coordinator.

Visiting Nurse Associations of America
3801 East Florida Avenue, Suite 900
Denver, CO 80210
1–800–426–2547 or 1–888–866–8773
Many of the more than 580 nonprofit community-based Visiting Nurse Associations (VNAs) offer in-home respite services for caregivers. Phone to find a nearby VNA office.

REGIONAL

Organizations on this list provide services in limited geographic areas. You may be able to find groups offering similar services in your relative's community.

AgeWell Resource Center
Westgate Mall
2341-M Schoenersville Road
Bethlehem, PA 18017
610–954–3999
Fax: 610–954–3525
For caregivers in the Lehigh Valley area of Pennsylvania, this center offers free personal counseling, support groups, and

a series of educational programs on aging, caregiving, legal and financial issues, community resources, and housing options.

Aging in America
1500 Pelham Parkway South
Bronx, NY 10461
718–824–4004

This nonprofit Bronx agency sponsors an Alzheimer's day care clinic, run by an affiliated nursing home, as well as a lecture series for caregivers.

CARIE (Coalition of Advocates for the Rights of the Infirm Elderly)
1315 Walnut Street, Suite 1000
Philadelphia, PA 19107
215–545–5728
Fax: 215–545–5372

CARIE's Caregiver Coalition is a nonprofit membership organization of individuals and agencies involved with caregiving in Pennsylvania. Phone for information on statewide caregiver resources and respite care services.

Counseling for Caregivers
Philadelphia Geriatric Center
5301 Old York Road
Philadelphia, Pa 19141
215–455–6320

This regional program provides information, referrals, education, and counseling to Philadelphia-area families who are caring for an elderly relative. Services are free and provided by experienced social workers via phone, office, and home visits. The emphasis is on helping clients maintain their own health and well-being while coping with the challenges of caregiving.

Fairview/Ebenezer Caregiver Support Program
3400 West Sixty-sixth Street, Suite 190
Edina, MN 55435
612–924–7039 or 612–924–7040

Through free eight-week educational and support programs, Minneapolis-area caregivers learn about community resources, legal and financial considerations, coping with stress and depression, choosing health plans and nursing homes, and related topics.

Well Spouse Foundation (WSF)
610 Lexington Avenue, Suite 814
New York, NY 10022
1–800–838–0879 or 212–644–1241
Fax: 212–644–1338
A membership organization of partners of the chronically ill and/or disabled, WSF provides emotional support to caregiving spouses through local support groups, personal letter and phone outreach, round-robin letter-writing chains, and a bimonthly newsletter. Annual membership fee: $20.00 (those unable to pay the full fee may pay whatever they can afford).

Other Helpful Free or Low-Cost Publications

The American Association of Retired Persons offers a number of free publications on caregiving topics. For a complete catalog or to order the following titles, contact: AARP Fulfillment, 601 E Street NW, Washington, DC 20049 (1–800–424–3410).

"Caregiving: A Money Management Workbook." Order #D13855. 55-page workbook with worksheets for budgeting caregiving expenses.

"A Path for Caregivers." Order #D12957.

"Caregivers Need Care Too!" Series of five brochures, including these titles: "Who Is a Caregiver?" "When You Need a Break," "You and Your Family," "A Caregiver's Resource Guide," "Taking Care of Yourself." $1.15 per set. Contact: National Association of Area Agencies on Aging, Publications Department, 1112 16th Street NW, Suite 100, Washington, DC 20036 (202–296–8130).

The Sandwich Generation. Quarterly magazine for family caregivers, providing information on health care needs, legal and financial issues, and the emotional effects of balancing the care of an aging relative with family and/or job responsibilities. One-year subscription: $15.00. Write: Sandwich Generation, Box 132, Wickatunk, NJ 07765–0132.

"Take Care!" 32-page booklet for caregivers, covering topics including coping with challenges and stress, changing unrealistic expectations, improving caregiver health and well-being, and relaxation techniques. $2.50. Contact: Amherst H. Wilder Foundation/CCR, 919 LaFond Avenue, St. Paul, MN 55104 (612–642–4060).

Appendix A

Parent
Profile

Filling out this form will help you assemble much of the information you'll need in seeking long-term care. You also can use the profile to pass on vital information to a caregiver who substitutes for you temporarily or on a regular basis. The more caregivers know about the care-receiver's personal history, needs, and interests, the more they will see your loved one as a unique individual deserving of special understanding and attention.

Use pencil to complete this form, and review and update it periodically as your loved one's needs and abilities change.

PARENT PROFILE	
Care-receiver's name	
Address	
Phone #	
Date of birth	
Place of birth	

PARENT PROFILE (CONTINUED)	
Family caregiver's name	
Address	
Home phone #	
Work phone #	

PROFESSIONAL CONTACTS		
	Name/address	Phone number
Physicians:		
Nurses/social workers:		

	Name/address	Phone number
Dentist:		
Pharmacy:		
Other professional contacts:		

PERSONAL CONTACTS *(family, friends, neighbors, etc.)*		
Name/address	Phone #s (home & work)	Relationship to care-receiver

NEEDS HELP WITH: *(describe assistance needed)*	
❏ Dressing/undressing	
❏ Keeping clean and presentable	
❏ Toileting	
❏ Bathing	
❏ Walking	
❏ Climbing steps	
❏ Getting in and out of bed	
❏ Making and/or receiving phone calls	
❏ Reading and/or writing	
❏ Housework	
❏ Transportation	
❏ Shopping	
❏ Taking medications	
❏ Eating	
❏ Cooking	

MEALS	
Special dietary needs:	
Special utensils:	
Favorite breakfast foods:	
Favorite lunch foods:	
Favorite dinner foods:	
Favorite snacks:	

INTERESTS & PREFERENCES	
Reading (or being read to):	
Music:	
Television programs:	
Radio programs:	
Crafts/hobbies:	

Gardening:	
Exercise:	
Musical instruments played:	
Languages spoken:	
Favorite conversation topics:	
Important life experiences:	
Memorable childhood experiences:	
Marriage & family:	
Travel experiences:	
Educational, military, work history:	

Religious/spiritual background:	
Other accomplishments::	
Other interests::	

HEALTH & ACTIVITY INFORMATION	
Time out of bed each day:	
Morning/afternoon nap?	
How often out of the house?	
Problems with vision:	
Problems with hearing:	
Problems with communication:	
Problems with behavior (e.g., aggressiveness, destructiveness, disturbing others):	
Other:	

SPECIAL APPLIANCES, AIDS, OR HEALTH CARE ITEMS

- ❑ Cane
- ❑ Walker
- ❑ Wheelchair
- ❑ Incontinence pads/adult diaper
- ❑ Urinal/bedpan
- ❑ Eyeglasses
- ❑ Hearing aid
- ❑ Dentures
- ❑ Special shoes/socks
- ❑ Wig/makeup
- ❑ Other: _____

MEDICATIONS SCHEDULE
(note special items needed, or difficulty swallowing medication)

Medication name:	
Form (liquid, tablet, capsule, etc.):	
Dosage:	
Taken:	_____ times a day ❑ with food ❑ without food
Special instructions:	

Medication name:	
Form (liquid, tablet, capsule, etc.):	
Dosage:	
Taken:	_____ times a day ❏ with food ❏ without food
Special instructions:	

Medication name:	
Form (liquid, tablet, capsule, etc.):	
Dosage:	
Taken:	_____ times a day ❏ with food ❏ without food
Special instructions:	

Medication name:	
Form (liquid, tablet, capsule, etc.):	
Dosage:	
Taken:	_____ times a day ❑ with food ❑ without food
Special instructions:	

Medication name:	
Form (liquid, tablet, capsule, etc.):	
Dosage:	
Taken:	_____ times a day ❑ with food ❑ without food
Special instructions:	

Appendix B

State Units
on Aging

Contact your State Unit on Aging for statewide referrals to programs and services for older adults and caregivers. Your state office also can give you the address and phone number of your local Area Agency on Aging (AAA). Local AAAs are an excellent source of free assistance and referrals to older adults and family caregivers. Services vary, but most AAAs either provide the following services directly or will direct you to other public or private organizations that do:

- Case management/geriatric care management
- Home-delivered meals and congregate meals
- Friendly visitors
- Telephone reassurance
- Chores and home repairs
- Light housekeeping and shopping assistance
- Transportation
- Referrals to Visiting Nurses, home health aides, and other medical service providers
- Unevaluated lists of adult care facilities
- Free legal and/or financial planning assistance
- Social and recreational activities programs
- Adult day care
- Senior employment programs
- Respite care

National Association of State Units on Aging
1225 I Street NW, Suite 725
Washington, DC 20005
202–898–2578

ALABAMA
Commission on Aging
RSA Plaza, Suite 470
770 Washington Avenue
Montgomery, AL 36130
334–242–5743
Fax: 334–242–5594

ALASKA
Division of Senior Services
Department of Administration
3601 C Street, #310
Anchorage, AK 99503
907–563–5654
Fax: 907–562–3040

ARIZONA
Aging and Adult Administration
Department of Economic Security
1789 West Jefferson, #950A
Phoenix, AZ 85007
602–542–4446
Fax: 602–542–6575

ARKANSAS
Division of Aging and Adult Services
Arkansas Department of Human Services
P.O. Box 1437, Slot 1412
7th and Main Streets
Little Rock, AR 72201
501–682–2441
Fax: 501–682–8155

CALIFORNIA
Department of Aging
1600 K Street
Sacramento, CA 95814
916–322–5290
Fax: 916–324–1903

COLORADO
Division of Aging and Adult Services
Department of Human Services
110 Sixteenth Street, Suite 200
Denver, CO 80203–1714
303–620–4147
Fax: 303–620–4189

CONNECTICUT
Department of Social Services
Elderly Services Division
25 Sigourney Street, 10th floor
Hartford, CT 06106–5033
860–424–5281
Fax: 860–424–4966

DELAWARE
Division of Services for Aging and Adults with
 Physical Disabilities
Department of Health and Social Services
1901 North DuPont Highway
New Castle, DE 19720
302–577–4791
Fax: 302–577–4793

DISTRICT OF COLUMBIA
Office on Aging
One Judiciary Square
441 Fourth Street NW, 9th floor
Washington, DC 20001
202–724–5622   Fax: 202–724–4979

FLORIDA
Department of Elder Affairs
Building B, Suite 152
4040 Esplanade Way
Tallahassee, FL 32399
904–414–2000
Fax: 904–414–2002

GEORGIA
Office of Aging
#2 Peachtree Street NE, 18th floor
Atlanta, GA 30303
404–657–5258
Fax: 404–657–5285

HAWAII
Executive Office on Aging
250 South Hotel Street, Suite 107
Honolulu, HI 96813–2831
1–800–332–2272 or 808–586–0100
Fax: 808–586–0185

IDAHO
Commission on Aging
700 West Jefferson, Room 108
P.O. Box 83720
Boise, ID 83720-0007
208–334–3833
Fax: 208–334–3033

ILLINOIS
Department on Aging
421 East Capitol Avenue
Springfield, IL 62701
217–785–2870
Fax: 217–785–4477

INDIANA
Bureau of Aging/In Home Services
402 West Washington Street, #E–431
Indianapolis, IN 46207–7083
317–232–7020
Fax: 317–232–7867

IOWA
Department of Elder Affairs
Clemens Building, 3rd Floor
200 Tenth Street
Des Moines, IA 50309-3609
515–281–5187
Fax: 515–281–4036

KANSAS
Department on Aging
Docking State Office Building, 122-S
915 Southwest Harrison
Topeka, KS 66612–1500
913–296–4986
Fax: 913–296–0256

KENTUCKY
Division of Aging Services
Cabinet for Human Resources
275 East Main Street, 6 West
Frankfort, KY 40621
502–564–6930
Fax: 502–564–4595

LOUISIANA
Office of Elderly Affairs
P.O. Box 80374
4550 North Boulevard, 2nd floor
Baton Rouge, LA 70806
504–925–1700
Fax: 504–925–1749

MAINE
Bureau of Elder and Adult Services
Department of Human Services
State House, Station #11
Augusta, ME 04333
207–624–5335
Fax: 207–624–5361

MARYLAND
Office on Aging
State Office Building, Room 1004
301 West Preston Street
Baltimore, MD 21201
410–767–1100
Fax: 410–333–7943

MASSACHUSETTS
Executive Office of Elder Affairs
1 Ashburton Place, 5th floor
Boston, MA 02108
617–727–7750
Fax: 617–727–6944

MICHIGAN
Office of Services to the Aging
P.O. Box 30026
Lansing, MI 48909
517–373–8230
Fax: 517–373–4092

MINNESOTA
Board on Aging
444 Lafayette Road
St. Paul, MN 55155–3843
612–296–2770
Fax: 612–297–7855

MISSISSIPPI
Council on Aging
Division of Aging and Adult Services
750 North State Street
Jackson, MS 39202
601–359–4929
Fax: 601–359–4370

MISSOURI
Division on Aging
Department of Social Services
P.O. Box 1337
615 Howerton Court
Jefferson City, MO 65102–1337
573–751–3082
Fax: 573–751–8687

MONTANA
Office on Aging
Senior and Long Term Care Division
Department of Health and Human Services
111 Sanders Street
P.O. Box 4210
Helena, MT 59604
406–444–7788
Fax: 406–444–6743

NEBRASKA
Department on Aging
P.O. Box 95044
301 Centennial Mall South
Lincoln, NE 68509
402–471–2306
Fax: 402–471–4619

NEVADA
Division for Aging Services
Department of Human Resources

1665 Hot Springs Road, Suite 158
Carson City, NV 89710
702–687–4210
Fax: 702–687–4264

NEW HAMPSHIRE
Division of Elderly and Adult Services
State Office Park South
115 Pleasant Street Annex Building #1
Concord, NH 03301–3843
603–271–4680
Fax: 603–271–4643

NEW JERSEY
Division on Aging
Department of Community Affairs
CN 807
South Broad and Front Streets
Trenton, NJ 08625–0807
1–800–792–8820 or 609–984–6693
Fax: 609–633–6609

NEW MEXICO
State Agency on Aging
La Villa Rivera Building
224 East Palace Avenue, 4th floor
Santa Fe, NM 87501
505–827–7640
Fax: 505–827–7649

NEW YORK
Office for the Aging
New York State Plaza
Agency Building #2
Albany, NY 12223
518–474–4425
Fax: 518–474–1398

NORTH CAROLINA
Division of Aging
CB 29531
693 Palmer Drive
Raleigh, NC 27626–0531
919–733–3983
Fax: 919–733–0443

NORTH DAKOTA
Aging Services Division
Department of Human Services
600 South Second Street, Suite 1C
Bismarck, ND 58504
701–328–8910
Fax: 701–328–8989

OHIO
Department of Aging
50 West Broad Street, 9th floor
Columbus, OH 43215–5928
614–466–5500
Fax: 614–466–5741

OKLAHOMA
Aging Services Division
Department of Human Services
P.O. Box 25352
312 Northeast Twenty-eighth Street
Oklahoma City, OK 73125
405–521–2327
Fax: 405–521–2086

OREGON
Senior and Disabled Services Division
500 Summer Street Northeast, 2nd floor
Salem, OR 97310–1015
503–945–5811
Fax: 503–373–7823

PENNSYLVANIA
Department of Aging
MSS Office Building
400 Market Street, 7th floor
Harrisburg, PA 17101–2301
717–783–1550
Fax: 717–783–6842

PUERTO RICO
Governor's Office for Elderly Affairs
Corbian Plaza Stop 23
Ponce De Leon Avenue #1603
U.M. Office C
San Ture, PR 00908
809–721–5710
Fax: 809–721–6510

RHODE ISLAND
Department of Elderly Affairs
160 Pine Street
Providence, RI 02903–3708
401–277–2858
Fax: 401–277–1490

SOUTH CAROLINA
Division on Aging
Office of the Governor
202 Arbor Lake Drive, #301
Columbia, SC 29223
803–737–7500
Fax: 803–737–7501

SOUTH DAKOTA
Office of Adult Services and Aging
700 Governors Drive
Pierre, SD 57501
605–773–3656
Fax: 605–773–4855

TENNESSEE
Commission on Aging
Andrew Jackson Building
500 Deaderick Building, 9th floor
Nashville, TN 37243–0860
615–741–2056
Fax: 615–741–3309

TEXAS
Department on Aging
P.O. Box 12786 Capitol Station
1949 IH 35 South
Austin, TX 78741–3702
512–424–6840
Fax: 512–424–6890

UTAH
Division of Aging and Adult Services
Department of Social Services
Box 45500
120 North, 200 West
Salt Lake City, UT 84145–0500
801–538–3910
Fax: 801–538–4395

VERMONT
Aging and Disabilities
103 South Main Street
Waterbury, VT 05676
802–241–2400
Fax: 802–241–2325

VIRGINIA
Department for the Aging
700 Centre, 10th floor
700 East Franklin Street
Richmond, VA 23219–2327
804–225–2271   Fax: 804–371–8381

WASHINGTON
Aging and Adult Services Administration
600 Woodland Square Loop SE
Lacey, WA 98503
360–493–2500
Fax: 360–438–8633

WEST VIRGINIA
Office of Aging
Department of Health and Human Resources
Holly Grove, State Capitol
Charleston, WV 25305
304–558–3317
Fax: 304–558–0004

WISCONSIN
Bureau of Aging
Division of Community Services
217 South Hamilton Street, Suite 300
Madison, WI 53707
608–266–2536
Fax: 608–267–3203

WYOMING
Division on Aging
Hathaway Building, Room 139
Cheyenne, WY 82002–0710
307–777–7986
Fax: 307–777–5340

Appendix C

State Long-Term Care Ombudsmen

Every state has an ombudsman program to provide assistance to residents and families of residents in nursing homes, assisted living facilities, and other long-term care facilities. Ombudsmen can provide lists of facilities in the state or local area as well as information on financial and legal issues related to long-term care. They will not recommend specific facilities but often will share information to steer you away from poor ones and to help you make an informed choice. Your ombudsman also will investigate and try to resolve complaints about services and quality of care.

Most ombudsman programs include a state office plus a network of county or local offices. Your state office may assist you directly or refer you to the local office closest to you or your relative.

Following is a directory of state ombudsman addresses and phone numbers. When writing to any of these addresses, mark your inquiries, "Attention: State Long-term Care Ombudsman."

ALABAMA
Commission on Aging
RSA Plaza, Suite 470
770 Washington Avenue
Montgomery, AL 36130
1–800–243–5463 or 334–242–5743
Fax: 334–242–5594

ALASKA
Alaska Commission on Aging
3601 C Street, Suite 260
Anchorage, AK 99503–5209
1–800–730–6393 or 907–563–6393
Fax: 907–561–3862

ARIZONA
Aging and Adult Administration
1789 West Jefferson, 950A
Phoenix, AZ 85007
602–542–4446
Fax: 602–542–6575

ARKANSAS
Department of Human Services
1417 Donaghey Plaza South, Slot 1412
Little Rock, AR 72203–1437
501–682–2441
Fax: 501–682–8155

CALIFORNIA
Department of Aging
Long Term Care Ombudsman Program
1600 K Street
Sacramento, CA 95814
1–800–231–4024 or 916–323–6681
Fax: 916–323–7299

COLORADO
The Legal Center
455 Sherman Street, Suite 130
Denver, CO 80203
1–800–332–6356 or 303–722–0300
Fax: 303–722–0720

CONNECTICUT
Department on Aging
Elder Rights Services Division
25 Sigourney Street, 10th floor
Hartford, CT 06106–5033
203–424–4200
Fax: 203–424–4966

DELAWARE
**Division of Services for the Aging and Adults with
    Physical Disabilities**
Department of Health and Social Services
256 Chapman Road
Oxford Building, Suite 200
Newark, DE 19702
1–800–223–9074 or 302–453–3820
Fax: 302–453–3836

DISTRICT OF COLUMBIA
AARP, Legal Counsel for the Elderly
601 E Street NW, 4th floor, Building A4
Washington, DC 20049
202–662–4933
Fax: 202–434–6464

FLORIDA
State Long Term Care Ombudsman Council
Carlton Building, Office of Governor
501 South Calhoun Street
Tallahassee, FL 32399–0001
904–488–6190
Fax: 904–488–5657

GEORGIA
Division of Aging Services
2 Peachtree Street NW, 18th floor
Atlanta, GA 30303
404–657–5319   Fax: 404–657–5285

373

HAWAII
Office of the Governor
Executive Office on Aging
335 Merchant Street, Room 241
Honolulu, HI 96813–2831
808–586–0100
Fax: 808–586–0185

IDAHO
Commission on Aging
700 West Jefferson, Suite 108
P.O. Box 83720
Boise, ID 83720–0007
208–334–3833
Fax: 208–334–3033

ILLINOIS
Department on Aging
421 East Capitol Avenue, #100
Springfield, IL 62701
217–785–3140
Fax: 217–785–4477

INDIANA
Division of Disability, Aging and Rehabilitative Services
P.O. Box 7083
402 West Washington Street, W–454
Indianapolis, IN 46207–7083
1–800–622–4484 or 317–232–7134
Fax: 317–232–7867

IOWA
Department of Elder Affairs
Clemens Building, 3rd floor
200 Tenth Street
Des Moines, IA 50319–3609
515–281–5187
Fax: 515–281–4036

KANSAS
Department on Aging
915 Southwest Harrison, #150
Topeka, KS 66612–1500
1–800–432–3535 or 913–296–4986
Fax: 913–296–0256

KENTUCKY
Division of Aging Services
275 East Main Street, 5th floor West
Frankfort, KY 40621
1–800–372–2291 or 502–564–6930
Fax: 502–564–4595

LOUISIANA
Governor's Office of Elderly Affairs
4550 North Boulevard, 2nd floor
Baton Rouge, LA 70806
504–925–1700
Fax: 504–925–1749

MAINE
State Long Term Care Ombudsman Program
P.O. Box 126
21 Bangor Street
Augusta, ME 04332
1–800–499–0229 or 207–621–1079
Fax: 207–621–0509

MARYLAND
Office of Aging
301 West Preston Street, Room 1004
Baltimore, MD 21201
410–767–1100
Fax: 410–333–7943

MASSACHUSETTS
Executive Office of Elder Affairs
1 Ashburton Place, 5th floor
Boston, MA 02108–1518
617–727–7750
Fax: 617–727–9368

MICHIGAN
Citizens for Better Care
416 North Homer Street, Suite 101
Lansing, MI 48912–4700
1–800–292–7852 or 517–336–6753

MINNESOTA
Office of Ombudsman for Older Minnesotans
444 Lafayette Road, 4th floor
St. Paul, MN 55155–3843
1–800–652–9747 or 612–296–0382
Fax: 612–297–7855

MISSISSIPPI
Division of Aging and Adult Services
Department of Human Services
750 North State Street
Jackson, MS 39202
601–359–4929
Fax: 601–359–4370

MISSOURI
Division of Aging
Department of Social Services
P.O. Box 1337
615 Howerton Court
Jefferson City, MO 65102–1337
1–800–292–3282 or 573–751-3082
Fax: 573–751–8687

MONTANA
Department of Public Health and Human Services
Division on Aging
P.O. Box 8005
Helena, MT 59604–8005
1–800–332–2272 or 406–444–5900
Fax: 406–444–7743

NEBRASKA
Department on Aging
301 Centennial Mall South
P.O. Box 95044
Lincoln, NE 68509–5044
402–471–2306
Fax: 402–471–4619

NEVADA
Department of Human Resources
Ombudsman Program
340 North Eleventh Street, Suite 203
Las Vegas, NV 89101
702–486–3545
Fax: 702–486–3572

NEW HAMPSHIRE
Division of Elderly and Adult Services
115 Pleasant Street Annex, Building 1
Concord, NH 03301–6508
1–800–442–5640 or 603–271–4375
Fax: 603–271–4643

NEW JERSEY
Division on Aging
Office of the Ombudsman
101 South Broad Street/ CN807, 7th floor
Trenton, NJ 08625–0807
1–800–792–8820 or 609–292–8016
Fax: 609–633–6609

NEW MEXICO
State Agency on Aging
228 East Palace Avenue
Santa Fe, NM 87501
1–800–432–2080 or 505–827–7640
Fax: 505–827–7649

NEW YORK
New York State Office for the Aging
Agency Building 2
2 Empire State Plaza
Albany, NY 12223–0001
518–474–0108
Fax: 518–474–0608

NORTH CAROLINA
Division of Aging
693 Palmer Drive
CB #29531
Raleigh, NC 27626–0531
919–733–3983
Fax: 919–733–0443

NORTH DAKOTA
Department of Human Services
Aging Service Division
600 South Second Street, Suite 1C
Bismarck, ND 58504
1–800–755–8521 or 701–328–8910
Fax: 701–328–8989

OHIO
Department of Aging
50 West Broad Street, 9th floor
Columbus, OH 43215–5928
1–800–282–1206 or 614–466–1221
Fax: 614–466–5741

OKLAHOMA
Department of Human Services
Aging Services Division
312 Northeast Twenty-eighth Street, Suite 109
Oklahoma City, OK 73105
405–521–6734
Fax: 405–521–2086

OREGON
Office of Long Term Care Ombudsman
2475 Lancaster Drive NE, #B–9
Salem, OR 97310
1–800–522–2602 or 503–378–6533
Fax: 503–373–0852

PENNSYLVANIA
Department of Aging
400 Market Street, 6th floor
Harrisburg, PA 17101–2301
717–783–7247
Fax: 717–783–6842

RHODE ISLAND
Department of Elderly Affairs
160 Pine Street
Providence, RI 02903–3708
401–277–2858
Fax: 401–277–2130

SOUTH CAROLINA
Office of Governor, Division on Aging
202 Arbor Lake Drive, Suite 301
Columbia, SC 29223–4535
803–737–7500
Fax: 803–737–7501

SOUTH DAKOTA
Office of Adult Services and Aging
Department of Social Services
700 Governors Drive
Pierre, SD 57501–2291
605–773–3656
Fax: 605–773–6834

TENNESSEE
Tennessee Commission on Aging
500 Deaderick Street, 9th floor
Andrew Jackson Building
Nashville, TN 37243–0860
615–741–2056
Fax: 615–741–3309

TEXAS
Department on Aging
P.O. Box 12786
Austin, TX 78711
1–800–252–9240 or 512–444–2727
Fax: 512–440–5252

UTAH
Department of Human Services
Division of Aging and Adult Services
120 North 200 West, Room 401
Salt Lake City, UT 84145–0500
801–538–3924
Fax: 801–538–4395

VERMONT
Ombudsman Project
18 Main Street
St. Johnsbury, VT 05819
1–800–642–5119 or 802–748–8721
Fax: 802–748–4612

380

VIRGINIA
Virginia Association of Area Agencies on Aging
530 East Main Street, Suite 428
Richmond, VA 23219
1–800–552–3402 or 804–644–2923
Fax: 804–644–5640

WASHINGTON
Washington State Long Term Care Ombudsman Program
South King County Multi-Service Center
1200 South 336th Street
Federal Way, WA 98003–7452
1–800–562–6028 or 206–838–6810
Fax: 206–874–7831

WEST VIRGINIA
Commission on Aging
1900 Kanawha Boulevard East
Holly Grove/Capital Complex
Charleston, WV 25305–0160
304–558–3317
Fax: 304–558–0004

WISCONSIN
Board on Aging and Long Term Care
214 North Hamilton Street
Madison, WI 53703–2118
608–266–8944
Fax: 608–261–6570

WYOMING
Senior Citizen Inc.
756 Gilchrist, P.O. Box 94
Wheatland, WY 82201
307–322–5553
Fax: 307–322–3419

Appendix D

Sources of State Inspection Reports for Long-Term Care Facilities

Nursing homes and other long-term care facilities are supposed to post copies of their latest state inspection reports. At many facilities, though, these reports are out of date, hard to read, or unavailable. It can be a chore tracking down an alternate source for current surveys. We contacted each state's long-term care ombudsman to find out where consumers should turn for help. Following are the phone numbers and addresses the ombudsmen provided for state licensing agencies and other sources of current state inspection reports. In a few cases the reports are available directly from the ombudsman's office, sometimes for a small fee based on the number of pages requested.

ALABAMA
Alabama Department of Public Health
Division of Licensure and Certification
434 Monroe Street
Montgomery, AL 36130–3017
334–240–3500

ALASKA
Health Facilities Licensing and Certification
Division of Medical Assistance
Department of Health and Social Services
4730 Business Park Boulevard, Suite 18

Anchorage, AK 99503
907–561–8081

ARIZONA
Arizona Department of Health Service
Office of Health Care Licenses—Long Term Care
1647 East Morten
Phoenix, AZ 85020
602–255–1244

ARKANSAS
Office of Long Term Care
Department of Human Services
532 South Louisiana
P.O. Box 8059, Slot 400
Little Rock, AR 72203–8059
501–682–8487

CALIFORNIA
State Licensing and Certification
Department of Health Services
1800 Third Street
Sacramento, CA 94234–7320
916–324–8625

COLORADO
State Health Department
4300 Cherry Creek Drive South
Denver, CO 80222
303–692–2800

CONNECTICUT
Department of Public Health
Division of Health Systems Regulations
410 Capitol Avenue, 2nd Floor
MS 112HFL, P.O. Box 340308
Hartford, CT 06134
860–509–7444

DELAWARE
Delaware Health and Social Services
3 Mill Road, Suite 308
Wilmington, DE 19806
302–577–6666

DISTRICT OF COLUMBIA
Service Facility Regulation and Administration
614 H Street NW
Washington, DC 20001
202–727–7190

FLORIDA
Agency for Health Care Administration
2727 Mahan Drive
Tallahassee, FL 32308
904–487–3513

GEORGIA
Office of Regulatory Services
Department of Human Resources
2 Peachtree Street NE, 21st floor
Atlanta, GA 30303
404–657–5726

HAWAII
Hospital and Medical Facilities Branch
1270 Queen Emma Street, 1100
Honolulu, HI 96813
808–586–4090

IDAHO
Bureau of Facility Standards
Idaho Department of Health and Welfare
450 West Second Street, 3rd floor
P.O. Box 83720
Boise, ID 83720–0036
208–334–6626

ILLINOIS
Illinois Department of Public Health
525 West Jefferson Street
Springfield, IL 62761
217–782–5180

INDIANA
Indiana State Department of Health
Division of Long Term Care
2 North Meridian Street, 4th floor
Indianapolis, IN 46204
317–233–7442

IOWA
Department of Inspections and Appeals
Lucas Building
Des Moines, IA 50319
515–281–4115

KANSAS
Health and Environment
Adult and Child Care
Landon State Office Building, Suite 1001
900 Southwest Jackson
Topeka, KS 66612
913–296–1240

KENTUCKY
Division of Licensing and Regulation
Cabinet of Health Services
275 East Main Street, 4th floor East
Frankfort, KY 40621
502–564–2800

LOUISIANA
Department of Health and Hospitals
Health Standards Section
P.O. Box 3767

Baton Rouge, LA 70821
504–342–0138

MAINE
Division of Licensing and Certification
Department of Human Services
Statehouse Station 11
Augusta, ME 04333
207–624–5443

MARYLAND
Licensing and Certification Administration
4201 Patterson Avenue, 4th floor
Baltimore, MD 21215
410–764–2747

MASSACHUSETTS
Department of Public Health
Public Information Office
10 West Street, 5th floor
Boston, MA 02111–1212
617–727–5860, ext. 337 or 343

MICHIGAN
Citizens for Better Care
416 North Homer Street, Suite 101
Lansing, MI 48912–4700
517–336–6753

MINNESOTA
Long Term Care Ombudsman
85 East Seventh Place, Suite 280
St. Paul, MN 55101
612–296–0382

MISSISSIPPI
Mississippi Department of Health
Division of Licensure and Certification

P.O. Box 1700
Jackson, MS 39215–1700
601–354–7300

MISSOURI
Long Term Care Ombudsman—Division of Aging
Box 1337, 615 Howerton Court
Jefferson City, MO 65102
1–800–309–3282 or 573–751–3082

MONTANA
Long Term Care Ombudsman
Department of Public Health and Human Services
Division on Aging
P.O. Box 4210
Helena, MT 59604–4210
406–444–5900

NEBRASKA
Nebraska Department of Health
Health Facility Licensure and Inspection
P.O. Box 95007
Lincoln, NE 68509–5007
402–471–2946

NEVADA
Bureau of Licensure and Certification
1550 College Parkway, Suite 158
Capitol Complex
Carson City, NV 87706-7921
702–687–4475

NEW HAMPSHIRE
Bureau of Health Facilities
Department of Health and Human Services
6 Hazen Drive
Concord, NH 03301–6508
603–271–4592

NEW JERSEY
New Jersey State Department of Health
Division of Health Facilities Evaluation and Licensing
CN367
Trenton, NJ 08625–0367
609–588–7809

NEW MEXICO
Health Facilities Licensing and Certification
Bureau
525 Camino de los Marquez, Suite 2
Santa Fe, NM 87501
505–827–4200

NEW YORK
New York State Department of Health
Bureau of Long Term Care
Empire State Plaza
Corning Tower
Albany, NY 12237
518–473–8033

NORTH CAROLINA
Long Term Care Ombudsman
Division of Aging
693 Palmer Drive
CB 29531
Raleigh, NC 27626–0531
919–733–3983

NORTH DAKOTA
Division of Health Facilities
North Dakota Department of Health
600 East Boulevard
Bismarck, ND 58505
701–328–2352

OHIO
Ohio Department of Health
Division of Quality Assurance
Bureau of Information and Operational Support
246 North High Street
P.O. Box 118
Columbus, OH 43215
614–466–4704

OKLAHOMA
Oklahoma State Department of Health
Special Health Services, Long Term Care
1000 Northeast Tenth Street
Oklahoma City, OK 73117
405–271–6868

OREGON
Human Resources Department
Senior and Disabled Services Division
500 Summer Street NE, 2nd floor
Salem, OR 97310–1015
1–800–232–3020 or 503–945–5811

PENNSYLVANIA
Division of Nursing Care Facilities
Health and Welfare Building, Room 526
Harrisburg, PA 17108
717–787–1816

RHODE ISLAND
Department of Health
Division of Facilities Regulation
3 Capitol Hill
Providence, RI 02908–5097
401–277–2566
Reports must be reviewed in the office; no information by
phone or mail.

SOUTH CAROLINA
Bureau of Certification
Department of Health and Environmental Control
2600 Bull Street
Columbia, SC 29201
803–737–7205

SOUTH DAKOTA
South Dakota Department of Health
Office of Health Care Facilities, Licensure, and
Certification
445 East Capitol Avenue
Pierre, SD 57501–3185
605–773–3364

TENNESSEE
Tennessee Department of Health
Division of Health Care Facilities
710 Ben Allen Road
Nashville, TN 37247–0530
615–650–7100

TEXAS
Texas Department of Human Services
Long Term Care Regulatory—Y976
P.O. Box 149030
Austin, TX 78714–9030
512–834–6774

UTAH
Utah Department of Health
Division of Health System Improvement
Bureau of Medicare/Medicaid Program Certification and
Resident Assessment
Box 142905
Salt Lake City, UT 84114–2905
801–538–6157

VERMONT
Department of Aging and Disability
Division of Licensing and Protection
103 South Main Street
Waterbury, VT 05671–2306
802–241–2345

VIRGINIA
Virginia Department of Health
Office of Health Facility Regulation
3600 West Broad Street, Suite 216
Richmond, VA 23230
804–367–2102

WASHINGTON
Washington Long Term-Care Ombudsman
South King County Multi-Service Center
P.O. Box 23699
Federal Way, WA 98093–0699
1–800–562–6028 or 206–838–6810

WEST VIRGINIA
West Virginia Department of Health and Human Resources
Office of Health Facilities Licensure and Certification
1900 Kanawha Boulevard East
Building 3, Room 550
Charleston, West Virginia 25305
304–558–0050

WISCONSIN
Bureau of Quality Assurance
Department of Health and Family Services
1 West Wilson Street, Room 131
P.O. Box 309
Madison, WI 53701–0309
608–266–3024

WYOMING
Office of Health Quality
2020 Carey Avenue
First Bank Building, 8th floor
Cheyenne, WY 82002
307–777–7123

Appendix E

Self-Help Clearinghouses

Mutual aid self-help groups can be a welcome source of comfort and emotional support for people facing chronic illness, disability, depression, bereavement, caregiving stress, and any number of other concerns. Support group leaders and members also may provide valuable information on local resources for medical care, financial and legal aid, and other services. Listed below are phone numbers for national and statewide clearinghouses that can help you or your loved one find a nearby self-help group for a specific concern. If no local group exists, many clearinghouses will provide assistance in starting one.

NATIONAL CLEARINGHOUSES

American Self-Help Clearinghouse
St. Clare's-Riverside Medical Center
25 Pocono Road
Denville, NJ 07834–2995
201–625–7101
TTY: 201–625–9053
Fax: 201–625–8848
E-mail (on CompuServe): 70275,1003
Via CompuServe Information Service: Health and Fitness
Forum ("go GoodHealth"), Self-Help Support Section

National Self-Help Clearinghouse
CUNY, Graduate School and University Center
25 West Forty-third Street, Room 620
New York, NY 10036
212–354–8525

REGIONAL CLEARINGHOUSES

ALABAMA—Birmingham	205–251–5912
ARIZONA	1–800–352–3792 or 602–231–0868
ARKANSAS—Northeast area	501–932–5555
CALIFORNIA	
Davis	916–756–8181
Modesto	209–558–7454
Sacramento	916–368–3100
San Diego	619–543–0412
San Francisco	1–800–273–6222 or 415–772–4357
CONNECTICUT	203–789–7645
ILLINOIS	
statewide	312–368–9070
Champaign	217–352–0099
Macon	217–429–4357
IOWA	1–800–952–4777 or 515–576–5870
KANSAS	1–800–445–0116 or 316–689–3843
MASSACHUSETTS	413–545–2313

MICHIGAN

statewide	1–800–777–5556 or 517–484–7373
Benton Harbor	1–800–336–0341 or 616–925–0594

MISSOURI

Kansas City	816–822–7272
St. Louis	314–773–1399

NEBRASKA 402–476–9668

NEW JERSEY 201–625–7101

NEW YORK

Brooklyn	718–875–1420
Broome	607–771–8888
Cattaragus	716–372–5800
Dutchess	914–473–1500
Erie	716–886–1242
Fulton	518–736–1120
Manhattan	212–586–5770
Monroe	716–256–0590
Montgomery	518–842–1900, ext. 286
Niagara	716–433–3780
Oneida	315–735–4463
Onondaga/Syracuse	315–474–7011
Orange/Sullivan	1–800–832–1200 or 914–294–7411
Rockland	914–639–7400, ext. 22
St. Lawrence	315–265–2422
Saratoga	518–664–8322
Schoharie	518–234–2568
Steuben	1–800–346–2211 or 607–936–4114
Tompkins	607–273–9250
Ulster	914–339–9090

Westchester	914–949–0788, ext. 237
Wyoming	716–786–0540

NORTH CAROLINA
Mecklenberg	704–331–9500

NORTH DAKOTA
Fargo	701–235–7335

OHIO
Dayton	513–225–3004
Toledo	419–475–4449

OREGON—
northwest Oregon/ southwest Washington	503–222–5555

PENNSYLVANIA
Pittsburgh	412–261–5363
Scranton	717–961–1234

SOUTH CAROLINA
Richland/Lexington	803–791–2800

TENNESSEE
Knoxville	423–584–9125
Memphis/Shelby	901–323–8485

TEXAS
statewide	512–454–3706
Dallas	214–871–2420
Houston	713–522–5161
San Antonio	210–826–2288
Tarrant	817–335–5405

UTAH
Salt Lake City	801–978–3333

Bibliography

Books and Booklets

Adams, Tom, and Kathryn Armstrong. *When Parents Age: What Children Can Do*. New York: Berkley, 1993.

Bathauer, Ruth M. *Parent Care: A Guide to Help Adult Children Provide Care and Support for Their Aging Parents*. Ventura, CA: Regal Books, 1990.

Blum, Laurie. *Free Money and Services for Seniors and Their Families*. New York: John Wiley, 1995.

Boughton, Jill A. *You and Your Aging Parent: The Practical Side of Love*. South Bend, IN: Greenlawn Press, 1994.

Carter, Rosalynn, with Susan K. Golant. *Helping Yourself Help Others*. New York: Times Books, Random House, 1994.

The Consumer's Guide to Health Insurance. Washington, DC: Health Insurance Association of America, 1992.

The Continuing Care Retirement Community: A Guidebook for Consumers. Washington, DC: American Association of Homes for the Aging, 1993.

Dolan, J. Michael. *How to Care for Your Aging Parents and Still Have a Life of Your Own!* Los Angeles: Mulholland Pacific, 1992.

Family Service America. *The Family Guide to Elder Care: Making the Right Choices.* Milwaukee: Family Service America, 1990.

Guide to Choosing a Nursing Home. Revised edition. Washington, DC: Health Care Financing Administration, 1994.

Hastings, Diana. *The Complete Guide to Home Nursing.* Woodbury, NY: Barron's, 1986.

Levin, Nora Jean. *How to Care for Your Parents: A Handbook for Adult Children.* Washington, DC: Storm King Press, 1987.

Mall, E. Jane. *Caregiving: How to Care for Your Elderly Mother and Stay Sane.* New York: Ballantine, 1990.

Medigap: Medicare Supplement Insurance. Revised edition. Washington, DC: American Association of Retired Persons, 1994.

Miles Away & Still Caring. Washington, DC: American Association of Retired Persons, 1994.

Moskowitz, Francine, and Robert Moskowitz. *Parenting Your Aging Parent.* Woodland Hills, CA: Key Publications, 1991.

1995 Guide to Health Insurance for People with Medicare. Washington, DC: Health Care Financing Administration, 1995.

Portnow, Jay, with Martha Houtmann. *Home Care for the Elderly: A Complete Guide.* New York: McGraw-Hill, 1987.

Pritikin, Enid, and Trucy Reece. *Parentcare Survival Guide: Helping*

Your Folks Through the Not-So-Golden Years. Hauppauge, NY: Barron's, 1993.

Rob, Caroline, with Janet Reynolds. *The Caregiver's Guide: Helping Elderly Relatives Cope with Health & Safety Problems.* Boston: Houghton Mifflin, 1991.

Safety for Older Consumers. Washington, DC: U.S. Consumer Product Safety Commission.

Schomp, Virginia. *The Better Business Bureau A to Z Buying Guide.* New York: Henry Holt, 1990.

Schwartz, Arthur N. *Survival Handbook for Children of Aging Parents.* Chicago: Follett, 1977.

Self-Help Sourcebook. 5th edition. Denville, NJ: American Self-Help Clearinghouse, 1995.

Staying at Home. Washington, DC: American Association of Retired Persons, 1994.

Susik, D. Helen. *Hiring Home Caregivers: The Family Guide to In-Home Eldercare.* San Luis Obispo, CA: Impact Publishers, 1995.

Tomorrow's Choices: Preparing Now for Future Legal, Financial, and Health Care Decisions. Washington, DC: American Association of Retired Persons, 1988.

Watt, Jill. *A Care-giver's Guide: Practical Solutions for Coping with Aging Parents or a Chronically Ill Partner or Relative.* 2nd edition. Bellingham, WA: Self-Counsel Press, 1994.

Werner, Anne P., and James P. Firman. *Home Care for Older People: A Consumer's Guide.* Washington, DC: United Seniors Health Cooperative, 1994.

Williams, Mark E. *The American Geriatrics Society's Complete Guide to Aging & Health.* New York: Harmony Books, Crown Publishers, 1995.

Your Medicare Handbook 1995. Washington, DC: Health Care Financing Administration, 1995.

Periodicals

"Baby Boomers and Their Parents." *USA Today.* Four-part series: July 17 to 20, 1995.

Consumer Reports. Three-part series: "Nursing Homes: When a Loved One Needs Care," August 1995. "Who Pays for Nursing Homes," September 1995. "Can Your Loved Ones Avoid a Nursing Home?" October 1995.

Goetting, Marsha A., and Vicki L. Schmall. "Talking with Aging Parents About Finances." *Journal of Home Economics,* Spring 1993. Pages 42–46.

Goleman, Daniel. "Depression in the Old Can Be Deadly, but the Symptoms Are Often Missed." *New York Times,* September 6, 1995.

O'Reilly, Brian. "How to Take Care of Aging Parents." *Fortune,* May 18, 1992. Pages 108–112.

Wilcox, Melynda Dovel. "Welcome to Generation S." *Kiplinger's Personal Finance Magazine,* June 1995. Pages 59–62.

Pamphlets and Brochures

Buying Your Medigap Policy. Washington, DC: National Committee to Preserve Social Security and Medicare, 1995.

Care Management: Arranging for Long Term Care. Revised edition. Washington, DC: American Association of Retired Persons, 1992.

Choosing Quality: Finding the Health Plan That's Right for You. Washington, DC: National Committee for Quality Assurance.

Helping You Choose . . . Quality Home Care. Washington, DC: Joint Commission on Accreditation of Healthcare Organizations, 1995.

How to Choose a Home Care Agency. Washington, DC: National Association for Home Care.

How to Select a Hospice. Miami Beach, FL: Hospice Foundation of America.

Law and Aging Series. Tucson, AZ: National Academy of Elder Law Attorneys, 1991.

Not-for-Profit Housing and Care Options for Older People. Washington, DC: American Association of Homes and Services for the Aging, 1994.

A Profile of Older Americans. Washington, DC: American Association of Retired Persons, 1995.

Questions & Answers When Looking for an Elder Law Attorney. Tucson, AZ: National Academy of Elder Law Attorneys, 1990.

A Reverse Mortgage Primer. Washington, DC: National Committee to Preserve Social Security and Medicare, 1995.

A Shopper's Guide to Long-Term Care Insurance. Revised edition. Kansas City, MO: National Association of Insurance Commissioners, 1993.

For Further Reading

Books for Older Adults and Caregivers

Avoiding Physical Restraint Use: New Standards in Care. Washington, DC: National Citizen's Coalition for Nursing Home Reform, 1994.
Guide for nursing home residents, families, and friends on laws regarding the use of physical restraints and ways to reduce their use. Contact: National Citizen's Coalition for Nursing Home Reform, 1424 Sixteenth Street NW, Suite 202, Washington, DC 20036–2211 (202–332–2275). $6.50.

Beresford, Larry. *The Hospice Handbook.* Boston: Little, Brown & Co., 1993.
Informative handbook discusses hospice philosophy, enrollment, financial and legal matters, pain management, and related issues. $12.95.

Boughton, Jill A. *You and Your Aging Parent: The Practical Side of Love.* South Bend, IN: Greenlawn Press, 1994.
A spiritual/Christian approach to caring for an aging loved one, with practical advice for full-time family caregivers. $10.95.

Carter, Rosalynn, with Susan K. Golant. *Helping Yourself Help Others.* New York: Times Books, Random House, 1994.

A compassionate personal narrative on caregiving, with practical advice on caring for a chronically ill or disabled parent, spouse, or child. $14.00.

Cervantes, Ellen, Jeanne Heid-Grubman, and Charlotte K. Schuerman. *Someone Who Cares: A Guide to Hiring an In-Home Caregiver.* Chicago: Center for Applied Gerontology, 1994.

Useful tips and resource information to help families recruit, hire, and supervise home care workers. $5.00 plus $2.50 shipping and handling. Contact: Center for Applied Gerontology, 3003 West Touhy Avenue, Chicago, IL 60645 (312–508–1075).

Griffin-Shirley, Nora, and Gerda Groff. *Prescriptions for Independence: Working with Older People Who Are Visually Impaired.* New York: AFB Press, 1993.

Practical, nontechnical suggestions for improving quality of life and promoting independence for an older person with visual impairments. $25.00. Contact: American Foundation for the Blind, c/o American Book Center, Brooklyn Navy Yard, Building No. 3, Brooklyn, NY 11205 (718–852–9873).

Hodgson, Harriet. *Alzheimer's: Finding the Words.* Minneapolis: Chronimed Publishing, 1995.

Practical guide for communicating with someone with Alzheimer's disease, drawn from research and examples from the author's experiences with her own mother. $10.95 plus $3.00 shipping and handling. Contact: Chronimed Publishing, P.O. Box 59032, Minneapolis, MN 55459 (1–800–848–2793).

The Johns Hopkins Medical Handbook: The 100 Major Medical Disorders of People Over the Age of 50. New York: Random House, 1992.

Written by the editors of the Johns Hopkins Medical Letter, Health Over 50. *$39.95.*

Lukens, Joan E., ed. *Affirmative Aging: A Creative Approach to*

Longer Life. Bethlehem, PA: Episcopal Society for Ministry on Aging, 1994.

A spiritual guidebook for older adults. $14.95 plus $3.00 shipping and handling. Contact: Episcopal Society for Ministry on Aging, 323 Wyandotte Street, Bethlehem, PA 18015–1527 (610–868–5400).

McConnell, Carol P. *This Is My Life—My Autobiography: A Guidebook for Writing Your Life History.* Chicago: Center for Applied Gerontology, 1995.

A nice gift for a loved one who would like to record her or his memories and life story but could use the guidance of helpful prompts and structure. $15.95 plus $2.50 shipping and handling. Contact: Center for Applied Gerontology, 3003 West Touhy Avenue, Chicago, IL 60645 (312–508–1075).

Mace, Nancy L., and Peter V. Rabins. *The 36-Hour Day: A Family Guide to Caring for Persons with Alzheimer's Disease, Related Dementing Illnesses, and Memory Loss Later in Life.* Revised edition. Baltimore: Johns Hopkins University Press, 1991.

This comprehensive standard guide is available through the Alzheimer's Association for $9.95 (pocket-sized edition, $6.95). Also available in Spanish. To order, phone 1–800–272–3900.

Miller, James E. *When You're Ill or Incapacitated/When You're the Caregiver: 12 Things to Remember in Times of Sickness, Injury, or Disability.* Fort Wayne, IN: Willowgreen Publishing, 1995.

A small handbook of advice and encouragement for both caregivers and care-receivers. $5.95. Contact: Willowgreen Publishing, 509 West Washington Boulevard, Fort Wayne, IN 46802 (219–424–7916).

Norris, Jane, ed. *Daughters of the Elderly: Building Partnerships in Caregiving.* Bloomington, IN: Indiana University Press, 1988.

This sensitively written book is addressed to daughters of aging parents and includes personal narratives plus useful information from professionals on caregiving options under various circumstances. $7.95. For ordering information, phone 1–800–842–6796.

Pritikin, Enid, and Trudy Reece. *Parentcare Survival Guide: Helping*

Your Folks Through the Not-So-Golden Years. Hauppauge, NY: Barron's, 1993.

A social worker and an occupational therapist give case-by-case examples of the best ways to deal with common emotional dilemmas of caregiving. $8.95.

Resources for Elders with Disabilities. 3rd edition. Lexington, MA: Resources for Rehabilitation, 1996.

Information about rehabilitation, legal issues, organizations, self-help groups, service providers, environmental adaptations, assistive devices, and other aids for everyday living for older people with hearing and vision loss, Parkinson's disease, stroke, arthritis, osteoporosis, and diabetes. $48.95. Contact: Resources for Rehabilitation, 33 Bedford Street, Lexington, MA 02173 (617–862–6455).

Rob, Caroline, with Janet Reynolds. *The Caregiver's Guide: Helping Elderly Relatives Cope with Health & Safety Problems.* Boston: Houghton Mifflin, 1991.

Excellent resource, written by a former geriatric nurse, to help caregivers assist an older person with medical and safety concerns and living arrangements. $12.95.

Rosenbluth, Vera. *Keeping Family Stories Alive: A Creative Guide to Taping Your Family Life and Lore.* Point Roberts, WA: Hartley & Marks, 1990.

Tips on interviewing, lists of questions, and other information for preparing an audio- or videotape of your parents as they talk about their lives. $11.95.

Scholen, Ken. *Your New Retirement Nest Egg.* Apple Valley, MN: National Center for Home Equity Conversion, 1995.

Comprehensive information on home equity conversion mortgages. $24.95 plus $4.50 shipping and handling. Contact: Bookmaster, P.O. Box 2039, Mansfield, OH 44905 (1–800–247–6553).

Sherman, James R. Caregiver Survival Series. Englewood, CO: National Stroke Association.

This continuing series includes a number of titles on different aspects of caregiving, including Creative Caregiving, Preventing Caregiver Burnout, Positive Caregiver Attitudes, and The Magic of Humor in Caregiving. Published in large print. $7.95 each plus $2.00 shipping and handling for orders under $20.00. Contact: National Stroke Association, 96 Inverness Drive East, Suite I, Englewood, CO 80112–5112 (1–800–787–6537).

Susik, D. Helen. Hiring Home Caregivers: The Family Guide to In-Home Eldercare. San Luis Obispo, CA: Impact Publishers, 1995.

A professional gerontologist's comprehensive, practical guide to seeking, evaluating, and hiring home caregivers. $11.95. For ordering information, phone 1–800–246–7228.

Thomsett, Kay, and Eve Nickerson. Missing Words: The Family Handbook on Adult Hearing Loss. Washington, DC: Gallaudet University Press, 1993.

Steps to help families adjust to hearing loss. $21.95. Contact: Self Help for Hard of Hearing People, 7910 Woodmont Avenue, Suite 1200, Bethesda, MD 20814 (301–657–2248).

Werner, Anne P., and James P. Firman. Home Care for Older People: A Consumer's Guide. Washington, DC: United Seniors Health Cooperative, 1994.

Helpful suggestions, solutions to common home care dilemmas, and sample documents and forms. $10.50. Contact: United Seniors Health Cooperative, 1331 H Street NW, Suite 500, Washington, DC 20005–4706 (202–393–6222).

Williams, Mark E. The American Geriatrics Society's Complete Guide to Aging & Health. New York: Harmony Books, Crown Publishers, 1995.

Comprehensive look at the medical aspects of aging, written for seniors and caregivers. Includes guidelines for developing a healthy lifestyle and coping with specific medical problems. $40.00.

Periodicals

"Baby Boomers and Their Parents." USA Today, July 17 to 20, 1995.

Special reprint of four-part series. $5.00. Contact: USA Today, *2240 Broadbirch Drive, Silver Spring, MD 20904 (1–800–872–0001).*

Consumer Reports, August to October 1995. Three-part series. Part 1: "Nursing Homes: When a Loved One Needs Care," August 1995 (includes ratings of facilities owned by nursing home chains or affiliated with religious groups). Part 2: "Who Pays for Nursing Homes?" September 1995 (discusses payment options). Part 3: "Can Your Loved Ones Avoid a Nursing Home?" October 1995 (examines assisted living facilities and home care).

$3.00 per article reprint. To order reprints, contact: Consumers Union, Reprints, 101 Truman Avenue, Yonkers, NY 10703–1057 (914–378–2000).

O'Reilly, Brian. "How to Take Care of Aging Parents." *Fortune,* May 18, 1992. Pages 108–12.

Advice on advance planning, choosing alternative housing, and home care.

Wilcox, Melynda Dovel. "Welcome to Generation S." *Kiplinger's Personal Finance Magazine,* June 1995. Pages 59–62.

Money management tips from a variety of sources regarding caring for an elderly parent at home and seeking alternative housing.

Directories

Most of the following are annually updated professional and association membership directories. Check your local library, senior center, or community resource center for copies, or contact the sponsoring organization for ordering information. Organization listings may be found in the Directory of Resources for the appropriate chapter.

AAHSA Directory of Members. Washington, DC: American Association of Homes and Services for the Aging.

Lists some five thousand nonprofit nursing homes, retirement communities, and senior housing facilities nationwide, with contact information, facility descriptions, and services provided.

ALFAA Membership Directory. Fairfax, VA: Assisted Living Facilities Association.

Lists about two thousand operators of assisted living facilities nationwide.

Case Management Resource Guide. Newport Beach, CA: Center for Healthcare Information.

Four-volume national health care directory with over ninety thousand entries covering forty categories of services, including home care providers, rehabilitation facilities, nursing homes, specialized care centers, hotlines, and databases.

Consumer's Directory of Continuing Care Retirement Communities. Washington, DC: American Association of Homes and Services for the Aging.

Two-volume directory of more than five hundred CCRCs nationwide, with information on settings, services, amenities, and fees.

Directory of Episcopal-Related Facilities for the Aging and/or Disabled. Bethlehem, PA: Episcopal Society for Ministry on Aging.

Lists 187 adult housing facilities by state, with descriptions of facilities and services.

Directory of Legal Aid and Defender Offices in the United States. Washington, DC: National Legal Aid and Defender Association.

Lists all U.S. civil legal aid, defender, and assigned counsel programs providing free legal assistance to indigents, with a section listing programs that specialize in services to senior citizens.

Directory of State and Area Agencies on Aging. Washington, DC: National Association of Area Agencies on Aging.

Lists local AAA offices throughout the country.

GCM Membership Directory. Tucson, AZ: National Association of Professional Geriatric Care Managers.

Lists about seven hundred geriatric care managers by geographic area and areas of expertise.

Guide to the Nation's Hospices. Arlington, VA: National Hospice Organization.

Lists more than 2,100 hospice programs in the fifty states and Puerto Rico.

National Directory for Eldercare Information and Referral: Directory of State and Area Agencies on Aging. Washington, DC: National Association of Area Agencies on Aging.

A hefty resource containing basic information on programs and services available to older people. Includes a directory of more than one thousand state and local organizations serving the elderly throughout the United States and its territories.

National Homecare & Hospice Directory. Washington, DC: National Association for Home Care.

Lists nearly twenty thousand home care organizations, hospices, and home care support service providers, with areas served and range of services.

Self-Help Sourcebook. Denville, NJ: American Self-Help Clearinghouse.

Information and contacts for over seven hundred national and model self-help groups, on-line computer support networks, and toll-free helplines, with ideas for starting a mutual aid self-help group.

Index

AAA Foundation for Traffic Safety, 297
ABLEDATA/Information for Independence, 37, 195–96
AMC Cancer Information and Counseling Line, 199
ATOD Resource Guide: Older Americans, 238
abnormal aortic aneurysm, 178
Accent on Living magazine, 264
accessory apartments, 57
activities, 290–91, 294–96;
    helpful publications; organizations, 298, 302, 304–5
adult day care, 25, 47; evaluating, 30–32; referrals, 16, 44, 48
adult foster care, 58, 68, 161
adult residential facilities, 85
Adventures in Movement for the Handicapped (AIM), 196
Advocates for Nursing Home Reform (ANHR), 86
age-related body changes, 168–70; organizations to help, 210
AgeWell Resource Center, 160, 262, 342–43
Aging in America, 18, 47, 86, 160, 304, 343
Aging Network Services (ANS), 17
Al-Anon Family Group Headquarters, 196–97
Alcohol Abuse Hotline, 282
Alcohol and Drug Helpline, 282
alcoholism: helpful publications, 197, 202, 238, 266;
    organizations, 196–97, 202, 238
Alcohol Rehabilitation for the Elderly, 282
Alzheimer's Association, 12, 197, 339
Alzheimer's Disease Education and Referral Center (ADEAR), 198–99
Alzheimer's disease and other dementias, 184–85; financial help, 206;
    helpful publications, 164, 198, 199, 206–7, 213, 249, 265, 339;
    organizations, 12, 197, 198, 207, 339; residential health care
    facilities, 94
American Academy of Allergy and Immunology, 282
American Academy of Dermatology, 199–200
American Academy of Family Physicians, 200
American Academy of Orthopaedic Surgeons, 200
American Academy of Physical Medicine and Rehabilitation, 200–201
American Association of Diabetes Educators, 201
American Association for Geriatric Psychiatry (AAGP), 12, 201
American Association of Homes & Services for the Aging (AAHSA), 12, 80

American Association of Kidney Patients (AAKP), 201
American Association of Oral and Maxillofacial Surgeons, 282
American Association of Retired Persons (AARP), 143, 297, 316
American Bar Association, 143–44
American Bible Society, 269
American Board of Medical Specialists, 202
American Brain Tumor Association, 282
American Cancer Society (ACS), 202
American College of Health Care Administrators, 81
American Council on Alcoholism (ACA), 202
American Council of the Blind (ACB), 203
American Deafness and Rehabilitation Association, 203
American Dental Association (ADA), 203
American Diabetes Association (ADA), 204
American Dietetic Association (ADA), 204
American Federation of Home Health Agencies (AFHHA), 37
American Foundation for Urologic Disease, 205–6
American Geriatrics Society (AGS), 13, 206
American Health Assistance Foundation, 206–7
American Health Care Association (AHCA), 81
American Hearing Research Foundation, 14, 207
American Heart Association (AHA), 207–8
American Institute for Cancer Research Nutrition Hotline, 283
American Kidney Fund (AKF), 209–10
American Leprosy Missions (Hansen's Disease), 283
American Liver Foundation, 283
American Lung Association, 210
American Lupus Society, 283
American Medical Alert Corporation, 51
American Mental Health Counselors Association, 210
American Nurses Association, 38
American Occupational Therapy Association (AOTA), 210
American Optometric Association, 211
American Osteopathic Association (AOA), 211
American Paralysis Association, 283
American Parkinson Disease Association (APDA), 212
American Physical Therapy Association (APTA), 212
American Podiatric Medical Association (APMA), 213
American Printing House for the Blind, 269
American Psychiatric Association, 213
American Psychiatric Nurses Association, 213–14
American Red Cross, 38, 144
American Self-Help Clearinghouse, 13
American Society for Dermatologic Surgery, 283
American Society of Hypertension, 214
American Speech-Language Hearing Association, 14, 214–15
American Tinnitus Association (ATA), 215
American Trauma Society, 283
Amyotrophic Lateral Sclerosis Association, 283
Ann Morris Enterprises, 277
annuities, 99–100
Anxiety Disorders Association of America (ADAA), 215–16

414

anxiety disorders: helpful publications, 213, 216, 249; organizations, 214
arthritis, 171–72; helpful publications, 196, 200, 216–17, 265;
     organizations, 216–17, 234–35
Arthritis Foundation, 216–17
Assistance Dog Institute, 217
assisted living facilities, 59–60; evaluating, 69–71; pros and cons, 68;
     referrals, 81–82, 83, 84, 89
Assisted Living Facilities Association of America (ALFAA), 12, 81–82
Associated Services for the Blind, 262
Asthma and Allergy Foundation of America, 283
Asthma Foundation Line, 283
attorneys, finding knowledgeable, 117; referrals, 144, 152, 156
Aurora Ministries, Bible Alliance, 269

Bankcard Holders of America (BHA), 144–45
Bassett HealthSource, 217–18
bathroom safety, 32
bedroom safety, 33–34
Better Hearing Institute, 218
Blinded Veterans Association (BVA), 218
Blindskills, 269
B'nai Brith, 38, 145; Center for Senior Housing and Services, 82
Books Aloud, 274–75
boredom of parent, 10. See also activities
Boston Center for Independent Living (BCIL), 262–63
bowel problems, helpful publications, 230–31
Braille Institute, 219
Braille Monitor magazine, 242–43
Brain Injury Association, 284
Brookdale Center on Aging, 145, 263

California Advocates for Nursing Home Reform (CANHR), 86–87, 160–61
cancer, 172–73; financial assistance, 219; helpful publications, 205, 220,
     259; organizations, 199, 202, 219–21, 230, 238–39, 257, 259;
     transportation for patients, 222
Cancer Care, 219
Cancer Control Society (CCS), 219–20
Cancer Information Service, 220
Can-Do Products, 278
cardiomyopathy, 178
cardiovascular problems: heart disease, 176–79; helpful publications, 207–8,
     245–46, 266; hypertension, 179–81, 214; normal system changes,
     168; organizations, 207–8, 233, 245
caregiver. See family caregiver
CARIE (Coalition of Advocates for the Rights of the Infirm Elderly), 47–48, 87,
     161, 343
Caring for the Caregiver: A Guide to Living with Alzheimer's Disease, 265
Caring Network, The, of B'nai Brith, 38–39
Carolyn's Products for Enhanced Living, 278
cataracts, 188
Catholic Charities USA, 39, 298
Catholic Golden Age, 146, 298

Center for the Study of Aging, 39, 299
Centers for Disease Control and Prevention (CDC), 298–99
Chemocare, 263
Children of Aging Parents (CAPS), 339–40
Choice in Dying, 12, 316–17
Choice Magazine Listening, 270
cholesterol, publications, 245, 246
chores, help with, 23, 38
Christian Record Services, 270
Christian Services for the Blind, 270
Christmas in April USA, 39–40
Citizen Advocates for Nursing Home Residents, 87–88
Citizens for Better Care, 48, 88, 161
Citizens for Quality Nursing Home Care, 88–89
cleaning and home maintenance, 11, 23, 38
clergy, 46, 86
clothing, modifying for ease in dressing, 45
Coalition of Institutionalized Aged and Disabled (CIAD), 89
Cochlear Implant Club International (CICI), 221
Communicating for Seniors, 146
Community Health Accreditation Program (CHAP), 40
Compeer, 221
congestive heart failure, 178
congregate housing, 58–59, 67
conservatorship, 119–20
Consumer Health, 264
Consumer Health Information Research Institute Hotline (CHIRI), 222
Consumer's Resource Handbook , 165
continuing care retirement community (CCRC), 60–62; evaluating, 71–73;
    lists of accredited, 12, 80; pros and cons, 68–69;
    publications on, 80, 82
coronary artery disease, 178
Coronary Club, 222
Corporate Angel Network (CAN), 222
Council of Better Business Bureaus (CBBB), 17, 40, 82, 146–47, 317
Council of Citizens with Low Vision International (CCLVI), 223
Council for Jewish Elderly (CJE), 18, 48, 89, 162
Counseling for Caregivers, 343
credit cards, low-rate and secured, 145
Crestwood Company, 278
Crohn's and Colitis Foundation of America, 284

Deafness Research Foundation, 223
death: advance directives, 308–10; dying at home, 14; helpful publications,
    316–22; hospice care, 310–12, 313–15; organizations, 316–21.
    See also funeral
Delta Society, 223
dental problems, low cost/free services, 203, 226
Department of Housing and Urban Development (HUD), 83, 147
Department of Veterans Affairs, 12, 147, 223–24
depression, 183–84; helpful publications, 213, 224, 268;
    organizations, 224, 244

DEPRESSION Awareness, Recognition, Treatment (D/ART), 224
Descriptive Video Service, 224–25
diabetes, 173–74; helpful publications, 204–5, 209, 240, 243;
    organizations, 204, 239–40, 243; referrals, 204
diabetic retinopathy, 189
Diabetics Division of the National Federation of the Blind, 243
Dietary Guidelines for Americans," 245
digestive system: helpful publications, 240–41; normal changes, 169;
    organizations, 240–41
Direct Marketing Association, 147–48
disabled adults, housing for, 84
Disabled American Veterans, 225
disability income, 113
dogs, guide and assistance, 217, 223, 227–28, 257
driving for seniors, 293; publications, 211, 297, 298
Dr. Leonard's HealthCare Catalog, 278
durable power of attorney. See power of attorney
Duraline Medical Products, 278–79

EAR Foundation, 225
ECHO Housing, 56–57
education for seniors, 291; organizations, 299–300, 303
Eldercare America, 340
Eldercare Locator, , 10, 11, 16, 40–41, 83, 148, 299, 340
Eldercraftsmen, 304–5
Elderhostel, 299–300
Electronic Industries Foundation/Assistive Devices Division, 225–26
emergency response systems (ERSs), 24, 50–51
emotional health: depression, 183–84: normal problems, 13, 169
employment for seniors, 292; organizations, 301, 302, 303–4
employer-sponsored or retirement plan health insurance, 112–13
Enrichments Product Catalog, 279
Epilepsy Foundation of America, 284
Episcopal Society for Ministry on Aging, 83
exercise: helpful publications, 208, 212, 265, 267
eye or eye problems. See vision changes

Fairview/Ebenezer Caregiver Support Program, 18, 343–44
falls, preventing, 52
Families USA Foundation, 148
family caregiver: burnout, 8–9; common feelings and concerns, xvii–xviii, 15;
    communication guidelines for, 2–3; follow-up to interviews/calls, 5–6;
    helpful publications, 339, 340, 344–45; information for, 38–39;
    intervening in problem, when to, 9–10, 15; "maintenance," 323–24;
    organizations, 339–44; organizing resource information, 5–6; phone
    calls for services, preparing for, 5–6; problems and solutions checklist,
    10–16; responsibilities, managing, 16; support plan, 3–4, 324–25;
    support groups for, 16, 326; support services for, 44, 325–26 tips,
    326–28, 329; "weekly planner," 330–38; worry about distant parent,
    16, 17, 328–29
Family Caregiver Alliance Association (FCA), 264
Family Friends, 300

417

family problems, counseling, in-home, 48
Family Service America (FSA), 341
Fannie Mae Public Information Office, 149
55 Alive/Mature Driving, 297
financial concerns: counseling, free, 155; consultants for hearing impaired,
    234; discounts and benefits on services or products, 143, 145, 146,
    153, 155, 157, 158, 159, 161, 163, 258; health care costs, 12; help
    for managing money or money problems, 15, 47; helpful publications,
    147, 148, 149–50, 153, 154, 158–59, 161–62, 163, 164, 166;
    long-term care costs, 12; inventory checklist, 121–22; money-saving
    options, checklist, 140–42; private sources of income, 99–103; public
    benefits as income, 97–99; records checklist, 126–32; records, locating,
    96; referrals, 148, 149, 162; representative payee, becoming your
    parent's, 99. See also insurance
food stamps, 98
foot problems, 169; helpful publications, 200, 213; organizations, 213;
    referrals, 213
Foundation of Dentistry for the Handicapped, 226
Foundation for Glaucoma Research, 226–27
Foundation for Hospice & Homecare, 11, 41, 317–18
Friends' Health Connection, 341
Friends and Relatives of Institutionalized Aged (FRIA), 89–90
Friends of Residents in Long Term Care, 90
funeral: burial instructions, 131; preplanning, 15, 312–13
Funeral Service Consumer Assistance Program, 15

gay men and lesbians, geriatric services, 49
Generations United, 41, 300
geriatric care manager: checking on quality of, 17; need for, 6; questions to
    ask, 7–8; referrals, 15, 16–19, 43–44
geriatrician referrals, 13
glaucoma, 188; helpful publications, 226–27, 231, 238;
    organization, 226, 237–38
Gleams newsletter, 226
government programs for at-home seniors, 36
Gray Panthers, 300–301
Grief Recovery Helpline, 284
guardianship, 119–20, 161
Guide Dog Foundation for the Blind, 227
Guide Dogs of America, 227–28
Guide Dogs for the Blind, 228

hair: age-related changes, 170; helpful publications, 199–200
Hansen's Disease Center, 284
Hardest Choice, The: Selecting a Nursing Home for an
    Alzheimer's Patient," 207
HDIS, 279
health care: community service agencies, 39, 40; physical complaints,
    normal, 13, 167–70; warning signs, 9–19, 170, 171–72, 173, 174,
    176, 179, 180–81, 182, 183–84, 186, 190
health insurance. See insurance
Health Insurance Counseling and Advocacy Programs (HICAP), 149

418

Healthy Living, 279
Hearing Aid Helpline, 228
hearing aids, 175, 207, 215; helpful publication, 228, 229, 247, 258
hearing impairments, 14, 169, 174–76; communication tips, 177;
    films/videos, 236–37; financial assistance, 218, 244; helpful publications,
        207, 214, 215, 228, 229, 247, 248–49, 258, 265; insurance, 244;
        organizations, 203, 207, 214, 215, 218, 221, 223, 225, 229,
        233–34, 236–37, 244, 246–47, 248, 257–58, 259–60; referrals to
        audiologists/speech language pathologists, 14, 214–15, 246, 247;
        referrals to clinics and specialists, 14, 214–15, 218, 223, 247; services,
        203, 214–15, 244, 247; technology products/devices, 195–96, 215,
        218, 225, 230, 244, 259–60
Hear-More, 279
Hear Now, 229
Hear You Are, 280
heart diseases. See cardiovascular problems
Helen Keller National Center for Deaf-Blind Youths and Adults, 229
H.E.L.P. for Seniors newsletter, 145
helplines, toll-free, 282–88
Histiocytosis Association, 284
HMO Hotline, 162
HMOs, PPOs, and physician networks; accreditation, 41, 154;
        managed care plans, 115–16
home care, 26; activities, 290–91, 294–96
        attendants, 47; community services, 21–26, 39, 40–41, 45;
        companies, checking on, 21; evaluating agencies, 26–28, 40, 41–42;
        hiring on your own, 28–30; service agencies, 37–50; training, 38
home energy assistance, 98, 160, 161
home equity: conversion mortgages, 100–101, 147, 149; loans, 102
home health care agencies, 49–50
homemakers, 25–26
home observation, 23
home repairs and modifications, 23, 39–41, 253, 255
home safety and security: brochure, 52; checklist, 32–36
home, scaling down to stay in, 55–56
homesharing, 57, 67; referrals, 89
Horizons for the Blind, 270
Hospice Association of America (HAA), 318
hospice care, 310–12
HospiceLink, 14, 318
hospices: evaluating and accrediting agencies, 41–42; helpful publications,
        317–18, 319; organizations, 317, 319, 320; referrals, 14; referrals to
        Medicare-certified, 14; selecting a program, 313–15
hospital indemnity insurance, 113
hospitals: accreditation, 41–42; helpful publications, 166
housing: alternatives, 12; emergency, 159
Huntington's Disease Society of America, 284
hypertension (high blood pressure), 179–81
        helpful publications, 210, 245–46; organizations, 214, 246

IBM Independence Series Information Center, 229–30
ID tags, emergency and medical, 231, 233, 261

419

Impotence World Association, 284
incontinence, 181–82; helpful publications, 206, 236, 251, 258, 266; organization, 235–36, 258
independent living facilities, referrals, 83
Institute of Certified Financial Planners, 12, 15, 149
insurance: claims management services, 151, 159; counseling, free, 149, 155, 160, 161, 162, 163; disability income, 113; employer-sponsored or retirement plan; health, 112–13; helpful publications, 143, 146, 147, 153, 159, 164, 165–66; hospital indemnity, 113; life, 113, 115; long-term care, 110–12, 134–39, 143; managed care plans, 115; Medicaid, 105–6; Medicare, 103–5; Medigap, 95, 104–5, 107–10, 112, 132–34; organizations and community groups issuing, 145, 146, 153, 155, 156; QMB, 106–7; rating insurance companies, 114; records checklist, 129–30; SLMB, 106–7; specified disease/"dread" disease insurance, 113
Integrated Health Services/First American Health Care, 50
Interim Services, 50
Internal Revenue Service (IRS), 150
International Association of Cancer Victors and Friends (IACVF), 230
International Association for Financial Planning (IAFP), 150–51
International Foundation for Functional Gastrointestinal Disorders, 230–31
International Senior Citizens Association, 301
In Touch Networks, 271
isolation, parent's feelings of, 10

JGB Cassette Library, 275
Jewish Association for Services for the Aged (JASA), 19, 48–49, 162, 305
Jewish Braille Institute of America, 271
Joint Commission on Accreditation of Health Care Organizations, 41–42, 83–84, 318
joint ownership accounts, 120
Johanna Bureau for the Blind and Physically Handicapped, 271
John Milton Society for the Blind, 271–72

Kansas Advocates for Better Care, 90–91
Kelly Assisted Living Services, 50
Kernal Books (for the blind), 243
kidney problems: helpful publications, 209–10, 250–51; organizations, 201, 209–10, 250
Kings Tape Library for the Blind, 275
kitchen safety, 32–33

Legal Assistance for Seniors (LAS), 162–63
legal concerns and problems, 12, 13, 47, 49, 116–20; advice, free or lowcost, 145, 151, 156, 161, 162–63; helpful publications, 144, 145–46, 164, 321; referrals, 148, 156, 160, 162
Legal Counsel for the Elderly (LCE), 151
letter of instruction, 118
Leukemia Society of America, 284
Life Extension Foundation, 284
life insurance, 113, 115

Lifeline Systems, 51
Lifesaver Charities, 231
Lighthouse Low Vision Products, 280
Lighthouse National Center for Vision and Aging (NCVA), 231–32
Lions Clubs International, 232
living with adult children, 54–55; pros and cons, 66–67
living alone, fears of emergencies/crime, 11, 23. See also home care
Living Is for the Elderly (LIFE), 91
living trusts, 118
living will, 308; helpful publications, 320
loneliness of parent, 10
long-term care facilities. See nursing homes
long-term care insurance, 110–12, 143, 161; choosing a policy
    checklist, 134–39
LS&S Group, 280
Lucent Technologies Accessible Communications Products Center, 280
Lung Line Information Service, 232
Lupus Foundation of America, 284
Lutheran Braille Workers, 272

macular degeneration, 189
Macular Degeneration International, 232–33
managed care plans, 115; evaluating checklist, 139–30
Martha Arney Library for the Blind, 276
Maxi Aids & Appliances for Independent Living, 281
meals: community nutrition programs, 22, 10, 38, 39, 40–41, 43, 44–45,
    47, 48–49; emergency food, 159; helpful publications, 204, 208, 245,
    265, 266; kosher, 48–49; nutrition counseling, 47; recipe cards, 246;
    tips for providing/preparing, 4, 265
Meat and Poultry Hotline, 284
Medicaid, 105–6
Medical Business Associates, 151
Medic Alert U.S., 233
Medical Rehabilitation Education Foundation, 285
Medicare, 103–5, 153; helpful publications, 143, 146, 148, 149, 154, 159
Medicare Hotline, 12, 14, 149, 151–52, 318–19
medication: helpful publications, 213, 239; managing, checklist, 191–92;
monitoring, 14; organizations, 239; record keeping, 193–94, 239
Medigap, 95, 104–5, 107–10, 112; choosing a policy checklist, 132–34;
    helpful publications, 143, 146, 154, 159, 166
memory/forgetfulness, 168, 182–86
Mended Hearts, 233
Meniere's disease, 225
Meniere's Network, 285
mental health: counselors, referrals, 210; helpful publications, 213, 214, 249,
    251–52; nurses, referrals, 213–14; organizations, 221, 234, 241, 244,
    249, 251; psychiatrist, referrals, 213, 244; support groups, 241, 244
Merrill Lynch Deaf/Hard-of-Hearing Investor Services, 233–34
Minnesota Alliance for Health Care Consumers, 91–92
money problems. See financial concerns
muscle and bone, aging and, 169; organization, 234
Myasthenia Gravis Foundation, 285

National Academy of Elder Law Attorneys, 12, 13
National Accessible Apartment Clearinghouse (NAAC), 84
National Adult Day Services Association, 16, 341
National AIDS Clearinghouse, 285
National Alliance of Breast Cancer Organizations, 285
National Alliance for the Mentally Ill (NAMI), 234
National Aphasia Association, 285
National Arthritis and Musculoskeletal and Skin Diseases Information
    Clearinghouse, 234–35
National Asian Pacific Center on Aging (NAPCA), 42, 235, 301
National Association for Continence (NAFC), 235–36
National Association for the Deaf (NAD), 236
National Association of Elder Law Attorneys (NAELA), 152
National Association for Hispanic Elderly, 301–2
National Association for Home Care (NAHC), 11, 42–43, 319
National Association of Hospital Hospitality Houses, 237
National Association of Insurance Commissioners (NAIC), 152–53
National Association of Meal Programs (NAMP), 43
National Association of Nutrition and Aging Services, 43
National Association of Professional Geriatric Care Managers
    (GCM), 15, 17, 43–44
National Association of Retired Federal Employees (NARFE), 153
National Association of Social Workers, 17, 44
National Association for Visually Handicapped (NAVH), 237–38
National Braille Association, 272
National Caucus and Center on Black Aged (NCBA), 84, 302
National Citizen's Coalition for Nursing Home Reform (NCCNHR), 85
National Clearinghouse for Alcohol and Drug Information (NCADI), 238, 285
National Coalition for Cancer Survivorship (NCCS), 238–39
National Committee to Preserve Social Security and Medicare, 153
National Committee for Quality Assurance (NCQA), 154
National Council on Aging (NCOA), 44
National Council on Alcoholism and Drug Dependence, 285
National Council on Patient Information and Education, 14, 239
National Council of Senior Citizens (NCSC), 154–55
National Diabetes Information Clearinghouse (FDIC), 239–40
National Digestive Diseases Information Clearinghouse, 240–41
National Drug Information Treatment and Referral Hotline, 286
National Empowerment Center (NEC), 241
National Eye Care Project (NECP), 241
National Eye Institute (NEI), 242
National Family Caregivers Association (NFCA), 341–42
National Federation of the Blind (NFB), 242, 281
National Foundation for Consumer Credit, 155
National Foundation for Depressive Illness, 244
National Fraternal Society of the Deaf, 244
National Headache Foundation, 286
National Health Information Center (NHIC), 244–45
National Heart, Lung and Blood Institute (NHLBI), 245
National Hospice Organization, 319
National Hypertension Association (NHA), 246
National Indian AIDS Hotline, 286

National Information Center on Deafness, 246–47
National Information Center on Hearing Loss, 247
National Information Center for Orphan Drugs and Rare Diseases, 286
National Institute on Aging (NIA), 247–48
National Institute on Deafness and Other Communicative Disorders Information Clearinghouse (NIDCD), 248
National Institute for Jewish Hospices (NIJH), 320
National Institute on Mental Health (MIMH), 249
National Institute of Neurological Disorders and Stroke (NINDS), 249
National Insurance Consumer Helpline, 155
National Kidney Foundation (NKF), 250
National Kidney and Urologic Diseases Information Clearinghouse (NKUDIC), 250–51
National Legal Aid and Defender Association (NLADA), 156
National Library Service for the Blind and Physically Handicapped, 272
National Lymphedema Network, 286
National Mental Health Association (NMHA), 251
National Mental Health Consumer's Self-Help Clearinghouse, 251–52
National Meals-on-Wheels Foundation, 10, 44–45
National Multiple Sclerosis Society, 286
National Organization for Rare Disorders, 286
National Osteoporosis Foundation (NOF), 252
National Parkinson Foundation, 252
National Psoriasis Foundation, 286
National Rehabilitation Information Center (NARIC), 252–53
National Resource Center for the Prevention of Alcohol, Tobacco, Other Drug Abuses, and Mental Illness in Women, 286
National Senior Service Corps, 10, 302, 342
National Spinal Cord Injury, 287
National Spinal Cord Injury Association Hotline, 287
National University Continuing Education Program, 303
National Women's Health Network, 254
New Eyes for the Needy, 264
Newsline talking newspaper, 243
New Vision Store, 281
New York Times Mail Subscriptions, 273
North Carolina Senior Citizens Association (NCSCA), 163
Nursing Home Hotline Patrol, 92
Nursing Home Information Service (NHIS) National Council of Senior Citizens, 85
nursing homes and other long-term care facilities, 62–63; activities, 76, 91; advocacy groups, 85, 86, 89, 90, 92–93; costs and payments, 79; evaluating and accrediting agencies, 41–42, 83–84; general issues, 73; levels of care, 63–64; physical environment, 78–79; policies, 74–75; problems, 53, 66; pros and cons, 69; publications on, 82, 85, 90, 92, 93–94, 245; referrals, 80, 81, 83, 84, 85, 89, 90, 91–92; resident care, 75–76; resident councils, 85, 89, 92; search and selection, 64–65; services, medical, 76–77; services, nonmedical, 77–78; staff, 74
nursing services, 11, 38, 40–41, 46–47
Nutrition Action Healthletter, 267

Office of Minority Health Resource Center, 287

Older Americans Act of 1965, 36
Older Women's League, 156
Oley Foundation, 287
Olsten Kimberly Quality Care, 50
osteoporosis, 186–88; helpful publications, 200, 252; organization, 252
Osteoporosis Report, 252
outdoors, safety checks, 34

panic disorders, 213
Paralyzed Veterans of America (PVA), 254–55
Parkinson's disease: helpful publications, 212, 256;
        organizations, 249, 252, 255
Parkinson's Disease Foundation (PDF), 255–56
Parkinson's Disease Foundation Newsletter, 256
PDQ (Physician's Data Query), 221
pension and profit-sharing plans, 103; helpful publications, 156, 164
Pension Rights Center, 156
peripheral arterial disease, 178
personal care: aides, 25–26, 41; assistance, 11; clothing modification for, 45
personal records: checklist, 122–25; where to get missing, 164
Persys Medical Division, 51
phobias, 213
Phoenix Society National Organizations for Burn Survivors, 287
phone calls, procedures for making to support resources, 5–6
physician referrals, 200–201, 202, 206, 211, 214, 223.
        See also specific disorders
Polycystic Kidney Foundation, 287
power of attorney, 119, 308–9, 321
Presbyterian Church USA, 45, 303
Prevent Blindness America, 256
PRIDE Foundation, 45, 256
products and devices for the home, 37, 230
prostate disease or cancer; helpful publications, 206; organizations, 205
psychiatrists: publications, 213; referrals, 213

R. A. Bloch Cancer Foundation, 257
Railroad Retirement Board, 157
Reader's Digest Fund for the Blind, 273
Readings for the Blind, 273
Recording for the Blind & Dyslexic, 276
relocating to new home or apartment, 55–56, 89
respiratory system, 169
Retired Officers Association (TROA), 157
retirement communities, 59, 68
retirement homes, referrals, 85, 86
retirement hotels and apartments, 58–59, 67
Retirement Office Information, 157
reverse mortgages, 100–101
Richmond Friends and Relatives, 92

SageNet (Senior Action in a Gay Environment), 49, 305
Sandwich Generation magazine, 345

Science Products, 281
Seafood Hotline, 287
Sears Home HealthCare Catalog, 281–82
Sears Mature Outlook, 157–58
Seeing Eye, 257
Self Help for Hard of Hearing People (SHHH), 257
senior centers, 25
Senior Community Service Employment Program, 303–4
senior companions, 24, 47
Senior Health Insurance Information Program (SHIIP), 163
September Days Clubs, 158
Shepherd's Centers of America, 45–46
shingles, 199
shopping help, 10, 41
Simon Foundation for Continence, 258
Sjogren's Syndrome Association, 287
skin: age-related changes, 170; helpful publications, 199–200, 235;
    organizations, 199–200, 234, 259
Skin Cancer Foundation, 259
sleep problems, 14, 191; publications, 249
smell, sense of, and aging, 169; publication, 248
smoking, helpful publications, 245
Social Security Administration, 158–59, 320
Social Security benefits, 97–98, 153–54, 158–59
Spondylitis Association of America, 287
SSI, 98; helpful publications, 146, 154
stairs and halls safety, 33
stroke: helpful publications, 208–9, 245, 253–54, 268;
    organizations, 208, 249, 253–54, 259
Stroke Clubs International (SCI), 259
Stroke Connection magazine, 209
Stroke of Luck newsletter, 209
stubbornness of parent, 10
substance abuse, 213; helpful publications, 238, 266; organization, 238
supervision/parent cannot be alone, 11
Supplemental Security Income. See SSI "Supplemental Security Income:
    Questions and Answers About a Program to Help Seniors," 154
Supportive Older Women's Network (SOWN), 49

TFI Engineering, 282
Taped Ministries NW, 276–77
taxes: credits, deductions, exclusions, 102–3; helpful publications, 150
Technical File, 267
technology products/devices, 195–96, 215, 225–26, 230, 243
Telecommunications for the Deaf (TDI), 259–60
Tele-Consumer Hotline, 260
telephone counseling, 48
telephone reassurance, 23, 41, 47
Texas Advocates for Nursing Home Residents (TANHR), 92–93
THEOS (They Help Each Other Spiritually), 320
Thorndike Press/G. K. Hall, 273
Thyroid Foundation of America, 288

touch, sense of, age-related changes, 170
Tourette Syndrome Association, 288
Transplant Recipients International Organization, 287
transportation services, 11, 22–23, 39, 40–41, 47; for cancer patients, 222; to VA medical facilities, 225

United Methodist Communications InfoService, 46, 86
United Ostomy Association (UOA), 260
United Scleroderma Foundation, 288
United Senior Action, 93, 305
United Senior Health Cooperative (USHC), 159
United Way of America, 46, 159, 260–61
urinary system: age-related changes, 170; helpful publications, 205–6, 236, 251; incontinence, 181–82; organizations, 205, 235–26, 250

valvular heart disease, 178
Vestibular Disorders Association, 288
veterans' benefits, 98–99, 144; organizations, 12, 147, 216, 223–24, 225, 254–55
vision changes/problems, 169–70, 188–90; free care, 241, 254, 256; helpful publications, 196, 211, 226–27, 231–32, 237–38, 241–42, 256, 265; lending libraries, 274–77; organizations, 203, 211, 217, 218, 219, 223, 224–25, 226, 229, 231–32, 237–38, 241, 254, 261, 269–74; research, 242; technology products/devices, 195–96, 219, 225–26, 230, 243
Vision Foundation, 261
Vision World Wide, 273–74
Visiting Nurse Associations of America, 11, 46–47, 320–21, 342
visitors, arranging for, 23–24
Voice of the Diabetic magazine, 243
volunteer programs for elders, 10, 292, 294; organizations, 300–301, 303, 305
Volunteers of America, 277

Wander Watch Alert 24, 261
Watt, Jill, 54
Well Spouse Foundation (WSF), 344
wills, 117
women: helpful publications, 166, 212, 235, 251; organizations, 49, 156, 254
Women & Aging newsletter, 166
World at Large, 274
Worst Pills Best Bills, 268

Xavier Society for the Blind, 274

Y-Me National Breast Cancer Organization, 288

VIRGINIA SCHOMP has written extensively on topics including consumer affairs, investments, notable Americans, state travel and history, and modern and ancient cultures. She is the author of *The Better Business Bureau A to Z Buying Guide*, selected as one of the top ten reference books of 1991 by the New York Public Library. Schomp lives in Monticello, New York, with her husband, Richard, and their son, Chip.